# COMPILER DESIGN

# COMPILER DESIGN

H. S. Mohan

## Alpha Science International Ltd.
Oxford, U.K.

**Compiler Design**
232 pgs.

**H. S. Mohan**
Professor and Head
Department of Information Science and Engineering
SJB Institute of Technology
Kengeri, Bangalore

Copyright © 2014

ALPHA SCIENCE INTERNATIONAL LTD.
7200 The Quorum, Oxford Business Park North
Garsington Road, Oxford OX4 2JZ, U.K.

www.alphasci.com

ISBN 978-1-84265-857-4

Printed in India

Dedicated
to
My Beloved Mother
Yashodha

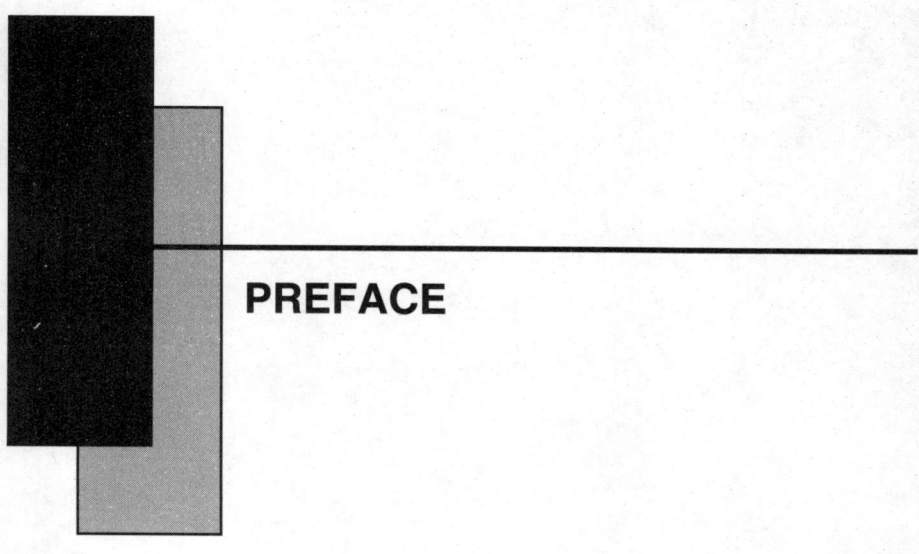

# PREFACE

Computer understands only Machine code. So it is necessary to have a intermediate to convert the source language into the machine code. So the design of compilers is very important in the engineering fields.

Overwhelming response from my students and other teachers of various engineering colleges who have referred my notes inspired me to write this book.

The book is written as a text, with problems and exercises. In every chapter of this book, more importance is given to the concepts and many problems are solved which covers all varieties of problems in a simpler and easier techniques.

The book covers the syllabus of Undergraduate and Postgraduate students of CSE and ISE branches of almost all universities.

Any suggestion for the improvement of the book will be acknowledged and well appreciated. Suggestions can be emailed to mohan_kit@yahoo.com

**H. S. Mohan**

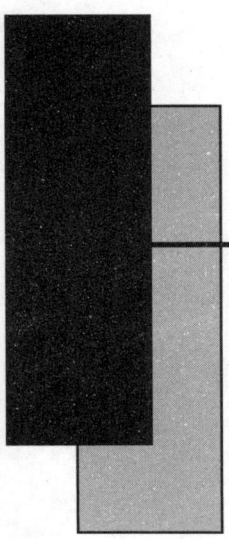

# ACKNOWLEDGEMENTS

The satisfaction and euphoria that accompany the successful completion of any task would be incomplete without the mention of people who made it possible because "Success is the abstract of hard work and perseverance, but steadfast of all is encouragement guidance". So I would like to acknowledge all those whose guidance and encouragement served as a beacon light and crowned my efforts with success.

I would like to express my pranam's to his Divine soul Padmabhushana Sri Sri Sri Dr. Balagangadharanatha Maha Swamiji and pranam's to his Holiness Sri Sri Sri Nirmalanandanatha Maha Swamiji, the president of Sri Adichunchanagiri shikshana trust ® for their Blessings.

I would like to express my profound grateful to Reverend Sri Sri Prakashnath Swamiji, Managing Director, SJBIT, Bangalore for his blessings.

I am grateful to Dr. Puttaraju, Principal for his kind co-operation and encouragement.

I am grateful to Dr. V. Rajappa, Founder, Director Prajwal Academy of Technical Educations and Neelakanta V. for their moral support and encouragement given to me for writing this book.

I would like to render my heartfelt gratitude to my parents, my wife Bindiya M.K. and My daughter Aditi Mohan and my son Adithya Mohan for their kind cooperation, valuable moral support and encouragement given to me and the role they have played in completing my book.

I am grateful to all my friends, collegues and others who are directly or indirectly involved for their inspiration, encouragement and support to successfully complete this book.

Finally I convey my thanks to publisher of this book, for their constructive critism and suggestions for improvement in the manuscript.

**H.S. Mohan**

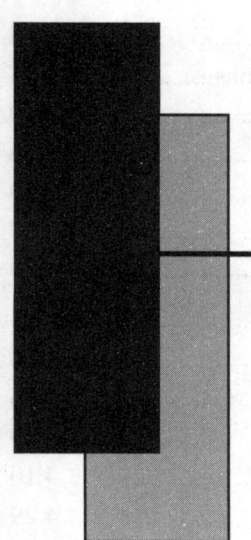

# CONTENTS

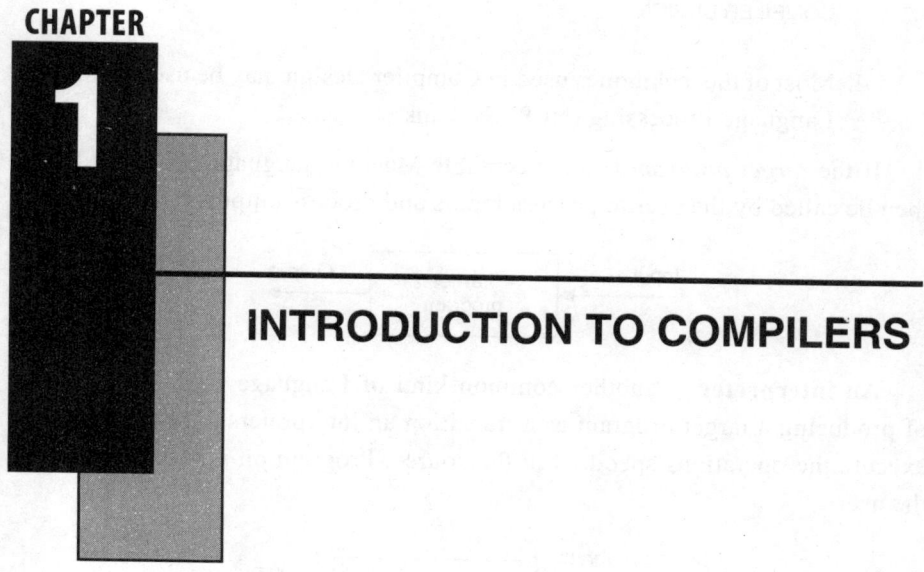

# INTRODUCTION TO COMPILERS

## 1.1 COMPILERS

A Compiler is a program, takes a program written in a source language and translates it into equivalent program in a target language.

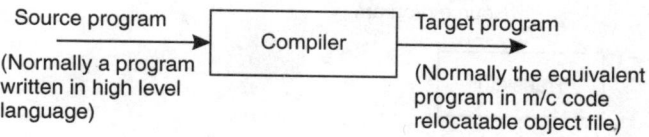

Source program
(Normally a program written in high level language)

Compiler

Target program
(Normally the equivalent program in m/c code relocatable object file)

## 1.2 OTHER APPLICATIONS

In addition to the development of Compiler, the techniques used in compiler design can be applicable to many problems in Computer Science.

1. Techniques used in Lexical Analyzer can be used in Text editors, information retrieval system and Pattern Recognition Programs.

2. Techniques used in a parser can be used in a query processing system such as SQL.

3. Many software having a complex front end may need techniques used in Compiler Design.

4. Most of the techniques used in Compiler Design may be used in Natural Language Processing (NLP) Systems.

If the *target program* is an executable Machine language program. It can then be called by the user to process inputs and process outputs.

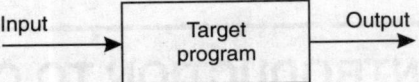

An **interpreter** is another common kind of Language Processor. Instead of producing a target program as a transition an interpreters appear to directly execute the operations specified in the source. Program on inputs supplied by the user.

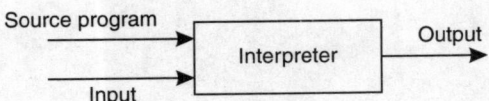

**Example**

A java language Processor combine compilation and interpretation.

A Java Source Program may first be compiled into an intermediate form called *Byte Code*. The Byte codes are then interpreted by a virtual machine.

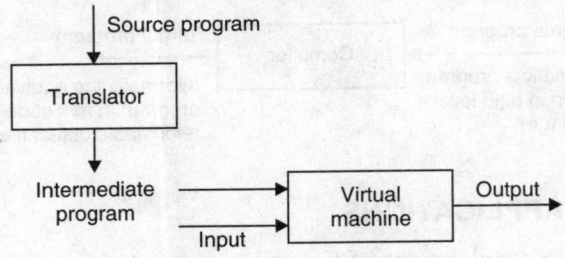

**Figure:** A hybrid compiler

## 1.3 A LANGUAGE PROCESSING SYSTEM

In addition to a compiler, several other Programs may be required to create an executable Target Program as shown in figure.

- A source program may be divided into modules stored in seperate files. The task of collecting the source program is sometimes entrusted to a seperate program called a *preprocessor*. The preprocessor may also expand shorthands called Macros.

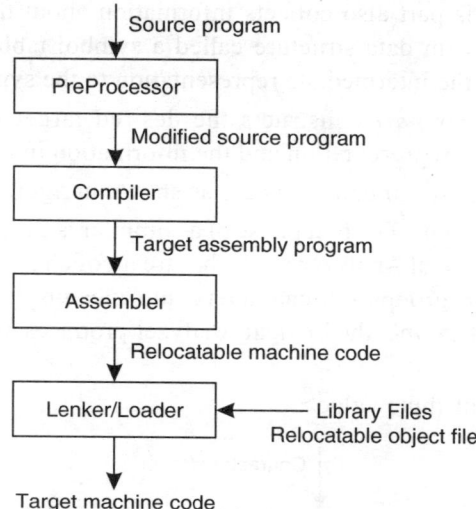

- The modified source Program is then fed into a *Compiler*. The compiler may produce an Assembly Language Program as its output because Assembly language is easy to produce output and is easier to debug.

- The Assembly Language is then processed by a program called *Assembles* that produces relocatable machine code as its output.

- Large programs are often compiled in pieces. So the *relocatable machine code* may have to be linked together with other relocatable object files and library files into the code that actually runs on the machine.

- The *Linker* resolves the external memory addresses where the code in one file may refer to location in another file.

- The *Loader* then puts together all of the executable object files into memory for execution.

## 1.4  THE STRUCTURE OF A COMPILER OR PHASES OF A COMPILER

There are two parts in the structure of a Compiler —  Analysis and (front end)

Synthesis (back end)

- The *Analysis part* breaks up the Source Program into costituent pieces and imposes a grammatical structure on them. It then used this structure to create an intermediate representation of the source program.

The analysis part also collects information about the source program and stores it in data structure called a symbol table, which is passed along with the intermediate representation to the synthesis part.

- The *synthesis part* constructs the desired target program from the intermediate representation and the information in the symbol table.

The different phases of compilers are as shown in figure below:

**1. Lexical Analyzer:** The first phase of a compiler is called Lexical Analysis or *Scanning*. The Lexical Analyzer reads the stream of characters making up the source program and groups the characters into meaningful sequences called *Lexemes*. For each Lexeme, the Lexical Analyzer produces as output, a token of the form.

&lt;token-name, attribute value&gt;

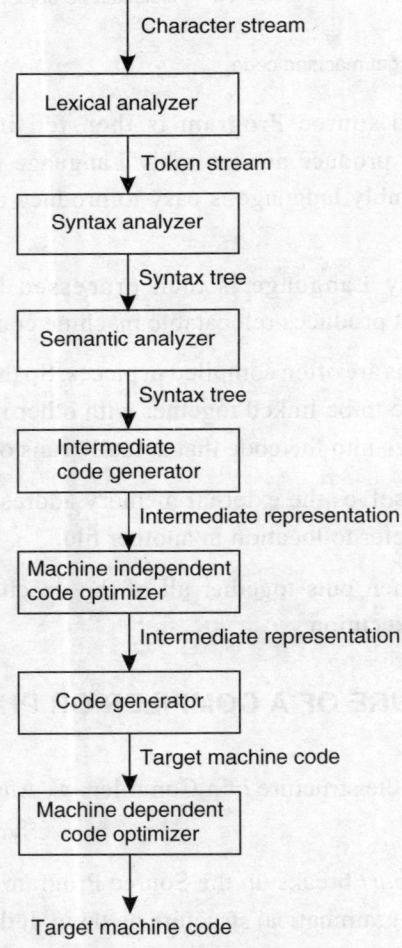

**Figure:** Different phase of a compiler

That is passes onto the subsequent phase. In the token the first component, *token name* is an abstract symbol that is used during Syntax Analysis and the Second Component *Attribute value* points to an entry in the Symbol table for this token.

**Example**

Suppose the source program contains a assignment statement,

$$position = initial + rate * 60;$$

(*i*) *Position* is a Lexeme, that would be mapped into a token <*id*, 1>. Where id is an abstract symbol standing for identifier and 1 points to the symbol table entry for position.

(*ii*) The assignment symbol '=' is a Lexeme, that is mapped into token <=>. Since this token needs no attribute value, we have omitted the second component.

(*iii*) *Initial* is a Lexeme, that would be mapped into token <*id*, 2>, where 2 points to the symbol table entry for initial.

(*iv*) + is a Lexeme, that is mapped into token <+>

(*v*) *Rate* is a Lexeme, that is mapped into token <*id*, 3> where 3 points to the symbol table entry for rate.

(*vi*) * is a Lexeme that is mapped into token <*>.

(*vii*) 60 is a Lexeme that is mapped into token <60>

80 After Lexical Analysis, the output is <*id*, 1> <=> <*id*, 2> <+> — <*id*, 3> <*> <60>

# NOTE:

1. **Syntax:** The form of structure of the expressions statements and program units.

2. **Semantics:** The meaning of expressions, statements and program units.

3. **Language:** A language is a set of sentence.

4. **Sentence:** It is a string of characters composed of Lexemas over some alphabet.

5. **Lexeme:** A Lexeme is the lowest level syntactic unit of a language described by a Lexical specification.

6. **Token:** A token is a category or abstraction of Lexemes.

**2. Syntax Analysis:** The second phase of the compiler is syntax analysis or *Parsing*.

The parser uses the first components of tokens produced by the Lexical analysis, create a tree like intermediate representation that shows the grammatical structure of the token stream.

A typical representation is a *Syntax Tree* in which each interior node represents an operation and the children of the node represents the argument of the operation.

**3. Semantic Analysis:** The Semantic Analyzer uses the Syntax tree and the information in the symbol table to check the source program for Semantic consistency with the Language Definition.

An important part of Semantic Analysis is *Type Checking*, where the Compiler checks that each operator has matching operands.

For *e.g.*, many programing language definitions require an array index to be an integer, the compiler must report an error if the floating point number is used to index an array.

**4. Intermediate Code Generation:** In the process of translating a source program into target code a Compiler may construct one or more intermediate representations which can have a variety of forms. Syntax Trees are a form of Intermediate representation, they are commonly used during Syntax and Semantic Analysis.

One possibility of intermediate form called 3 address code which consists of a sequence of assembly like instructions with three operand per instruction. Each operand can act like a Register.

The output of the intermediate code generator consists of 3 address code.

$$t_1 = \text{into float } (60)$$
$$t_2 = id_3 * t_1$$
$$t_3 = id_2 * t_2$$

**5. Code Optimization:** The machine independent code optimization phase attempts to improve the intermediate code so that better target code will result.

Usually better means Faster, but other objectives may be designed such as shorter code or target code that consumes less power.

Code optimization is a good way to generate target code. The optimizer can deduce the conversion of 60 from integer to floating point can be done once and for all at compile time. So the int to float operation can be eliminated by replacing the integer 60 by floating point 60.0

$$t_1 = id_3 * 60.0$$

$$id_1 = id_2 + t_1$$

**6. Code Generation:** The code generation takes an input an intermediate representation of the source program and maps it into target language. If the target language is machine code. Registers or memory locations are selected for each of the variables used by the program. Then the intermediate instructions are translated into sequence of machine instructions that perform the same task.

$$\begin{aligned}
&\text{LDF} && R_2, id_3 \\
&\text{MULF} && R_2, R_2, \#60.0 \\
&\text{LDF} && R_1, id_1 \\
&\text{ADDF} && R_1, R_1, R_2 \\
&\text{STF} && id_1, R_1
\end{aligned}$$

## Symbol Table Management

An essential function of a compiler is to record the variable names used in the source program and collect information about various attributes of each name.

These attributes can provide the information about storage allocated for a name, its type, its scope and in case of procedure name such as number and types of its arguments the method of passing each argument and the type returned.

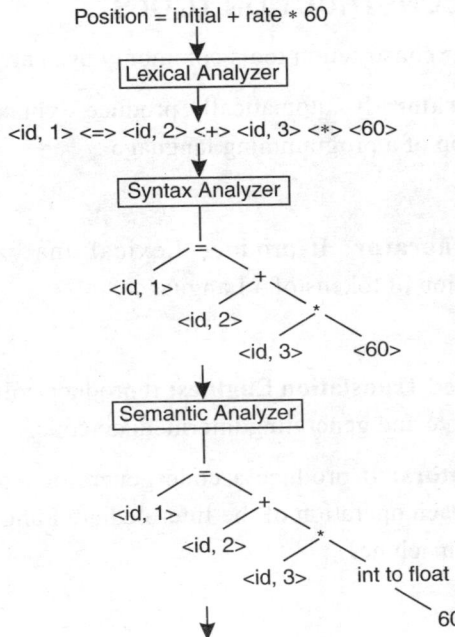

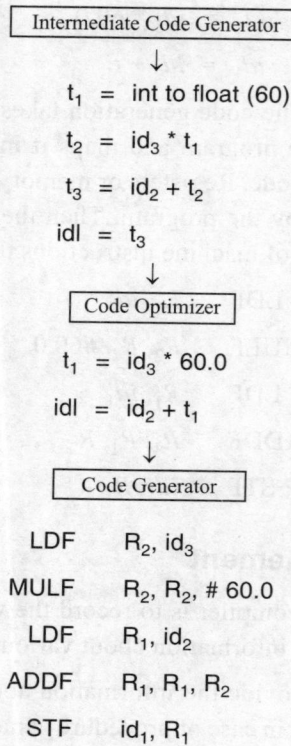

$$\boxed{\text{Intermediate Code Generator}}$$
$$\downarrow$$

$$t_1 \; = \; \text{int to float (60)}$$
$$t_2 \; = \; id_3 * t_1$$
$$t_3 \; = \; id_2 + t_2$$
$$idl \; = \; t_3$$
$$\downarrow$$

$$\boxed{\text{Code Optimizer}}$$

$$t_1 \; = \; id_3 * 60.0$$
$$idl \; = \; id_2 + t_1$$
$$\downarrow$$

$$\boxed{\text{Code Generator}}$$

$$LDF \qquad R_2, id_3$$
$$MULF \qquad R_2, R_2, \# \, 60.0$$
$$LDF \qquad R_1, id_2$$
$$ADDF \qquad R_1, R_1, R_2$$
$$STF \qquad id_1, R_1$$

## 1.5 COMPILER CONSTRUCTION TOOLS

Some of the compiler construction tools commonly used are:

**1. Parser Generator:** It automatically produce Syntax Analysers from a gramatical description of a programming language

Example: YACC

**2. Scanner Generator:** It produce Lexical analyzers from regular expressions, description of tokens of a Language.

Example: LEX

**3. Syntax-directed Translation Engines:** It produce collection of Routines for walking a parse tree and generating intermediate code.

**4. Code Generators:** It produce a code generator from a collection of rules for translating each operation of the Intermediate Language into machine language for a target machine.

**5. Data-flow Analysis Engines:** It facilitate the gathering of information about values are transmitted from one part of a program to each other part. Data analysis is the key part of Code Optimization.

**6. Compiler Construction Toolkits:** It provides on integrated set of routines for constructing various phases of a compiler.

## 1.6 THE EVOLUTION OF PROGRAMMING LANGUAGES

The first electronic computers appeared in 1940's and were programmed in Machine Language by sequence of 0's and 1's that explicitly told the computer what operations to execute and in what order.

The operations themselves were very low level, move data from one location to other, add the contents of two registers, compare two values and so on. So this kind of programming was slow, tedious and once written the programs were hard to understand and modify.

## The Move to Higher Level Languages

Today there are thousands of programming languages. They can be classified in variety of ways.

One classification is by generation.

(*i*) First Generation are the Machine Languages.

(*ii*) Second Generation are the Assembly Languages.

(*iii*) Third Generation are the high-level languages like FORTRAN, COBAL, LISP, C.

(*iv*) Fourth Generation Languages are languages designed for specific applications for report generation, SQL for database.

(*v*) Fifth Generation Languages has been applied to logic and constraint based Languages like Prolog.

Another classification of Languages uses the term *imperative* for languages in which a program specifies how a computation is to be done and *declarative* for languages in which a program specifies what computation is to be done.

Languages such as C, C++, Java are imperative languages.

## 1.7 APPLICATIONS OF COMPILER TECHNOLOGY

The important interactions and applications of the Compiler technology are:

### 1. Implementation of High-level Programming Languages:

- A High-level Programming Languages defines a programming abstraction, the programmer expresses an algorithm using the language and the compiler must translate that program to the target language.
- Generally Higher level programming languages are easier to program that are less efficient *i.e.,* Target program runs slowly.

**2. Optimizations for Computer Architecture:** The rapid evolution of Computer Architecture has created a great demand for new Compiler Technology. Almost all high performance systems take advantage of the two basic techniques. Parallelism and Memory Hirarchies.

### 3. Design of New Computer Architecture:

- In the early days of Computer architecture design, compilers were developed after the machines were built.
- One of the best known example of how compilers influenced the design of computer architecture was the invention of RISC (Reduced Instruction Set Computer) Machines.

**4. Program Translators:** The following are some of the important applications of program translating techniques:

(*i*) **Binary Translation:** Compiler Technology can be used to translate the binary code for one machine to that of another allowing a machine to run programs originally compiled for another instruction set.

(*ii*) **Hardware-Synthesis:** Not only is most software written in high-level languages even hardware designs are mostly designed in hardware description languages like verilog and VHDL.

(*iii*) **Database Query Interpreters:** Besides specifying, Software and Hardware Languages Compilers are useful in many other applications. For example, query languages especially SQL are used to search databases.

(*iv*) **Software Productivity Tools:** The software productivity tools are:

(*a*) **Type-checking:** It is an effective and well established technique to catch inconsistencies in programs. It can be used to catch errors.

(*b*) **Bounds Checking:** It is easier to make mistakes when programming in lower level language than a higher level one. C does not have array bounds check, it is upto the user to ensure that arrays are not accessed out of bounds.

## CHAPTER

# 2

## LEXICAL ANALYSIS

## 2.1 ROLE OF THE LEXICAL ANALYZER

Lexical Analyzer is the first phase of a compiler, the main task of the lexical analyzer is to read the input characters of the source program, group them into lexemas and produces as output the *sequence of tokens* as for each lexema in the source program.

The stream of tokens is sent to the parser for syntax analysis. It is common for lexical analyzer to interact with the symbol table. When the Lexical analyzer identifies a lexema constituting an identifier, it needs to enter that lexema into the Symbol table.

The call suggested by the 'get next token' command shown in figure causes the lexical analyzer to read characters from its input until it can identify the next lexema and produce for it the next token, which it returns to the parser.

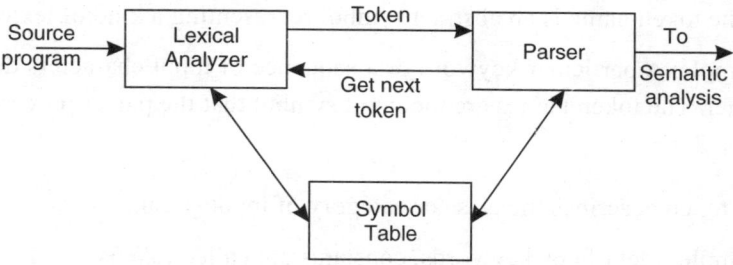

Apart from Token identification Lexical Analyzer also performs following functions:

(*i*) It produces stream of tokens.

(*ii*) It eliminates blanks and comments.

(*iii*) It generates symbol table which stores the information about identifiers, constants encountered in the input.

(*iv*) It keeps track of line numbers.

(*v*) It reports the error encountered while generating the tokens.

## Lexical Analysis v/s Parsing

There are number of reasons why the analysis portion of a compiler is separated into lexical and parsing (Syntax analysis phase):

**1. Simplicity of design is the most important consideration:** The seperation of Lexical and Syntatic analysis often allows us to simplify atleast one of these tasks.

For example, a parser that had to deal with comments and white spaces as syntatic units would be considerably more complex than one can assume while space and comments have already been removed by the lexical analyzer.

**2. Compiler efficiency is improved:** A Seperate Lexical Analyzer allows us to apply specialized techniques that serve only the Lexical task, not the job of parsing.

**3. Compiler portability is enhanced:** Input device specific pecularities can be restricted to the lexical analyzer.

## 2.2  TOKENS, PATTERNS AND LEXEMES

**Token:** A Token is a pair consisting of a token name and an optional attribute value. The token name is an abstract symbol representing a kind of lexical unit.

Example: A particular keyword or a sequence of input characters denoting a identifier. The token names are the input symbol that the parser process.

Or

The token describes the class or category of input stream.

Example: Identifiers, keywords, constants are called tokens.

**Patterns:** is a description of the form that the Lexemas of a token may take.

In case of a *keyword* as a token, the pattern is just the sequence of characters that form the keyword.

For *identifiers* and some other tokens, the pattern is a more complex structure that is matched by many string.

Or

Set of rules that describes the token.

**Lexemas:** is a sequence of characters in the source program that matches the pattern for a token and is identified by the Lexical Analyzer as an instance of that token.

**Example:**

(*i*) printf ("Total=%d\n", Score);

Here,

printf and score are Lexemas matching the pattern for token *identifier* and "Total=%d\n" is a Lexema matching *Literals*.

(*ii*)    if (*a* < *b*)

Here,

if, (*a* , < , *b* ,) are all Lexemas

and    if is a keyword

'C' is a opening paranthesis

*a* is a identifier

< is a operator

and so on are all *Tokens*.

| Sample Lexemes | Token |
|---|---|
| if | if |
| else | else |
| <=, != | comparision operator |
| 3.1415 | constant |
| "core dumped" | Literals |

## 2.3 INPUT BUFFERING

- The amount of time taken to process characters and the large number of characters that must be processed during the compilation of a large source program, specialized by buffering techniques have been developed to reduce the amount of overhead required to process a single input character.

- An important scheme involves *two buffers* that are alternatively relocate. Each buffer is of the same size $n$ and $n$ is usually the size of a disk block.

**Example:** 4096 bytes

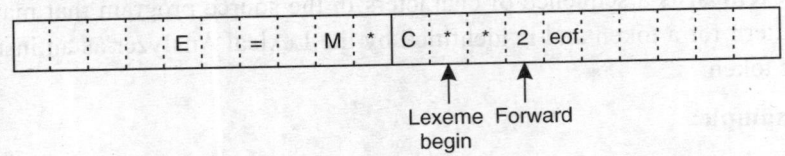

- If fewer than N character remain in the input file, then a special character represented by EOF marks the end of the source file.
- Two pointers to the inputs are maintained.

1. Pointer *Lexeme begin*, makes the beginning of the current Lexema whose extent we are attempting to determine.

2. Points *Forward*, scans ahead until a pattern match is found.

- Once the next Lexema is determined, forward is set to the character at its right end, then after the Lexema is recorded as an attribute. Value of a token returned to the parser, Lexema begin is set to the character immediately after the Lexema just found.

In the above example, forward has passed the end of the next Lexema **2.

## 2.4  SPECIFICATION OF TOKENS

To specify tokens, regular expressions are used. When a pattern is matched by some regular expression, then token can be recognized.

**Example :** The Token names and associated attribute values for statement.

$$E = m * c ** 2 \text{ are written below:}$$

< *id*, pointer to the symbol table entry for *E*>

<assignment-operator>

<*id*, pointer to the symbol table entry for *m*>

<multiplication-operator>

<*id*, pointer to the symbol table enter for *c*>

<exponential-operator>

<number, integer value 2>

## Strings and Languages

*String* is a collection of finite number of alphabets or letters.

*Language* is a collection of strings defined on $\Sigma$.

## Regular Expressions

Some rules that describe definitions of Regular Expressions over the input set denoted by $\Sigma$

1. $a$, $\phi$, $\lambda$ are all primitive Regular Expressions

2. If $R_1$ and $R_2$ are Regular Expressions then, $R = R_1 + R_2$ is also Regular Expression $(R = R_1/R_2)$

3. If $R_1$ and $R_2$ are Regular Expression then, $R = R_1 . R_2$ is also Regular Expression.

4. If $R_1$ is a Regular Expression then $R_1^*$ is also Regular Expression.

A language denoted by Regular Expression is said to be Regular Language.

Let $S = \{a, b\}$

1. The Regular Expression $a/b$ or $(a + b)$ denotes the language,

   $L = \{a, b\}$

2. $(a/b) (a/b)$ denotes. $L = \{aa, ab, ba, bb\}$...

   The language of all strings of length two over the alphabet $\Sigma$.

3. $a^*$ denotes the language consisting of all strings of zero or more $a$'s

   *i.e., $L = \{\lambda, a, aa, aaa, ....\}$*

4. $(a/b) *$ denotes the set of all strings consisting of 0 or more instances of $a$ or $b$.

   *i.e.,* All strings of $a$'s and $b$'s

   $L = \{\lambda, a, b, aa, bb, ab, ba, aaa, ....\}$

5. $a/a^*b$

   denotes $L = \{a, b, ab, aab, aaab, ....\}$

   *i.e.,* all strings consistings of zero or more $a$'s ending with $b$.

## 2.5 REGULAR DEFINITIONS

For notational convinience we may give names to certain Regular Expressions and use those names is subsequent expressions.

If $\Sigma$ is an alphabet of basic symbols, then the regular definition is a sequence of definitions of the form,

$$d \rightarrow r_1$$
$$d_2 \rightarrow r_2$$
$$.$$
$$.$$
$$.$$
$$d_n \rightarrow r_n$$

Where,

1. Each $d_i$ is a new symbol, not is $\Sigma$ and not the same as any other of the $d$'s.

2. Each $r_i$ is a Regular Expression over the alphabet $\Sigma U\{d_1, d_2, d_3, ....d_{i-1}\}$

## EXAMPLE 1

$C$ identifiers are strings of letters, digits and underscore (–). The regular definition for the language of C identifiers are

$$\text{Letter} \rightarrow A|B|C| ... z|a|b| ... z|\_$$
$$\text{digit} \rightarrow 0|1|2| ... 9$$
$$id \rightarrow \text{letter\_(letter\_|digit)*}$$

## EXAMPLE 2

Unsigned numbers (integer or Floating point) are strings such as 5280, 0.01234, 5.336E4 or 1.89E–4

The regular definition are :

$$\text{digit} \rightarrow 0|1| ... 9$$
$$\text{digits} \rightarrow (\text{digit}) (\text{digit})*$$
$$\text{optional fraction} \rightarrow \text{digits} | \varepsilon$$
$$\text{optional exponent} \rightarrow (E (+|-|\varepsilon) \text{digits})|\varepsilon$$
$$\text{number} \rightarrow (\text{digits}) (\text{optional fraction}) (\text{optional exponent})$$

## Extensions of Regular Expressions

**1. One or More Instances:** The Unary postfix operator '+' represents the positive closure of a Regular Expression *i.e.* if $r$ is a Regular Expression, then $(\gamma)^+$ denotes the Language $(L(\gamma))^+$.

The operator '+' has the same precedence and associativity as the operator '*'.

Two Laws

$$\gamma* \;=\; r^+ \mid \varepsilon$$
$$\gamma^+ \;=\; \gamma \cdot \gamma* = \gamma* \cdot \gamma$$

**2. Zero or One Instance:** The unary postfix operator '?' means zero or one occurence, that is,

$r$? is equivalent to $r/\varepsilon$

and $\qquad L(\gamma?) \;=\; L(\gamma)\; U\{\varepsilon\}$

The ? operator has the same precedence and associativity as $*$ and $+$.

**3. Character Classes:** A Regular Expressions $a_1|a_2|\ldots a_n$

Where $a_i$'s are each symbols of the alphabet, can be replaced by short hands.

$[a_1\; a_2 \ldots a_n]$

**4.** $[a\; b\; c]$ is shorthand for $a|b|c$

$[a-z]$ is shorthand for $a|b|c|\ldots|z$

## EXAMPLE 3

Using the shorthands rewrite the regular definition given in Example 1

$$\text{letter} \;\rightarrow\; [A-z\; a-z]$$
$$\text{digit} \;\rightarrow\; [0-9]$$
$$\text{id} \;\rightarrow\; \text{letter (letter/digit)}*$$

## EXAMPLE 4

Using the shorthands rewrite the regular definition given in Example 2

$$\text{digit} \;\rightarrow\; [0-9]$$
$$\text{digits} \;\rightarrow\; \text{digit} +$$
$$\text{number} \;\rightarrow\; \text{digits (.digits)? (E } [+-]\text{? digits)?}$$

## Recognition of Tokens

We know how to express patterns using Regular Expressions now we need to know how to take the patterns for all needed tokens and build a piece of code that examines the input string and finds a prefix *i.e.,* a lexima matching one of the patterns.

Consider a Grammar for branching statement

$$\text{Stmt} \rightarrow \text{if expr then stmt}$$
$$|\underline{\text{if}} \text{ expr } \underline{\text{then}} \text{ stmt } \underline{\text{else}} \text{ stmt}$$
$$|\varepsilon$$
$$\text{expr} \rightarrow \text{term } \underline{\text{relop}} \text{ term}$$
$$|\text{term}$$
$$\text{term} \rightarrow \underline{\text{id}|\text{number}}$$

The terminals of the Grammar, which are if, then, else, relop, *id* and number are the names of tokens. The patterns for these tokens are described using Regular definition.

$$\text{digit} \rightarrow [0-9]$$
$$\text{digits} \rightarrow \text{digit} +$$
$$\text{number} \rightarrow \text{digits (.digits)? (E [+ -]? digits)?}$$
$$\text{letter} \rightarrow \text{letter (letter/digit)*}$$
$$\text{if} \rightarrow \text{if}$$
$$\text{else} \rightarrow \text{else}$$
$$\text{then} \rightarrow \text{then}$$
$$\text{relop} \rightarrow <|>|<=|>=|=|<>$$

In the addition, we assign the Lexical Analyzer the job of stripping out white space by recognizing the token ws defined by

$$\omega s \rightarrow (\text{blank}|\text{tab}|\text{newline})^+$$

| Lexemes | Token name | Attribute value |
|---|---|---|
| Any ws | — | — |
| if | if | — |
| then | then | — |
| else | else | — |
| Any *id* | id | pointer to table entry |
| Any number | number | pointer to table entry |
| Any *id* | id | pointer to table entry |
| Any number | number | pointer to table entry |
| < | relop | LT |
| < = | relop | LE |
| > | relop | GT |
| >= | relop | GE |
| = | relop | EQ |
| <> | relop | NE |

## Transition Diagrams

As an intermediate step the construction of a lexical analyzer will first convert patterns into transition diagrams.

Transition diagram have a collection of node or circles called states each state represents a condition that could occur during the process of scanning the input, looking for a lexima that matches one of several patterns.

Edges are directed from state of the transition diagram to other. Each edge is labelled by a symbol or set of symbols. It should also know lexima **begin pointer** and the **forward pointer.** Certain states are said to be accepting or final indicated by double circle.

## PROBLEM 1

Construct a transition diagram for the following.

(*i*) Relational operators or relop.

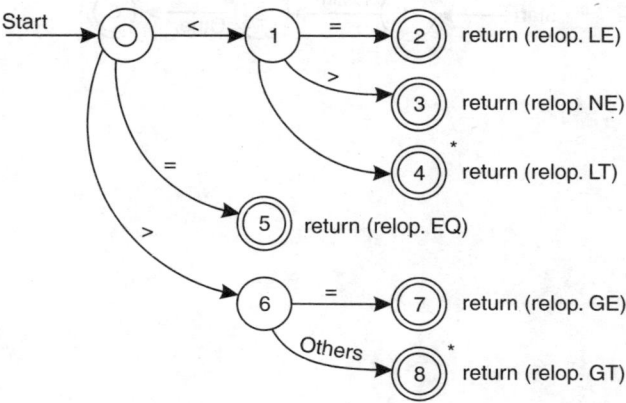

(*ii*) Transition diagram for identifiers/keywords

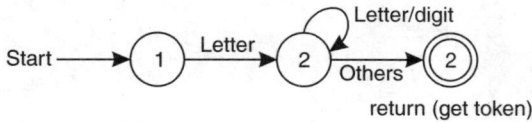

## (iii) Transition diagram for unsigned numbers.

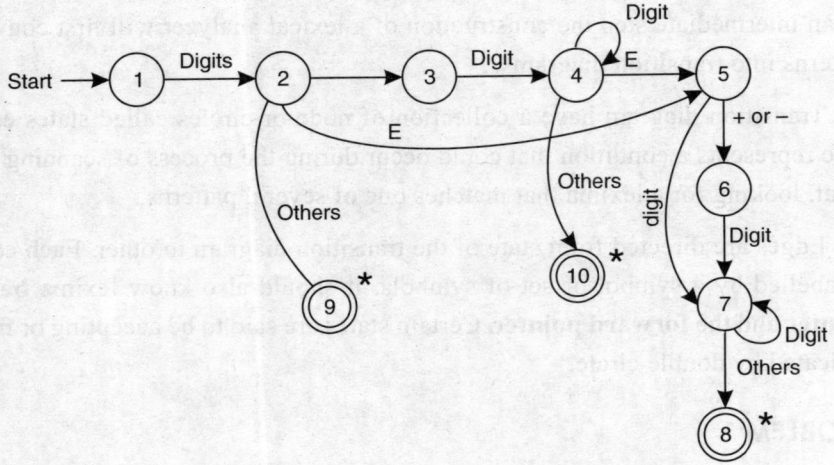

## (iv) Transition diagram for white space.

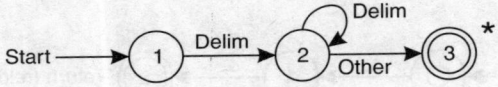

# 3

# SYNTAX ANALYSIS–I

## 3.1 INTRODUCTION

**Syntax Analysis is the second phase** in Compilation. The Syntax Analyzer (Parser) checks the syntax of the language.

A Syntax Analyzer takes the token from the Lexical Analyzer and groups them in such a way that some programming structure (syntax) can be recognized.

After grouping the tokens, if at all any syntax cannot be recognized then syntactic error will be generated. This overall process is called syntax checking of the language.

## Definition of Parser

A parsing or Syntax analysis is a process which takes the input string $w$ and products either a parse tree (syntatic structure) or generates the syntactic errors.

**Example**

$$a = b + 10$$

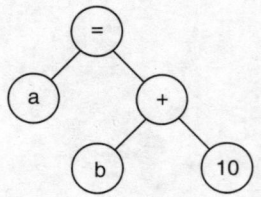

## Role of the Parser

In the process of compilation the parser and Lexical Analyzer work together that means when parser requires string of tokens, it involves Lexical Analyzer.

The parser obtains a string of tokens from the Lexical Analyzer and verifies that the string of token names can be generated by the Grammar for the source program.

We expect the parser to report any syntax errors in an intelligible fashion and to recover from commonly occuring errors to continue processing the remainder of the program.

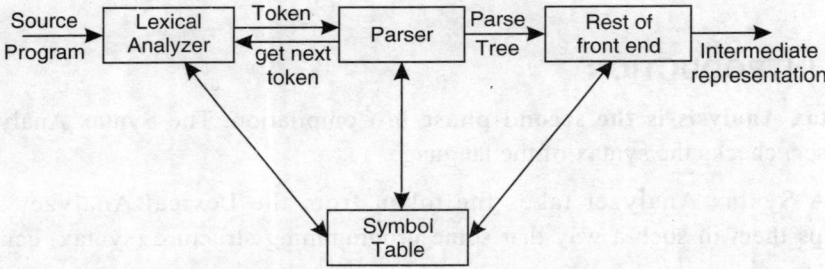

There are three general types of Parsers for Grammars:

- Universal.
- Top-down.
- Bottom-up approach.

The Top-down and bottom-up are commonly used. As implied by their names, the top-down method build parse tree from top (root) down method build parse tree from top (root) to bottom (leaves), while bottom-up method starts from the leaves and work their way upto the root. In either case input is scanned from left to right, one symbol at a time.

### NOTE:

Lexical and Syntax Analyzer are separated out because

(*i*) It accelarates the process of compilation.

(*ii*) The errors in the source input can be identified precisely.

## 3.2  CONTEXT-FREE GRAMMAR: (CFG)

A CFG consists of terminals, Non-terminal (variables), a start symbol and production.

$$G = (V, T, S, P)$$

where, Terminals are the basic symbols from which strings are formed.

Variables are non-Terminals are syntatic variable that denote sets of strings.

$S$ is the start symbol and the set of strings it denotes is the language generated by the grammar.

P is the production of the form.

$$A \rightarrow x$$

where $A \in V$ and $x \in (VUT)^*$

## EXAMPLE 1

Stmt→if (expr) stmt else stmt

Here,    if, else (,) are terminals

expr, Stmt are non terminals or Variables

stmt is the start variable.

## EXAMPLE 2

The Grammar for simple arithmetic operations.

$$Expression \rightarrow Expression + term$$

$$Expression \rightarrow Expression - term$$

$$term \rightarrow term * factor$$

$$term \rightarrow term/factor$$

$$term \rightarrow factor$$

$$factor \rightarrow (Expression)$$

$$factor \rightarrow id$$

Here, $id$, +, –, *, (,), | are terminals

Expression, term, factor are non terminals

Expression is the start symbol.

## EXAMPLE 3

$$S \rightarrow aB$$
$$B \rightarrow cD$$
$$D \rightarrow \lambda$$

where,

$$V = \{S, B, D\}$$
$$T = \{a, c\}$$
$$S = \{S\}$$

## PROBLEM 1

Obtain context free Grammar to generate 0 or more number of A's.

## SOLUTION

Suppose, consider

$$A \rightarrow aA|a|\varepsilon$$
$$A \rightarrow aA$$
$$\rightarrow aaA$$
$$\rightarrow aa$$

where

$$V = \{A\}$$
$$T = \{a\}$$
$$S = \{A\}$$

and $p$ as shown above.

## PROBLEM 2

Obtain context free Grammar to generate strings of $a$'s and $b$'s of any length.

## SOLUTION

$$A \rightarrow aA|bA|\in$$

Suppose, consider

$$A \Rightarrow abA$$
$$\Rightarrow abaA \Rightarrow aba$$

Where,

$$V = \{A\}$$
$$T = \{a, b\}$$
$$S = \{A\}$$

and $p$ as shown above

## PROBLEM 3

Write a context free Grammar to generate strings of $a$'s and $b$'s starting with $ab$.

## SOLUTION

$$S \rightarrow ab\ A$$
$$A \rightarrow aA|bA|$$

Suppose

Consider,
$$S \rightarrow abA$$
$$\Rightarrow abaA$$
$$\Rightarrow ababA$$
$$\Rightarrow abab$$

where,
$$V = \{S, A\}$$
$$T = \{a, b\}$$
$$S = \{S\} \text{ and } p \text{ as shown above}$$

## PROBLEM 4

Obtain a CFG to generate $a$'s and $b$'s ending with $ab$.

## SOLUTION

$$S \rightarrow A\ ab$$
$$A \rightarrow aA|bA|\lambda.$$

Consider,
$$S \rightarrow Aab$$
$$\Rightarrow bAab$$
$$\Rightarrow baAab$$
$$\Rightarrow baab$$

where,
$$V = \{S, A\}$$
$$T = \{a, b\}$$
$$S = \{S\} \text{ and } P \text{ as shown above.}$$

## PROBLEM 5

Find a context free Grammar to generate a strings of $a$ and $b$ palindrome where

$$= \{a, b,\} \text{ [or } \{0, 1\}]$$

**OR**

Find a CFG for the Language

$$L(G) = \{WW^R : \text{we } \{a, b\}^*\}$$

## SOLUTION

$$S \rightarrow aSa|bsb|\in$$

**OR**

$$S \rightarrow aSa|bSb|\in$$
$$S \rightarrow a|b|\in$$

Suppose,

$$S \rightarrow asa$$
$$\Rightarrow absba$$
$$\Rightarrow abbsbba$$
$$\Rightarrow abbasabba$$
$$\Rightarrow abbaabba, \text{ which is in palindrome}$$

Here,     $V = \{S\}$
$$T = \{a, b\}$$
$$S = \{S\}$$

## PROBLEM 6

Obtain a context free Grammar to generate strings of $a$'s and $b$'s having substring $ab$.

## SOLUTION

First construct a DFA that accepts all strings with substring $ab$.

$$\delta(q_0, a) = q_1$$
$$\delta(q_0, b) = q_0$$
_____
$$\delta(q_1, a) = q_1$$
$$\delta(q_1, b) = q_2$$

$$\delta(q_2, a) = q_2$$
$$\delta(q_2, b) = q_2$$

The DFA can be rewritten as

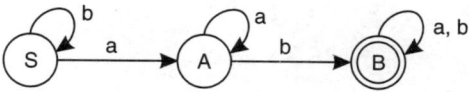

For above context free Grammar can be written as

$$S \rightarrow aA|bs$$
$$A \rightarrow aA|bB$$
$$B \rightarrow aB|bB|\lambda$$

where,    $V = \{S, A, B\}$

$T = \{a, b\}$

$S = \{S\}$

and $P$ as shown above

Consider,

$$S \rightarrow bs$$
$$\Rightarrow baA$$
$$\Rightarrow babB$$
$$\Rightarrow babaB$$
$$\Rightarrow baba, \text{ that has substring } ab.$$

## 3.3 LEFTMOST AND RIGHTMOST DERIVATIONS

In context free Grammars that **are** not linear (only one variable on the Right hand Side), a derivation may involve sentential form with more than one variable. In such cases. We have a choice in the order in which variable are replaced.

There are two types of derivations; Leftmost and Rightmost derivations.

A derivation is said to be **Leftmost,** if in each step, the leftmost variable in the sentential form is replaced.

A derivation is said to be **Rightmost,** if in each step, the right most variable in the sentential form is replaced.

**Example :**

Consider the Grammar,

$$S \rightarrow aAB$$
$$A \rightarrow bBb$$
$$B \rightarrow A|\lambda$$

Then

$$S \rightarrow a\underline{A}B$$
$$\Rightarrow ab\underline{B}bB$$
$$\Rightarrow abb\underline{B}$$
$$\Rightarrow abb$$

is the Leftmost derivation

$$S \rightarrow aA\underline{B}$$
$$\Rightarrow a\underline{A}$$
$$\Rightarrow a, b\underline{B}b$$
$$\Rightarrow abb$$

is the Rightmost derivation.

## Derivation Trees (Parse Tree)

A second way of showing derivations, independent of the order in which productions are used, by a derivation tree.

A derivation tree is an ordered tree is which nodes are labelled with the left side of the production and in which the children of a node represents its corresponding right side.

**Example :**

Figure shows a part of derivation tree for the productions

$$A \rightarrow abABC$$

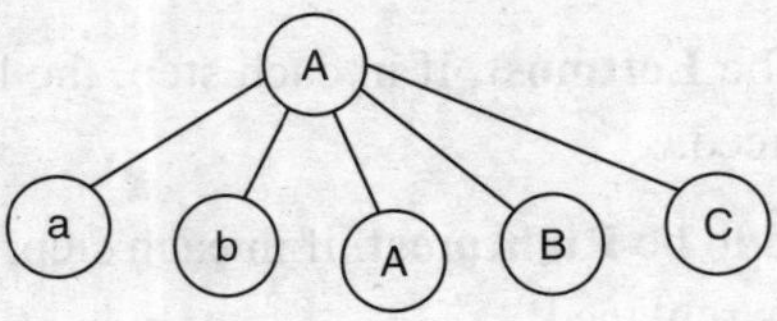

Leaf should be a terminal symbols for a **complete derivation tree,** otherwise it is a **partial derivation tree**.

The strings of symbols obtained by reading the leafs of the tree from left to right by omitting the $\lambda$'s encountered is said to be yield of a tree.

Consider the Grammar with productions.

$$S \rightarrow aAB$$

$$A \rightarrow bBb$$

$$B \rightarrow A|\lambda$$

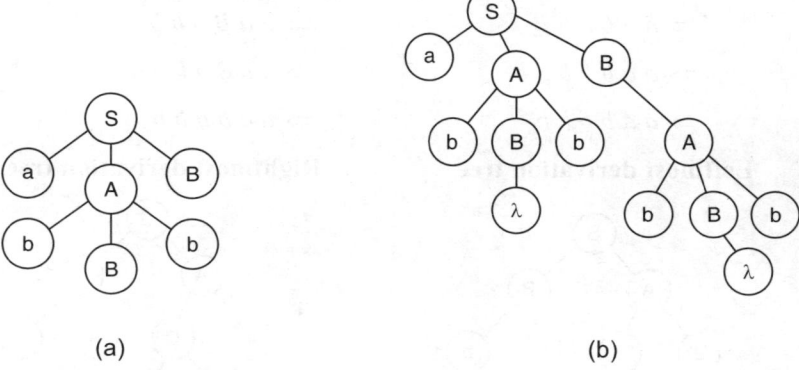

(a)  (b)

The tree in Figure (a) is a partial derivation tree, white the tree in Figure (b) is a complete derivation tree.

The string **abBbB** which is the yield of first tree is a **Sentential form** of G.

The yield of second tree, **abbbb** is a **Sentence** of G.

## PROBLEMS

### PROBLEM 1

*Obtain the Leftmost and Rightmost derivation for the String aabbbb with Grammer given below. Also write the derivation tree/Parse tree.*

$$S \rightarrow AB|\lambda$$

$$A \rightarrow aB$$

$$B \rightarrow Sb$$

## SOLUTION

| Leftmost derivation | Rightmost derivation |
|---|---|
| $S \rightarrow AB$ | $S \rightarrow A\underline{B}$ |
| $\Rightarrow a \underline{B} B$ | $\Rightarrow A \underline{S} b$ |
| $\Rightarrow a \underline{S} b B$ | $\Rightarrow \underline{A} b$ |
| $\Rightarrow a \underline{A} B b B$ | $\Rightarrow a \underline{B} b$ |
| $\Rightarrow a a \underline{B} B b B$ | $\Rightarrow a \underline{B} b b$ |
| $\Rightarrow a a \underline{S} b B b B$ | $\Rightarrow a A \underline{B} b b$ |
| $\Rightarrow a a b \underline{B} b B$ | $\Rightarrow a A \underline{B} b b b$ |
| $\Rightarrow a a b b b \underline{B}$ | $\Rightarrow a a \underline{B} b b b$ |
| $\Rightarrow a a b b b \underline{S} b$ | $\Rightarrow a a \underline{S} b b b b$ |
| $\Rightarrow a a b b b b$ | $\Rightarrow a a b b b b$ |

| Leftmost derivation tree | Rightmost derivation tree |
|---|---|

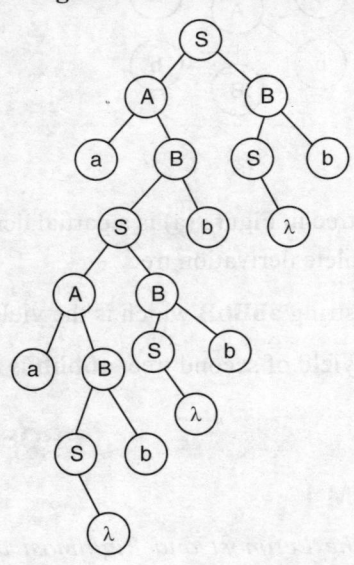

## PROBLEM 2

Obtain the Leftmost and Rightmost derivation for the Grammar.

$$S \rightarrow AS | \varepsilon$$

$$A \rightarrow aa | ab | ba | bb$$

for the string– (*i*) *aabbba*

(*ii*) *baabab*

and also obtain the derivation tree (Parse Tree)

## SOLUTION:

(*i*) For the string *aabbba*

| **Leftmost derivation** | **Rightmost derivation** |
|---|---|
| $S \rightarrow \underline{A}S$ | $S \rightarrow A\underline{S}$ |
| $\Rightarrow a\,a\,\underline{S}$ | $\Rightarrow A\,A\,\underline{S}$ |
| $\Rightarrow a\,a\,\underline{A}\,S$ | $\Rightarrow A\,A\,A\,\underline{S}$ |
| $\Rightarrow a\,a\,b\,b\,\underline{A}\,S$ | $\Rightarrow A\,\underline{A}\,b\,a$ |
| $\Rightarrow a\,a\,b\,b\,b\,a\,\underline{S}$ | $\Rightarrow \underline{A}\,b\,b\,b\,a$ |
| $\Rightarrow a\,a\,b\,b\,b\,a$ | $\Rightarrow a\,a\,b\,b\,b\,a$ |

| **Leftmost derivation Tree** | **Rightmost derivation tree** |
|---|---|

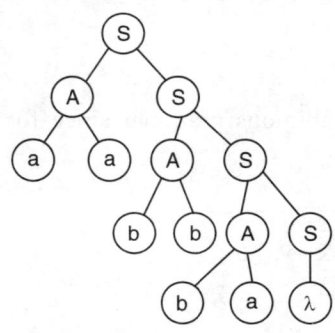
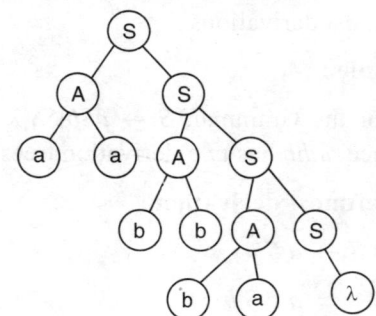

(*ii*) For the string *b a a b a b*

| **Leftmost derivation** | **Rightmost derivation** |
|---|---|
| $S \rightarrow \underline{A}\,S$ | $S \rightarrow A\,\underline{S}$ |
| $\Rightarrow b\,a\,\underline{S}$ | $\Rightarrow A\,A\,\underline{S}$ |
| $\Rightarrow ba\,\underline{A}\,S$ | $\Rightarrow A\,A\,A\,\underline{S}$ |
| $\Rightarrow b\,a\,a\,b\,\underline{S}$ | $\Rightarrow A\,A\,\underline{A}$ |
| $\Rightarrow b\,a\,a\,b\,\underline{A}\,S$ | $\Rightarrow A\,\underline{A}\,a\,b$ |
| $\Rightarrow b\,a\,a\,b\,a\,b\,\underline{S}$ | $\Rightarrow \underline{A}\,a\,b\,a\,b$ |
| $\Rightarrow b\,a\,a\,b\,a\,b$ | $\Rightarrow b\,a\,a\,b\,a\,b$ |

**Leftmost derivation tree**     **Rightmost derivation tree**

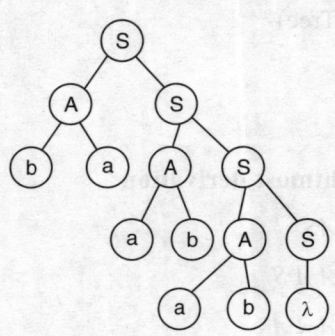 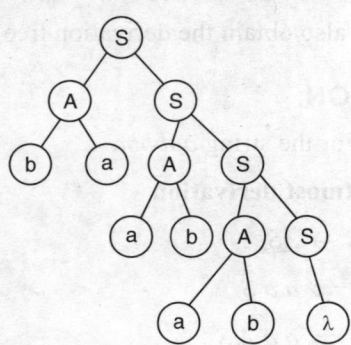

## Ambigious Grammar

**Definition:** A context free Grammar $G$ is said to be ambigious, if there exists some $\omega \in L(G)$ which has atleast two distint derivation trees.

Alternatively ambiguity implies the existence of two or more Leftmost or Rightmost derivations.

**Example :**

For the Grammar, $S \rightarrow aSb|SS|\lambda$ is as ambigious grammar since for the sentence *aabb* has two derivation trees.

**Leftmost derivation**

$(i)\ S \rightarrow a \underline{S} b$

$\quad \Rightarrow a a \underline{S} b b$

$\quad \Rightarrow a a b b$

$(ii)\ S \rightarrow \underline{S} S$

$\quad \Rightarrow a \underline{S} b S$

$\quad \Rightarrow a a \underline{S} b b S$

$\quad \Rightarrow a a b b \underline{S}$

$\quad \Rightarrow a a b b$

**Leftmost derivation trees**

$(i)$ 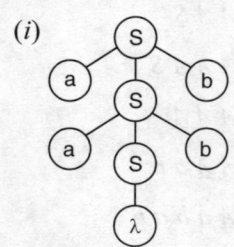      $(ii)$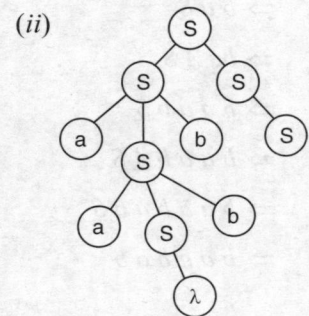

## PROBLEM 1

Consider a Grammer shown below from which any arithmetic expression can be obtained.

$$E \rightarrow E + E$$
$$E \rightarrow E - E$$
$$E \rightarrow E * E$$
$$E \rightarrow E/E$$
$$E \rightarrow id$$

Show that the Grammar is ambigious for the sentence $id + id * id$.

## SOLUTION

Leftmost derivation

(i)  $E \rightarrow E * E$

$\Rightarrow \underline{E} + E * E$

$\Rightarrow id + \underline{E} * E$

$\Rightarrow id + id * \underline{E}$

$\Rightarrow id + id * id$

(ii)  $E \rightarrow \underline{E} + E$

$\Rightarrow id + \underline{E}$

$\Rightarrow id + \underline{E} * E$

$\Rightarrow id + id * E$

$\Rightarrow id + id * id$

**Leftmost derivations trees**

(i)                          (ii)

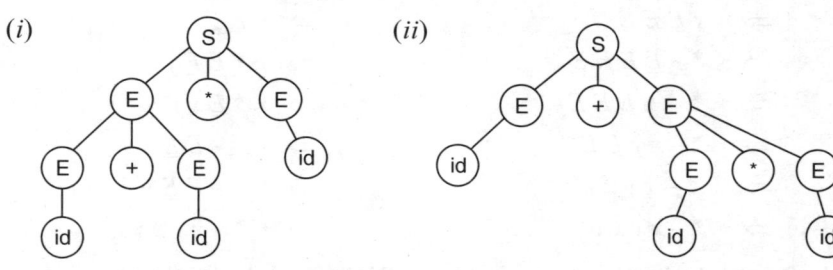

**Rightmost derivations**

(i)  $E \rightarrow E * \underline{E}$

$\Rightarrow \underline{E} * id$

$\Rightarrow E + \underline{E} * id$

$\Rightarrow \underline{E} + id * id$

$\Rightarrow id + id * id$

(ii)  $E \rightarrow E + \underline{E}$

$\Rightarrow E + E * \underline{E}$

$\Rightarrow E + \underline{E} * id$

$\Rightarrow \underline{E} + id * id$

$\Rightarrow id + id * id$

### Rightmost derivation trees

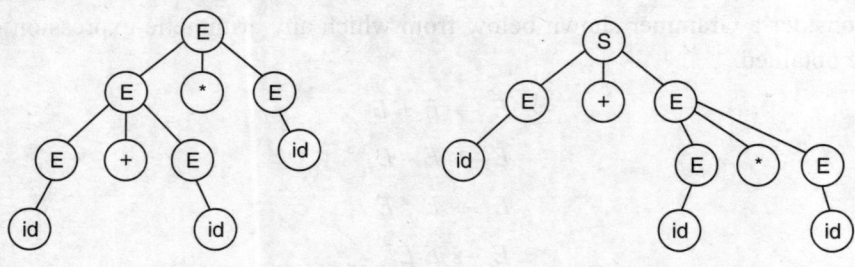

Since there exists two leftmost derivation and two Rightmost derivation, the given Grammar is ambigious.

## PROBLEM 2

The following Grammar generates the prefix expressions with operands $x$ and $y$ and binary operators +, -- and *. Production is given by

$$E \rightarrow + EE \mid * EE \mid - EE \mid x \mid y$$

Find the Leftmost and Rightmost derivations and the derivation tree for the string $+ * - x y x y$.

## SOLUTION

| Leftmost derivation | Rightmost derivation |
|---|---|
| $E \rightarrow + \underline{E} E$ | $E \rightarrow + E \underline{E}$ |
| $\Rightarrow + x \underline{E} E$ | $\Rightarrow + \underline{E} y$ |
| $\Rightarrow + * - \underline{E} E E E$ | $\Rightarrow + * E \underline{E} y$ |
| $\Rightarrow + * - x \underline{E} E E$ | $\Rightarrow + * \underline{E} x y$ |
| $\Rightarrow + * - x y \underline{E} E$ | $\Rightarrow + * - E \underline{E} x y$ |
| $\Rightarrow + * - x y x \underline{E}$ | $\Rightarrow + * - E \underline{E} x y$ |
| $\Rightarrow + * - x y x y$ | $\Rightarrow + * - x y x y$ |

**Leftmost derivation tree**

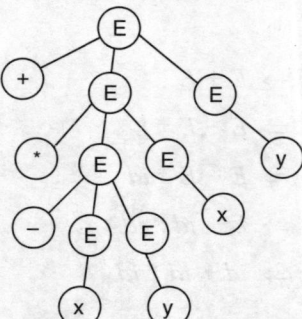

**Rightmost derivation tree**

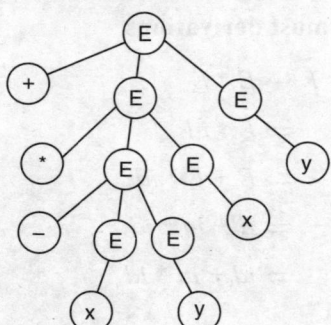

## PROBLEM 3

Consider the Grammar,

$$E \rightarrow E + E| \ E * E| - E|(E)| \ id$$

Obtain the Leftmost and Rightmost derivation for the string $-(id + id)$

## SOLUTION

**Leftmost derivation**

$E \rightarrow -E$
$\Rightarrow - (E)$
$\Rightarrow -(E + E)$
$\Rightarrow - (id + \underline{E})$
$\Rightarrow -(id + id)$

**Rightmost derivation**

$E \rightarrow - E$
$\Rightarrow - (E)$
$\Rightarrow -(E + E)$
$\Rightarrow -(\underline{E} + id)$
$\Rightarrow -(id + id)$

**Leftmost derivation tree**

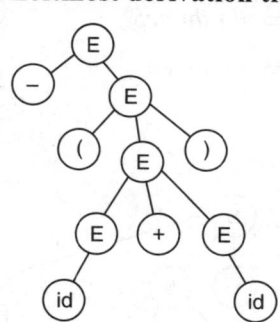

**Rightmost derivation tree**

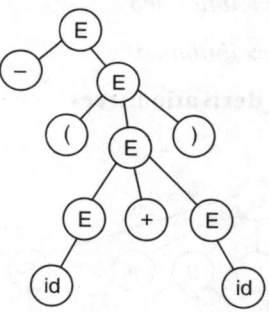

## 3.4    CONTEXT FREE GRAMMAR VERSUS REGULAR EXPRESSIONS

Grammars are more powerful notation than Regular Expression. Every construct that can be described by a Regular Expression can be described by a Grammar but not vice versa.

Alternatively every language is a Context Free Language but not vice versa.

**Example**

Consider the Regular Expression $(a/b)* \ abb$.

The Grammar is given by.

$$A_0 \rightarrow a \ A_0|bA_0|aA_1$$
$$A_1 \rightarrow bA_2$$
$$A_2 \rightarrow bA_3$$
$$A_3 \rightarrow \varepsilon$$

## PROBLEM 4

Show that the following Grammer is ambigious.

$$S \rightarrow ictS|ictSeS|a$$
$$C \rightarrow b$$

for the string *ibtibtaea*.

## SOLUTION

### Leftmost derivation

(i)   $S \rightarrow i \underline{c} t\ SeS$
       $\Rightarrow ibt\ \underline{SeS}$
       $\Rightarrow ibt\ i\underline{c}t\ SeS$
       $\Rightarrow ibtibt\ \underline{SeS}$
       $\Rightarrow ibtibt\ ae\underline{S}$
       $\Rightarrow ibtibtaea$

(ii)   $S \rightarrow i\underline{c}tS$
        $\Rightarrow ibt\underline{S}$
        $\Rightarrow ibt\ i\underline{c}t\ SeS$
        $\Rightarrow ibt\ ibt\ \underline{SeS}$
        $\Rightarrow ibt\ ibt\ ae\underline{S}$
        $\Rightarrow ibtibtaea$

### Leftmost derivation trees

(*i*)

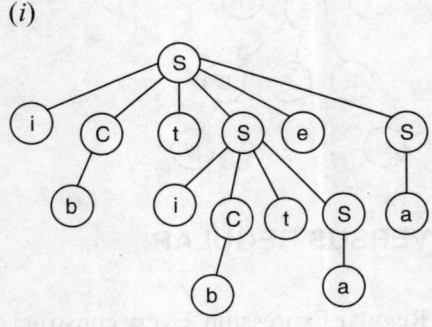

(*ii*)

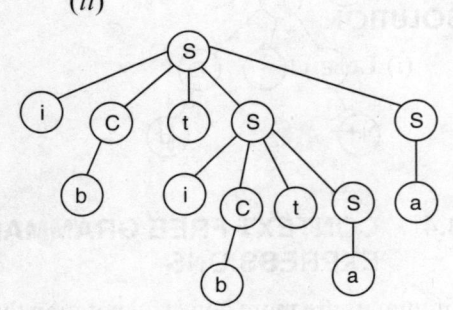

### Rightmost derivation

$S \rightarrow + ictSe\underline{S}$
$\Rightarrow ict\ \underline{Sea}$
$\Rightarrow ictict\ \underline{Sea}$
$\Rightarrow ict\ i\underline{c}taea$
$\Rightarrow i\underline{c}t\ ibtaea$
$\Rightarrow ibtibtaea$

$S \rightarrow ict\underline{S}$
$\Rightarrow ictictSe\underline{S}$
$\Rightarrow ictict\ \underline{Sea}$
$\Rightarrow icti\underline{c}taea$
$\Rightarrow i\underline{c}tibtaea$
$\Rightarrow ibtibtaea$

**Rightmost derivation trees**

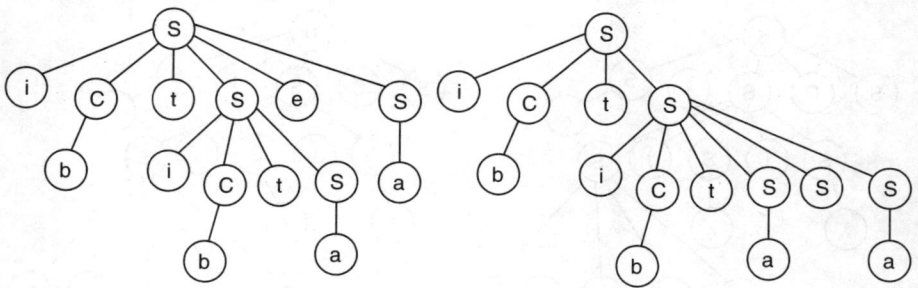

## PROBLEM 5

Given Grammar is

$$S \rightarrow S(S)S|\varepsilon \text{ for the string } (()())$$

    (*i*) Find the Leftmost derivation.

    (*ii*) Find the Rightmost derivation.

    (*iii*) Draw a parse tree.

## SOLUTION

| (*i*) Leftmost derivation | (*ii*) Rightmost derivation |
|---|---|
| $S \rightarrow \underline{S}(S)S$ | $S \rightarrow S(S)\underline{S}$ |
| $\Rightarrow (\underline{S})S$ | $\Rightarrow S(\underline{S})$ |
| $\Rightarrow (\underline{S}(S)S)S$ | $\Rightarrow S(S(S)\underline{S})$ |
| $\Rightarrow ((\underline{S})S)S$ | $\Rightarrow S(S\ (S)\ S(S)\ \underline{S})$ |
| $\Rightarrow (()\ \underline{S})S$ | $\Rightarrow S(S(S)\ S(\underline{S}))$ |
| $\Rightarrow (()\ \underline{S}(S)S)S$ | $\Rightarrow S(S(S)\ \underline{S}\ ())$ |
| $\Rightarrow (()\ (\underline{S})S)S$ | $\Rightarrow S(S(\underline{S})\ ())$ |
| $\Rightarrow (()\ ()\ \underline{S})\ S$ | $\Rightarrow S(\underline{S}\ ()\ ())$ |
| $\Rightarrow (()\ ())\underline{S}$ | $\Rightarrow \underline{S}\ (()\ ())$ |
| $\Rightarrow (()\ ())$ | $\Rightarrow (()\ ())$ |

**(ii) Leftmost derivation tree**    **(ii) Rightmost derivation tree**

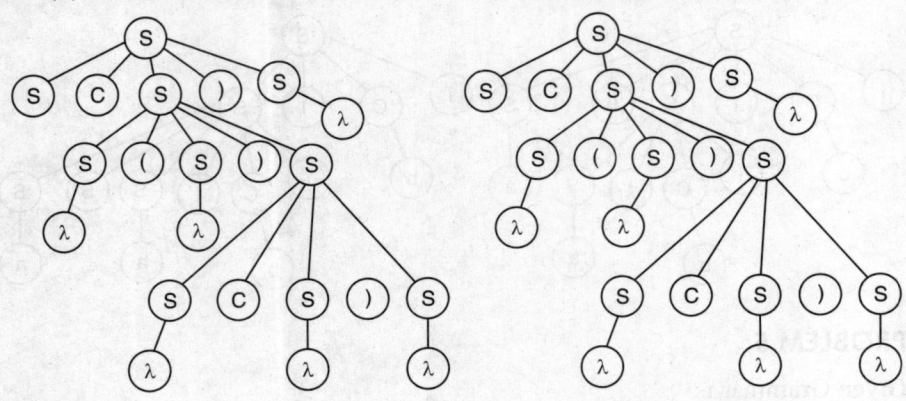

## Eliminating Ambiguity

Consider the Grammar

$$\text{Stmt} \rightarrow \text{if expr then stmt|}$$

$$\text{if expr then stmt else stmt|}$$

$$\text{other}$$

The grammar is ambigious, since the string if $E_1$ then if $E_2$ then $S_1$ else $S_2$ has two parse trees.

The two distinct Leftmost derivations and their corresponding parse trees are shown below.

(i)         Stmt $\rightarrow$ if <u>expr</u> then Stmt

$\Rightarrow$ if $E_1$ then <u>Stmt</u>

$\Rightarrow$ if $E_1$ then if <u>expr</u> then Stmt else Stmt

$\Rightarrow$ if $E_1$ then if $E_2$ then <u>Stmt</u> else Stmt

$\Rightarrow$ if $E_1$ then if $E_2$ then $S_1$ else <u>Stmt</u>

$\Rightarrow$ if $E_1$ then if $E_2$ then $S_1$ else $S_2$.

(*ii*)                    Stmt → if <u>Expr</u> then Stmt else Stmt

⇒ if $E_1$ then <u>Stmt</u> else stmt

⇒ if $E_1$ then if <u>expr</u> then Stmt else Stmt

⇒ if $E_1$ then if $E_2$ then <u>Stmt</u> else Stmt

⇒ if $E_1$ then if $E_2$ then $Si$ else <u>Stmt</u>

⇒ if $E_1$ then if $E_2$ then $Si$ else $S_2$

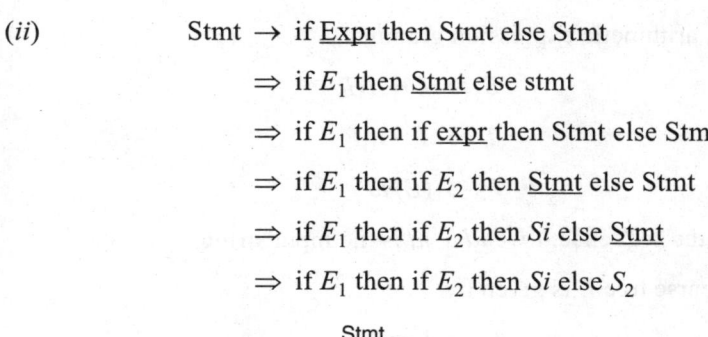

We can rewrite the following ambigus Grammar. The idea is that a statement appearing between a **then** and an else must be **matched**. The interior statement must not end with unmached or open statement.

A **Matched Statement** is either an if–then–else statement containing no open statements or it is any other kind of unconditional statement.

| Stmt | → matched–Stmt\|open-Stmt |
|------|---------------------------|
| matched–Stmt. | → if expr then matched–Stmt |
|  | else matched–Stmt\|Others. |
| Open–Stmt | → if expr then Stmt\| |
|  | if expr then matched–Stmt else open–Stmt |

**Note:** An ambigious grammar can be made nonambigious if the **left recursion** is removed from the grammar and **left factoring** is done.

## 3.5  LEFT RECURSION

**Elimination of Left Recursion:** A grammar is left-recursive if it has a non-terminal A such that there is a derivation.

A ⇒ A α for some string α.

Top down parsing methods cannot handle left recursive method. So a transformation is needed to eliminate it.

Consider, arithmetic expression grammar.

$$E \rightarrow E + T|T$$

$$T \rightarrow T * F|F$$

$$F \rightarrow (E)|id$$

Consider the sequence, $id + id + id$ is the input string.

Possible parse tree $E$ is given by.

$$E \rightarrow E + T$$

$$\Rightarrow E + T + T \text{ (replace } E \text{ by } E + T)$$

$$\Rightarrow E + T + T + T \text{ (replace } E \text{ by } E + T)$$

That is, it never reaches a match. So we never move on from the first token. Thus the grammar is Left Recursive.

The general form of Left Recursive Grammar is shown below.

$$A \rightarrow A\alpha \ |\beta \qquad\qquad ...(i)$$

Then we can eliminate Left Recursion by rewriting Left Recursion by rewriting the production as,

$$A \rightarrow \beta A' \qquad\qquad ...(ii)$$

$$A' \rightarrow \alpha A'|\varepsilon$$

We can also verify. Whether the modified grammar is equivalent to original or not.

Consider, $\beta \ \alpha \ \alpha \ \alpha$

From ($i$) we can have from ($ii$) we have

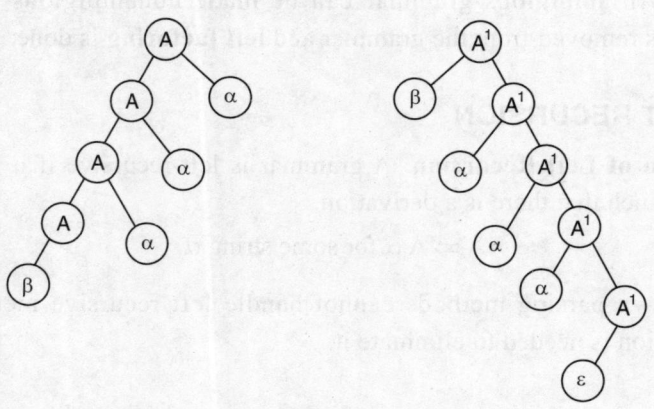

## PROBLEMS

## PROBLEM 1

Eliminate the Left Recursion from the following Grammar.

$$E \rightarrow E + T|T$$

$$T \rightarrow T * F|F$$

$$F \rightarrow (E)|id$$

## SOLUTION

We can map this grammar with the rule

$$A \rightarrow A \alpha |\beta'$$

Then using,

$$A \rightarrow \beta A'$$

$$A' \rightarrow A'|\varepsilon$$

We can say for

$$E \rightarrow E + T|T$$

Here        $A = E, \alpha = + T, \beta = T$

Then according to rule becomes.

$$E \rightarrow TE' \qquad \qquad ...(1)$$

$$E' \rightarrow + TE'|\varepsilon \qquad \qquad ...(2)$$

Similarly for, $T \rightarrow T * F|F$ becomes.

$$T \rightarrow FT' \qquad \qquad ...(3)$$

Here,        $A = T$

$$\alpha = *F$$

$$\beta = F$$

$$T \rightarrow *FT'|\in \qquad \qquad ...(4)$$

and            $F \rightarrow (E)|id$

Therefore after elimination of Left Recursion.

The equivalent grammar is,

$$E \rightarrow TE'$$

$$E' \rightarrow + TE'|\varepsilon$$

$$T \rightarrow FT'$$

$$T' \rightarrow *FT'|\varepsilon$$
$$F \rightarrow (E)|id$$

## PROBLEM 2

Eliminate the Left Recursion in the following Grammar

$$S \rightarrow Aa|b$$
$$A \rightarrow Ac|Sd|\varepsilon$$

## SOLUTION

There is no immediate Left Recursion among $S$ production. So nothing changes for productions.

The second production is replaced by.

$$A \rightarrow Ac|Aad|bd|\varepsilon \qquad ...(5)$$

and $\qquad S \rightarrow Aa|b \qquad\qquad ...(6)$

To eliminate Left Recursion among $A$ productions we apply the rules.

$$A \rightarrow bdA'|\varepsilon \qquad\qquad ...(7)$$

Here,    $\beta = bd$

$\qquad \alpha = c|ad$

$\qquad A = A$

$$A' \rightarrow CA'|adA'|\varepsilon \qquad ...(8)$$

Therefore after elimination of left recursion the equivalent grammar is.

$$S \rightarrow Aa|b$$
$$A \rightarrow bdA'/\varepsilon$$
$$A' \rightarrow CA'|adA'|\varepsilon$$

## PROBLEM 3

Remove the Left Recursion from the following grammar.

$$exp \rightarrow exp\ addop\ term/term$$
$$addop \rightarrow +/-$$
$$term \rightarrow term\ mulop\ factor/factor$$
$$mulop \rightarrow *$$
$$factor \rightarrow (exp)/number$$

## SOLUTION

Consider

$$exp \rightarrow exp \; addop \; term | term$$

Here,    $A$ = exp

$\alpha$ = addop term

$\beta$ = term

So,                $exp \rightarrow term \; exp'$

$exp' \rightarrow addop \; term \; exp' | \varepsilon$

Consider,

$$term \rightarrow term \; mulop \; factor | factor.$$

$term \rightarrow factor \; term'$        $A$ = term

$term' \rightarrow mulop \; factor \; term' | \varepsilon$    $\alpha$ = mulop factor

$\beta$ = factor

Therefore, after elimination of Left Recursion the equivalent grammar is,

$$exp \rightarrow term \; exp'$$

$$exp' \rightarrow addop \; term \; exp' | \varepsilon$$

$$addop \rightarrow + | -$$

$$term \rightarrow factor \; term'$$

$$term' \rightarrow mulop \; factor \; term' | \varepsilon$$

$$mulop \rightarrow *$$

$$factor \rightarrow (exp) | number$$

## PROBLEM 4

Eliminate Left Recursion from the following Grammar

$$lexp \rightarrow atom | list$$

$$atom \rightarrow number | identifier$$

$$list \rightarrow (lexp - Seq)$$

$$lexp–Seq \rightarrow lexp\text{-}Seq \; lexp | lexp$$

## SOLUTION

Consider,        $lexp–Seq \rightarrow lexp–seq \; lexp | lexp$

So,            $lexp–Seq \rightarrow lexp \; (lexp–seq)'$

$$(lexp–seq)' \rightarrow lexp \, (lexp – seq)'|\varepsilon$$

Therefore, after elminating Left Recursion the equivalent grammar is.

$$lexp \rightarrow atom|list$$

$$atom \rightarrow number|identifier$$

$$list \rightarrow lexp–Seq$$

$$lexp–Seq \rightarrow lexp \, (lexp–Seq)'$$

$$(lexp–Seq)' \rightarrow lexp \, (lexp–Seq)'|\varepsilon$$

**Note:**

Consider a Left Recursive Grammar,

$$A \rightarrow A\alpha,|A\alpha_2|A\alpha_3|... A\alpha_n|\beta_1|\beta_2...|\beta_m$$

The equivalent Left Recursion free Grammar is,

$$A \rightarrow \beta_1 \, A'|\beta_2 \, A'| .... \beta_m \, A'$$

$$A' \rightarrow \alpha_1 \, A'|\alpha_2 \, A'|... \alpha_n \, A'|\varepsilon$$

## PROBLEM 5

Remove Left Recursion from the following Grammar.

$$A \rightarrow Ba|Aa|C$$

$$B \rightarrow Bb|Ab|d$$

## SOLUTION

Consider,                          $A \rightarrow Ba|Aa|C$

Here,        $\alpha = a$

$\beta_1 = Ba$

$\beta_2 = C$

$$A \rightarrow BaA'|CA'$$

$$A' \rightarrow aA'|\in$$

Consider,          $B \rightarrow Bb|Ab|d$

$\Rightarrow$          $B \rightarrow Bb|BaA'b|CA'b|d$

Here,      $A = B$                                    [Replace $A$ by]

$\alpha_1 = b$                                        $A \rightarrow BaA'|CA']$

$\alpha_2 = aA'b$

$$\beta_1 = CA'b$$

$$\beta_2 = d$$

So,    $$B \rightarrow CA'b\ B'|dB'$$

$$B' \rightarrow bB'|aA'bB'|\varepsilon$$

Therefore, after eliminating Left Recursion, the equivalent grammar is,

$$A \rightarrow BaA'|CA'$$

$$A' \rightarrow aA'|\varepsilon$$

$$B \rightarrow CA'bB'|dB'|dB'$$

$$B' \rightarrow bB'|aA'bB'|\varepsilon$$

## 3.6  LEFT FACTORING

If the Grammar is left factored, then it becomes suitable for use.

Left factoring is used when it is not clear that which of the two alternatives is used to expand the Non-terminals.

In General, if $A \rightarrow \alpha\beta_1|\alpha\beta_2$

is a production, then it is not possible for us to take a decision whether to choose first or second. In such a situation, the above grammer can be left factored as.

$$A \rightarrow \alpha\ A'$$

$$A' \rightarrow \beta_1|\beta_2$$

## PROBLEM 1

Left factor the following Grammar.

$$E \rightarrow iEtS|iEtSeS|a$$

$$E \rightarrow b$$

## SOLUTION

$$E \rightarrow iEtSE'|a$$

$$E' \rightarrow eS|\varepsilon$$

$$E \rightarrow b$$

## PROBLEM 2

Left Factor the following Grammar

$$Exp \rightarrow term + exp|term.$$

## SOLUTION

$$Exp \rightarrow term. \; Exp'$$
$$Exp \rightarrow + exp|\varepsilon$$

## PROBLEM 3

Left factor the following Grammar

$$lexp \rightarrow atom|list$$
$$atom \rightarrow number|identifier$$
$$list \rightarrow (lexp\text{--}seq)$$
$$lexp\text{--}seq \rightarrow lexp, lexp\text{--}seq|lexp$$

## SOLUTION

$$lexp \rightarrow atom|list$$
$$atom \rightarrow number|identifier$$
$$list \rightarrow (lexp\text{--}seq)$$
$$lexp\text{--}seq \rightarrow lexp \; (lexp\text{--}Seq)'$$
$$(lexp\text{--}Seq)' \rightarrow , lexp\text{--}Seq|\varepsilon$$

## PROBLEM 4

Consider the Grammar,

$$E \rightarrow E + T|T$$
$$T \rightarrow id|id \; []| \; id \; [X]$$
$$X \rightarrow E, E|E$$

(a) Eliminate Left Recursion.

(b) Eliminate Left Factoring.

## SOLUTION

(a) Consider, $E \rightarrow E + T/T$

Here,

$$A = E \qquad\qquad A \rightarrow Aa|b$$
$$\alpha = +T \qquad\qquad \Downarrow$$
$$\beta = T \qquad\qquad A \rightarrow \beta A''$$
$$\qquad\qquad\qquad A' \rightarrow \alpha A/\varepsilon''$$

So,                              $E \rightarrow TE'$

$E' \rightarrow + TE'|\varepsilon$

Consider,              $T \rightarrow id|id \;[]| \; id \;[x]$    It remains same.

$X \rightarrow E, E|E$                It remains same.

So after elimination of Left Recursion, the equivalent grammar is,

$E \rightarrow TE'$

$E' \rightarrow +TE'|\varepsilon$

$T \rightarrow id|id \;[]| \; id \;[x]$

$X \rightarrow E, E|E$

### (b) Step 2

$E \rightarrow TE'$

$E' \rightarrow +TE'|\varepsilon$

$T \rightarrow id \; T'$

$T' \rightarrow [T''|\varepsilon$

$T'' \rightarrow ]|X]$

$X \rightarrow EX'$

$X' \rightarrow E|E$

## PROBLEM 5

Consider the Grammar,

$rexpr \rightarrow rexpr + rterm|rterm$

$rterm \rightarrow rterm \; rfactor|rfactor$

$rfactor \rightarrow rfactor * |rprimary$

$rprimary \rightarrow a|b$

(a) Left factoring

(b) Left Recursion from original grammar.

## SOLUTION

### (a) Left factoring:

$rexpr \rightarrow rexpr' \; rterm.$

$rexpr' \rightarrow rexpr + |\varepsilon$

$rterm \rightarrow rterm' \; rfactor$

$$rterm' \rightarrow rterm$$
$$rfactor \rightarrow rfactor * |rprimary$$
$$rprimary \rightarrow a|b$$

## (b) Left Recursion:

Consider.

$$rexpr \rightarrow rexpr + rterm|rterm$$

Here,     $A$ = rexpr
$\alpha$ = + rterm
$\beta$ = rterm

So,                    rexpr $\rightarrow$ rterm rexpr'
rexpr' $\rightarrow$ + rterm rexpr'|$\varepsilon$

Consider,

$$rterm \rightarrow rterm\ rfactor|rfactor$$

Here,     $A$ = rterm
$\alpha$ = rfactor
$\beta$ = rfactor

So,                    rterm $\rightarrow$ rfactor rterm'
rterm' $\rightarrow$ rfactor rterm'|$\varepsilon$

Consider,

$$rfactor \rightarrow rfactor*|rprimary$$

Here,     $A$ = rfactor
$\alpha$ = *
$\beta$ = rprimary

So,                    rfactor $\rightarrow$ rprimary rfactor'
rfactor' $\rightarrow$ *rfactor'|$\varepsilon$

Therefore after Eliminating Left Recursion the equivalent Grammar is,

$$rexpr \rightarrow rterm\ rexpr'$$
$$rexpr' \rightarrow + rterm\ rexpr'|\varepsilon$$
$$rterm \rightarrow rfactor\ rterm'$$
$$rterm' \rightarrow rfactor\ rterm'|\varepsilon$$
$$rfactor \rightarrow rprimary\ rfactor'$$
$$rfactor' \rightarrow * rfactor'|\varepsilon$$
$$rprimary \rightarrow a|b$$

## 3.7  PARSING TECHNIQUES

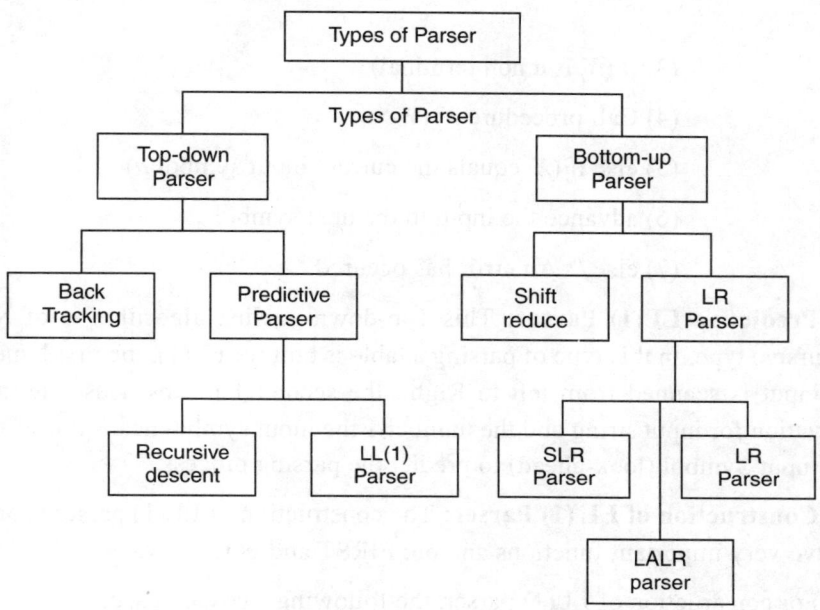

## Top-down Parser

**Predictive Parser:** As the name suggests, the predictive parser tries to predict the next construction using one or more look-ahead symbols from input string.

There are two types of predictive parsers:

1. Recursive Descent.

2. LL (1) Parser [Non-Recursive Descent].

*(i)* **Recursive Descent:** A parser that uses collection of recursive procedures for parsing the given input string is called recursive descent.

In this type of parser, the CFG is used to build the recursive routines. The RHS of the production rule is directly converted to a program. For each non-terminal (variable), a separate procedure is written.

## Algorithm for Recursive Descent

Void $A()$

{

(1) Choose a $A$-production, $A \rightarrow x_1, x_2, .... x_k$

(2) for ($i = 1$ to $k$)

    {

          (3) if ($X_i$ is a non terminal)

          (4) Call procedure $X_i$ ();

          (5) else if ($X_i$ equals the current input symbol $a$)

          (6) advance the input to the next symbol;

          (7) else /* An error has occured */

**Predictive LL(1) Parser:** This Top-down parsing algorithm is of Non-Recursive type. In this type of parsing a table is buit for LL(1), the first L means the input is scanned from left to Right, the second 1 means it uses leftmost derivation for input string and the number 1 the input symbol neans it uses only one input Symbol (look-ahead) to predict the parsing process.

**Construction of LL (1) Parser:** The construction of LL(1) parser is based on two very important functions and on: FIRST and FOLLOW.

For construction of LL(1) parser, the following steps are used.

1. Computation of FIRST and FOLLOW functions.

2. Construct the predictive parsing table using FIRST and FOLLOW functions.

3. Parse the input string with the help of predictive parsing table.

## First and Follow Functions

**FIRST:** First ($\alpha$) is a set of **terminal symbols** that are first symbols appearing at RHS in derivation of $\alpha$.

If $\alpha \overset{*}{\Rightarrow} \epsilon$, Then $\epsilon$ is also in FIRST ($\alpha$).

To compute FIRST ($X$) for all the grammar symbols $X$, apply the following rules, until no more terminals or $\epsilon$ can be added to any first set.

1. If $X$ is a terminal, then FIRST ($X$) = {$X$}

2. If $X \rightarrow \epsilon$ is a production, then FIRST ($X$) = {$\epsilon$}

3. If $X$ is a non terminal and $X \rightarrow Y_1, Y_2, ... Y_k$ then FIRST ($X$) = FIRST ($Y_1$), U FIRST ($Y_2$)U....FIRST ($Y_K$)

# FOLLOW

FOLLOW $(A)$ is defined as the set of terminal symbols appear immediately to the Right of $A$. To compute Follow $(A)$ for all **Non terminals** $A$, apply the following rules until nothing can be added to any FOLLOW Set.

1. For the start symbol $S$, place $ in FOLLOW $(S)$

2. If there is a production,

    $A \to \alpha\ B\beta$

    Then everything in FIRST$(\beta)$ without $\varepsilon$ is to be placed in FOLLOW$(B)$

3. If there is a production.

    $A \to \alpha\ B\beta$ or $A \to \alpha B$ and FIRST $(\beta) = \{\varepsilon\}$ then, FOLLOW $(A)$ = FOLLOW $(B)$

**or**

$$\text{FOLLOW } (B) = \text{FOLLOW } (A)$$

That means, everything in FOLLOW$(A)$ is in FOLLOW$(B)$

## PROBLEM 1

For the following Grammar

$$E \to TE'$$
$$E \to +TE'|\varepsilon$$
$$T \to FT'$$
$$T' \to *FT'|\varepsilon$$
$$F \to (E)|id$$

Find the FIRST and FOLLOW Sets.

## SOLUTION

**Step 1:** First find FIRST and FOLLOW set.

**FIRST(E):** As $E \to TE'$ is a rule in which the first symbol at RHS is $T$

Now $T \to FT'$, in which the first symbol at RHS is $F$

And $F \to (E)/id$

$\therefore$ FIRST $(E)$ = FIRST $(T)$ = FIRST $(F)$

As $F \to (E)|id$

Hence FIRST $(E)$ = FIRST $(T)$ = FIRST $(F)$ = {(, $id$}

FIRST $(T')$ = {*, $\varepsilon$}, FIRST $(E')$ = {+, $\varepsilon$)

FOLLOW Set:

**FOLLOW** $(E)$ As there is a rule.

$$F \rightarrow (E)|id$$

The symbol ')' immediately to the right of $E$

Hence, ')' will be FOLLOW $(E)$

($i$) The computation rule is, $\alpha\,B\,\beta$

we can map this rule with $F \rightarrow (E)|id$

Then,                        $A = F$

$\alpha = ($

$B = E$

$\beta = )$

$\therefore$             Follow $(B)$ = FIRST $(\beta) - \varepsilon$

*i.e.,*        FOLLOW$(E)$ = FIRST $()) - \varepsilon$

= {)}

Since $E$ is a start symbol, add \$ to the FOLLOW $(E)$.

Hence, FOLLOW $(E)$ = {), \$}

**FOLLOW (E')**

($i$) Consider, $E \rightarrow TE'$

we can map this rule with $A \rightarrow \alpha B\beta$

Here,      $A = E$

$\alpha = T$

$B = E'$

$\beta = \varepsilon$

$\therefore$              FOLLOW $(E')$ = FOLLOW $(E)$

= {), \$}

($ii$)   Consider $E' \rightarrow + TE'|\varepsilon$

We can map this with rule $A \rightarrow \alpha B\beta$

Here,     $A = E'$

$\alpha = +T$

$B = E'$

$\beta = \varepsilon$

$\therefore$         Follow $(E')$ = FOLLOW $(E')$

= $\{), \$\}$

## FOLLOW (T)

(i) Consider, $E \rightarrow TE'$

We can map it with rule $A \rightarrow \alpha B\beta$

Here     $A = E$

$\alpha = \varepsilon$

$B = T$

$\beta = E'$

So,          FOLLOW $(T)$ = FIRST $(E') - \varepsilon$

= $\{+, \varepsilon\} - \{\varepsilon\}$

= $\{+\}$

(ii) Consider, $E' \rightarrow + TE'|\varepsilon$

We can map this with the rule, $A \rightarrow \alpha B\beta$

Where,                    $A = E'$

$\alpha = +$

$B = T$

$\beta = E'$

So,          FOLLOW $(T)$ = FIRST $(E') - \varepsilon$

= $\{+, \varepsilon\} - \{\varepsilon\}$

= $\{+\}$

(ii) Again consider, $E' \rightarrow + TE'|\varepsilon$

Since $E' \rightarrow \varepsilon$ put $E'$ as $\varepsilon$ in $E' \rightarrow + TE'$

$\therefore$                    $E' \rightarrow +T$

Now we can map this with rule, $A \rightarrow \alpha B\beta$

Here,     $A = E'$

$$\alpha = +$$
$$B = T$$
$$\beta = \varepsilon$$

So          FOLLOW $(T)$ = FOLLOW$(E')$ = {), \$}

$\therefore$          FOLLOW $(T)$ = {+, ), \$}

## FOLLOW $(T')$

(i) Consider, $T \to FT'$

Here          FOLLOW $(T')$ = FOLLOW $(T)$

$$= \{+, ), \$\}$$

(ii) Consider $T' \to *FT'|\varepsilon$

FOLLOW $(T')$ = FOLLOW $(T')$

$$= \{+, ), \$\}$$

## FOLLOW $(F)$

(i) Consider, $T \to FT'$

Now,          FOLLOW $(F)$ = FIRST $(T') - \varepsilon$

$$= \{*, \varepsilon\} - \{\varepsilon\}$$

$$= \{*\}$$

(ii) Consider, $T' \to *FT'|\varepsilon$

Now,          FOLLOW $(F)$ = FIRST $(T') - \varepsilon$

$$= \{*, \varepsilon\} - \{\varepsilon\}$$

$$= \{*\}$$

(ii) Now, again consider,   $T' \to *FT'$

Substituting $\varepsilon$ for $T'$ we get

$$T' \to *F$$

$\therefore$          FOLLOW $(F)$ = FOLLOW $(T')$

$$= \{+, ), \$\}$$

$\therefore$          FOLLOW $(F)$ = {*, +, ), \$}

To summarize the above computations

FIRST $(E)$ = {(, $id$}

$$\text{FIRST } (E') = \{+, \varepsilon\}$$

$$\text{FIRST } (T) = \{(, id\}$$

$$\text{FIRST } (T') = \{*, \varepsilon\}$$

$$\text{FIRST } (F) = \{(, id\}$$

$$\text{FOLLOW } (E) = \{), \$\}$$

$$\text{FOLLOW } (E') = \{), \$\}$$

$$\text{FOLLOW } (T) = \{+, ), \$\}$$

$$\text{FOLLOW } (T') = \{+, ), \$\}$$

$$\text{FOLLOW } (F) = \{+, *, ), \$\}$$

## Constructing the Predictive Parsing Table using First and Follow Functions

**Algorithm for Predective Parsing Table:** The construction of predective parsing table is an important activity in predictive parsing method this algorithm requires FIRST and FOLLOW functions.

input : The Context Free Grammar $G$

output : Predictive Parsing Table $M$

**Algorithm:** For the rule $A \rightarrow \alpha$ of the grammar $G$.

1. For each '$a$' in FIRST $(\alpha)$ create entry.

   $$M[A, a] = A \rightarrow \alpha$$

   where '$a$' is a terminal symbol.

2. For $\varepsilon$ in FIRST $(\alpha)$ create entry,

   $$M[A, b] = A \rightarrow \alpha$$

   where '$b$' is the symbols from FOLLOW $(A)$.

3. If $\varepsilon$ is in FIRST $(\alpha)$ and $\$$ is in FOLLOW$(A)$ then create entry in the table $M[A, \$] = A \rightarrow \alpha$

4. All the remaining entries in the table $M$ are empty and set to $M[A, a]$ to Error.

**Step 2:** Now to Fill the entries in the table, consider the production one by one.

(1) $E \rightarrow TE'$

Compare it with value    $A \rightarrow \alpha$

Here,    $A = E$

$\alpha = TE'$

FIRST $(TE')$ if $E' = \varepsilon$

Then    FIRST $(T) = \{(, id\}$

$M[E, (] = E \rightarrow TE'$

$M[E, id] = E \rightarrow TE'$

(2) $E' \rightarrow + TE'$

Compare it with rute $A \rightarrow \alpha$

Here,    $A = E'$

$\alpha = +TE'$

FIRST $(+TE') = \{+\}$

$M[E', +] = E' \rightarrow +TE'$

(3) $E' \rightarrow \varepsilon$

Compare it with rule $A \rightarrow \alpha$

Here,    $A = E'$

$\alpha = \varepsilon$

$\therefore$    FOLLOW $(E') = \{), \$\}$

$M[E', )] = E' \rightarrow \varepsilon$

$M[E', \$] = E' \rightarrow \varepsilon$

(4) $T \rightarrow FT'$

Compare it with rule $A \rightarrow \alpha$

Here,    $A = T$

$\alpha = FT'$

$\therefore$ FIRST$(FT') = $ FIRST $(F) = \{\langle, id\}$

$\therefore$    $M[T, (] = T \rightarrow FT'$

$M[T, id] = T \rightarrow FT'$

(5) $T' \rightarrow *FT'$

Compare it with rule $A \rightarrow \alpha$

Here,    $A = T'$

$\alpha = *FT'$

$$\text{FIRST } (*FT') = \{*\}$$

$$M[T', *] = T' \rightarrow *FT'$$

(6) $T' \rightarrow \varepsilon$

Compare it with the rule $A \rightarrow \alpha$

Here,    $A = T'$

$\alpha = \varepsilon$

$$\text{FOLLOW } (T') = \{+, ), \$\}$$

$$M[T', +] = T' \rightarrow \varepsilon$$

$$M[T', )] = T' \rightarrow \varepsilon$$

$$M[T', \$] = T' \rightarrow \varepsilon$$

(7) $F \rightarrow (E)$

Compare it with the rule $A \rightarrow \alpha$

Here,    $A = F$

$\alpha = (E)$

$$\text{FIRST } ((E)) = \{(\}$$

$\therefore$        $M[F, (] = F \rightarrow (E)$

(8) $F \rightarrow id$

Compare it with the rule $A \rightarrow \alpha$

Here,    $A = F$

$\alpha = id$

$$\text{FIRST } (id) = \{id\}$$

$\therefore$        $M[F, id] = F \rightarrow id$

| Non Terminal | Input Symbols | | | | | |
|---|---|---|---|---|---|---|
| | id | + | * | ( | ) | $ |
| $E$ | $E \rightarrow TE'$ | | | $E \rightarrow TE'$ | | |
| $E'$ | | $E' + TE'$ | | | $E' \rightarrow \varepsilon$ | $E' \rightarrow \varepsilon$ |
| $T$ | $T \rightarrow FT'$ | | | $T \rightarrow FT'$ | | |
| $T'$ | | $T' \rightarrow \varepsilon$ | $T' \rightarrow *FT'$ | | $T' \rightarrow \varepsilon$ | $T' \rightarrow \varepsilon$ |
| $F$ | $F \rightarrow id$ | | | $F \rightarrow (E)$ | | |

**Step 3:** Parse the input string with the help of predictive parsing table.

Consider the input string.

$$id + id * id \$$$

## Procedure

At the beginning the stack contains the start symbol and $ at the bottom. The input string is parsed for each of its input symbol.

| Matched | Stack | Input | Action |
|---------|-------|-------|--------|
| | E$ | id + id * id $ | — |
| | TE' $ | id + id * id $ | $E \rightarrow TE'$ |
| | FT' E' $ | id + id * id $ | $T \rightarrow FT'$ |
| | id T'E'$ | id + id * id $ | $F \rightarrow id$ |
| id | T'E'$ | + id * id $ | Match id |
| id | E'$ | + id * id $ | $T' \rightarrow \varepsilon$ |
| id | + TE'$ | ± id * id $ | $E' \rightarrow + TE'$ |
| id + | TE'$ | id * id $ | Match + |
| id + | FT'E'$ | id * id $ | $T \rightarrow FT'$ |
| id + | idT'E'$ | id * id$ | $F \rightarrow id$ |
| id + id | T'E'$ | *id$ | Match id |
| id + id | * FT' E' $ | * id$ | $T' \rightarrow * FT'$ |
| id + id* | FT' E' $ | id$ | Match* |
| id + id* | id T' E' $ | id $ | $F \rightarrow id$ |
| id + id * id | T' E' $ | $ | Match id |
| id + id * id | E'$ | $ | $T' \rightarrow \varepsilon$ |
| id + id * id | $ | $ | $E' \rightarrow \varepsilon$ |

In the first step, the top element on the stack is $E$ and the first input symbol is id Thus the parsing table is searched for $M[E, id]$ which gives the production, $E \rightarrow TE'$. This tells us that $E$ is replaced by $TE'$.

In the second step, the top element on the stack is T and the input symbol is id, is searched for a production, *i.e.,* $M[T, id] = T \rightarrow FT'$. Thus $FD'$ is pushed replacing $T$.

In the third step, top element is $F$ and the input symbol is again id, thus $M[F, id] = F \rightarrow id$. Thus a terminal id is pushed onto stack replacing $F$.

In the fourth step, the topelement is id and the input symbol in the input string is also id, thus they are matched and are popped out of stack.

Similarly the production is searched in the parsing table in each grammar symbol in given input symbol.

Finally, when $ is in top element and input string is also $ we say that given input is accepted by the grammar.

## PROBLEM 2

Obtain the FIRST and FOLLOW for the following Grammar.

$$exp \rightarrow exp\ addop\ term$$
$$exp \rightarrow term$$
$$addop \rightarrow +$$
$$addop \rightarrow -$$
$$term \rightarrow term\ mulop\ factor$$
$$term \rightarrow factor$$
$$mulop \rightarrow *$$
$$factor \rightarrow (exp)$$
$$factor \rightarrow number.$$

## SOLUTION

$$FIRST\ (exp) = FIRST\ (term) = FIRST\ (factor)$$
$$= \{(, number\}$$
$$FIRST\ (addop) = \{+, -\}$$
$$FIRST\ (mulop) = \{*\}$$

**FOLLOW Set:**

**FOLLOW (exp):**

(*i*) Consider $\qquad exp \rightarrow exp\ addop\ term$

$$FOLLOW\ (exp) = FIRST\ (addop) - \varepsilon$$
$$= \{+, -\} - \{\varepsilon\}$$
$$= \{+, -\}$$

Since exp is the first production add $

(*ii*) Consider $\qquad Factor \rightarrow (exp)$

$$FOLLOW\ (exp) = \{)\}$$
$$\therefore \qquad FOLLOW\ (exp) = \{+, -, ), \$\}$$

**FOLLOW (addop):**

Consider, $exp \rightarrow exp\ addop\ term$

$$\therefore \qquad FOLLOW\ (addop) = FIRST\ (term) - \varepsilon$$
$$= \{(, number\} - \{\varepsilon\}$$
$$FOLLOW\ (addop) = \{(, number\}$$

## FOLLOW (term):

(*i*) Consider           exp $\rightarrow$ term

∴            FOLLOW (term)  =  FOLLOW (exp)

∴            FOLLOW (term)  =  {+, −, ), $}

(*i*) exp $\rightarrow$ exp addop term

            FOLLOW (term)  =  FOLLOW (exp) = {+, −, ), $}

(*ii*) term $\rightarrow$ term mulop factor

            FOLLOW (term)  =  FIRST (mulop) − {ε}

                    =  {*}

∴            FOLLOW (term)  =  {*, +, −, ), $}

## FOLLOW (mulop):

term $\rightarrow$ term mulop factor

∴            FOLLOW (mulop)  =  FIRST (factor) − ε

                    =  {(, number} − {ε}

                    =  {(, number}

## FOLLOW (factor):

(*i*) Consider term $\rightarrow$ term mulop factor

∴            FOLLOW (factor)  =  FOLLOW (term)

                    =  {*, +, −, ), $}

(*ii*) term $\rightarrow$ factor

            FOLLOW (factor)  =  FOLLOW (term)

                    =  {*, +, −, ), $}

To Summarize the above computations:

## FIRST Set:

                FIRST (exp)    =  {(, number}

                FIRST (addop)  =  {+, −}

                FIRST (term)   =  {(, number}

                FIRST (mulop)  =  {*}

                FIRST (factor) =  {(, number}

**FOLLOW Set:**

$$\text{FOLLOW (exp)} = \{+, -, ), \$\}$$
$$\text{FOLLOW (addop)} = \{\langle, \text{number}\}$$
$$\text{FOLLOW (term)} = \{*, +, -, ), \$\}$$
$$\text{FOLLOW (mulop)} = \{\langle, \text{number}\}$$
$$\text{FOLLOW (factor)} = \{*, +, -, ), \$\}$$

## PROBLEM 3

Obtain FIRST and FOLLOW Set for the given Grammar

$$\text{Statement} \rightarrow \text{if\_stmt|other.}$$
$$\text{if\_stmt} \rightarrow \text{if (exp) statement else part}$$
$$\text{else-part} \rightarrow \text{else statement|}\varepsilon$$
$$\text{exp} \rightarrow 0|1$$

## SOLUTION

**First Set:**

$$\text{FIRST (Statement)} = \text{FIRST (if\_stmt)} = \{\text{if, Other}\}$$
$$\text{FIRST(else\_part)} = \{\text{else, }\varepsilon\}$$
$$\text{FIRST (exp)} = \{0, 1\}$$

**FOLLOW Set:**

**FOLLOW (Statement):**

(*i*) if_stmt → if (exp) statement else-part

∴    FOLLOW (Statement) = FIRST (else-part) – ε

= {else}

(*i*) else_ part → else statement

∴ FOLLOW (Statement) = FOLLOW (else_part)

**FOLLOW (else-part):**

if_stmt → if (exp) Statement else-part

∴    FOLLOW (else-part) = FOLLOW (if_Stmt)

**FOLLOW (if_Stmt):**

Statement → if_stmt|other

**FOLLOW (exp):**

$$\text{if\_Stmt} \rightarrow \text{if (exp) Statement else\_part}$$

$$\text{Follow (exp)} = \{)\}$$

## PROBLEM 4

Consider the Grammar

$$S \rightarrow AaAb$$

$$S \rightarrow BbBa$$

$$A \rightarrow \varepsilon$$

$$B \rightarrow \varepsilon$$

Show that the grammar is LL(1)

## SOLUTION

**Step 1:** Find the FIRST and FOLLOW set

**FIRST Set:**

FIRST $(S)$ = FIRST $(A)$ = $\{\varepsilon\}$, When $A = \varepsilon$, FIRST $(S)$ = $\{a\}$

FIRST $(S)$ = FIRST $(B)$ = $\{\varepsilon\}$ When $B = \varepsilon$, FIRST $(S)$ = $\{b\}$

$\therefore$            FIRST $(S)$ = $\{a, b, \varepsilon\}$

**FOLLOW Set:**

$$\text{FOLLOW } (A) = \{a, b\}$$

$$\text{FOLLOW } (B) = \{b, a\}$$

$$\text{FOLLOW } (S) = \{\$\}$$

The above computations are summarized are

$$\text{FIRST } (S) = \{a, b, \varepsilon\}$$

$$\text{FIRST } (A) = \{\varepsilon\}$$

$$\text{FIRST } (B) = \{\varepsilon\}$$

$$\text{FOLLOW } (S) = \{\$\}$$

$$\text{FOLLOW } (A) = \{a, b\}$$

$$\text{FOLLOW } (B) = \{b, a\}$$

**Step 2:** Construct the predective parsing table.

| Non-terminals | Inputs | | |
|:---:|:---:|:---:|:---:|
| | a | b | $ |
| S | $S \rightarrow AaAb$ | $S \rightarrow BbBa$ | |
| A | $A \rightarrow \varepsilon$ | $A \rightarrow \varepsilon$ | |
| B | $B \rightarrow \varepsilon$ | $B \rightarrow \varepsilon$ | |

(*i*) Consider $S \rightarrow AaAb$

Compare it with $\qquad A \rightarrow \alpha$

Here, $\quad A = S$

$\qquad \alpha = AaAb$

$\qquad \qquad$ FIRST$(AaAB) = \{a\}$

$\qquad \qquad \qquad M[S, a] = S \rightarrow AaAb$

(*ii*) Consider $S \rightarrow BbBa$

Compare it with $\qquad A \rightarrow \alpha$

$\qquad \qquad$ Here $A = S$

$\qquad \qquad \qquad \alpha = BaBa$

$\qquad \qquad$ FIRST $(BbBa) = \{b\}$

$\qquad \qquad \qquad M[S, b] = S \rightarrow BbBa$

(*iii*) Consider $\qquad A \rightarrow \varepsilon$

Compare with $\qquad A \rightarrow \alpha$

Here, $\quad A = A$

$\qquad \alpha = E$

$\qquad \qquad$ FOLLOW $(A) = \{a, b\}$

∴ $\qquad \qquad M[A, a] = A \rightarrow \varepsilon$

$\qquad \qquad M[A, b] = A \rightarrow \varepsilon$

(*iv*) Consider $\qquad B \rightarrow \varepsilon$

Compare with $\qquad A \rightarrow \alpha$

Here, $\quad A = B$

$\qquad \alpha = \varepsilon$

$\qquad \qquad$ FOLLOW $(B) = \{b, a\}$

$$\therefore \qquad M[B, b] = B \to \varepsilon$$

$$M[B, a] = B \to \varepsilon$$

**Step 3:** To parse the string ba using predective parsing table.

| Matched | Stack | Input | Action |
|---------|-------|-------|--------|
| | S $ | b a $ | — |
| | B b B a $ | b a $ | S → Bb Ba |
| | bB a$ | ba $ | B → ε |
| b | B a $ | a $ | matched b |
| b | ¯a$ | a$ | B → ε |
| ba | $ | $ | matched a |

This shows the above grammar is LL(1)

## PROBLEM 5

Construct *LL*(1) prasing table for the Grammar

$$S \to aB|\ aC|\ sd|se$$

$$B \to bBc|f$$

$$C \to g$$

and verify the above grammar is *LL*(1) or not.

## SOLUTION

**Step 1:** Find FIRST and FOLLOW set.

**FIRST Set:**    FIRST (S) = {a}

FIRST (B) = {b, f}

FIRST (C) = {g}

**FOLLOW Set:**

(i)        Consider, S → Sd

FOLLOW (S) = {d}

(ii)       Consider S → Se

FOLLOW (S) = {e}

∴        FOLLOW (S) = {d, e, $}

**FOLLOW (B):**

(*i*)            Consider $S \rightarrow aB$

∴            FOLLOW (B) = FOLLOW (S) = {d, e, $}

(*ii*)            Consider $B \rightarrow bBc$

∴            FOLLOW (B) = {c}

∴            FOLLOW (B) = {c, d, e, $}

**FOLLOW (C)**

Consider $S \rightarrow aC$

∴            FOLLOW (C) = FOLLOW (S)

= {d, e, $}

**Step 2:** Construct predective parsing table.

| Non Terminals | Input | | | | | | | |
|---|---|---|---|---|---|---|---|---|
| | **a** | **b** | **c** | **d** | **e** | **f** | **S** | **$** |
| S | $S \rightarrow ab$ $S \rightarrow aC$ $S \rightarrow sd$ $S \rightarrow sc$ | | | | | | | |
| B | | $B \rightarrow bBC$ | | | | $B \rightarrow F$ | | |
| C | | | | | | | $C \rightarrow g$ | |

(*i*)            Consider, $S \rightarrow aB$

Compare it with $A \rightarrow \alpha$

Here,    $A = S$

$\alpha = aB$

∴            FIRST (aB) = {a}

∴            M[S, a] = $S \rightarrow aB$

(*ii*)            Consider $S \rightarrow aC$

Compare with $A \rightarrow \alpha$

Here,    $A = S$

$\alpha = aC$

FIRST (ac) = {a}

∴            M[S, a] = $S \rightarrow aC$

(*iii*) Consider $S \rightarrow Sd$

Compare with $\qquad\qquad A \rightarrow \alpha$

Here,    $A = S$

$\qquad\qquad\quad \alpha = Sd$

$\therefore \qquad\qquad$ FIRST $(Sd) = \{a\}$

$\therefore \qquad\qquad\quad M[S, a] = S \rightarrow Sd$

(*iv*) Consider $S \rightarrow Se$

Compare it with $\qquad\qquad A \rightarrow \alpha$

Here,    $A = S$

$\qquad\qquad\quad \alpha = Se$

$\therefore \qquad\qquad$ FIRST $(Se) =$ FIRST $(S) = \{a\}$

$\therefore \qquad\qquad\quad M[S, a] = S \rightarrow Se$

(*v*) Consider $B \rightarrow bBC$

Compare it with $\qquad\qquad A \rightarrow \alpha$

Here,    $A = B$

$\qquad\qquad\quad \alpha = bBC$

$\therefore \qquad\qquad$ FIRST $(bBC) = \{b\}$

$\therefore \qquad\qquad\quad M[B, b] = B \rightarrow bBC$

(*vi*) Consider $B \rightarrow f$

Compare it with $\qquad\qquad A \rightarrow \alpha$

Here,    $A = B$

$\qquad\qquad\quad \alpha = f$

$\therefore \qquad\qquad$ FIRST$(F) = \{f\}$

$\therefore \qquad\qquad\quad M[B, F] = B \rightarrow F.$

(*vii*) Consider $\qquad\qquad C \rightarrow g$

Compare it with $\qquad\qquad A \rightarrow \alpha$

Here,    $A = C$

$\qquad\qquad\quad \alpha = g$

$\therefore \qquad\qquad$ FIRST $(g) = \{g\}$

$\qquad\qquad\quad M[C, S] = C \rightarrow g$

The above table shows multiple entries for $M[s, a]$. This shows that the given grammer is not LL(1)

## 3.8  ERROR RECOVERY IN PREDICTIVE PARSING

An error is detected during predective parsing, when the terminal on top of the stack doesnot match the next input symbol (or) when nonterminal A is on top of the stack, a is the next input symbol and $M[A, a]$ is error [*i.e.,* The parsing table entry is empty].

**Panic Mode:** Panic Mode error recovery is based on the idea of skipping symbols on the input until a token in a selected set of synchronizing tokens appear.

**Some of the Rules are:**

1. As a starting point, place all symbols in FOLLOW(A) into the synchronizing set of non-terminal 'A'. If we skip tokens until an element of FOLLOW (A) is seen and popped 'A' from the stack, it is likely that parsing can continue.

## PROBLEM 1

Consider, the Grammar

$$E \rightarrow TE'$$
$$E' \rightarrow + TE'|\varepsilon$$
$$T \rightarrow FT'$$
$$T' \rightarrow *FT'|\varepsilon$$
$$F \rightarrow (E)|id$$

## SOLUTION

We have

$$\text{FOLLOW } (E) = \{), \$\}$$
$$\text{FOLLOW } (E') = \{), \$\}$$
$$\text{FOLLOW } (T) = \{+,), \$\}$$
$$\text{FOLLOW } (T') = \{+, ), \$\}$$
$$\text{FOLLOW } (F) = \{+, *, ), \$\}$$

| Non terminals | Input Symbols | | | | | |
|---|---|---|---|---|---|---|
| | id | + | * | ( | ) | $ |
| $E$ | $E \rightarrow TE'$ | | | $E \rightarrow TE'$ | Synch | Synch |
| $E'$ | | $E' \rightarrow TE'$ | | | $E' \rightarrow \varepsilon$ | $E' \rightarrow \varepsilon$ |
| $T$ | $T \rightarrow FT'$ | Synch | | $T \rightarrow *FT'$ | Synch | Synch |
| $T'$ | | $T' \rightarrow \varepsilon$ | $T' \rightarrow FT'$ | | $T' \rightarrow \varepsilon$ | $T' \rightarrow \varepsilon$ |
| $F$ | $F \rightarrow id$ | Synch | Synch | $F \rightarrow (E)$ | Synch | Synch |

The above table shows the synchronization tokens added to predective parsing table.

Using FIRST and FOLLOW symbols as synchronizing tokens parsing table is constructed with "synch" indicating synchronizing tokens obtained from the FOLLOW set of non-terminal.

Observe in the parsing table, if the parser look up entry $M[A, a]$ and finds that it is blank, then the input symbol '$a$' is skipped.

If the entry is "Synch" then the non terminal on top of the Stack is popped in an attempt to resume parsing.

If a taken on top of the stact doesnot match the input symbol, then we pop the token from the Stack.

On the Errorneous input ) $id * + id$, The parser and Error Recovery mechanism is given below.

| Stack | Input | Remark |
|---|---|---|
| $E\$$ | $) id * + id \$$ | Error, Skip $\rangle$ |
| $E\$$ | $id * + id \$$ | |
| $TE'\$$ | $id * + id \$$ | |
| $FT'E'\$$ | $id * + id \$$ | |
| $id\ T'\ E'\ \$$ | $id * + id \$$ | |
| $T'E'\ \$$ | $* + id \$$ | |
| $*\ FT'\ E'\ \$$ | $* + id \$$ | |
| $FT'\ E'\ \$$ | $+id \$$ | Error, $M[F, +]$ = Synch, $F$ has been popped |
| $T'E'\$$ | $+ id \$$ | |
| $E'\$$ | $+id \$$ | |
| $+TE'\$$ | $+id \$$ | |
| $TE'\$$ | $id \$$ | |
| $FT'\ E'\ \$$ | $id \$$ | |
| $id\ T'\ E'\ \$$ | $id \$$ | |
| $T'\ E'\ \$$ | $\$$ | |
| $E'\ \$$ | $\$$ | |
| $\$$ | $\$$ | |

## PROBLEM 2

For the following Grammar find out $LL(1)$ Parse

$$\text{lexp} \rightarrow \text{number}|(\text{op lexp-seq})$$

$$\text{op} \rightarrow |-| *$$

$$\text{lexp-seq} \rightarrow \text{lexp-seq lexp}|\text{lexp}$$

## SOLUTION

**Step 1.** Find the FIRST and FOLLOW sets.

**FIRST Set:**

$$\text{FIRST (lexp)} = \{\text{number, (}\}$$

$$\text{FIRST (OP)} = \{+, -, *\}$$

$$\text{FIRST (lexp-seq)} = \text{FIRST (lexp)}$$

$$= \{\text{number, (}\}$$

**FOLLOW Set:**

**FOLLOW (lexp–seq):**

(*i*) Consider, lexp $\rightarrow$ number|(OP lexp–seq)

$\therefore$       FOLLOW (lexp–seq) = $\{)\}$

(*ii*) Consider       lexp–seq $\rightarrow$ lexp–seq lexp|lexp

$\therefore$       FOLLOW (lexp–seq) = FIRST (lexp)–$\{\varepsilon\}$

$$= \{\text{number, (}\}$$

$\therefore$       FOLLOW (lexp–Seq) = $\{\text{number, (, )}\}$

**FOLLOW (lexp):**

(*i*) Consider,       lexp–Seq $\rightarrow$ lexp–seq lexp

$\therefore$             FOLLOW (lexp) = FOLLOW (lexp-seq)

$$= \{\text{number, (, )}\}$$

(*ii*) Consider,       lexp–seq $\rightarrow$ lexp

FOLLOW (lexp) = FOLLOW (lexp–seq)

$$= \{\text{number, (, )}\}$$

Since lexp is starting production,

$$\text{FOLLOW (lexp)} = \{\text{number, (, ), \$}\}$$

**FOLLOW (OP)**

Consider,                    lexp → (op lexp–seq)

$\therefore$              FOLLOW (OP)  =  FIRST (lexp-seq) – {ε}

=  {number, (} – {ε}

=  {number, (}

To Summarize above, we have.

$$\text{FIRST (lexp)} = \{\text{number, (}\}$$

$$\text{FIRST (op)} = \{+, -, *\}$$

$$\text{FIRST (lexp–seq)} = \{\text{number, (}\}$$

$$\text{FOLLOW (lexp)} = \{\text{number, (, ), \$}\}$$

$$\text{FOLLOW (OP)} = \{\text{number, (}\}$$

$$\text{FOLLOW (lexp–seq)} = \{\text{number, (, )}\}$$

**Step 2:**

Construct predictive parsing table from FIRST and FOLLOW set.

(*i*) Consider lexp → number

Compare with                    $A \rightarrow \alpha$

Here,      $A$ = lexp

$\alpha$ = number

FIRST (number)  =  {number}

$\therefore$          M[lexp, number]  =  lexp → number

(*ii*) Consider lexp → (OP lexp–seq)

Compare with                    $A \rightarrow \alpha$

Here,      $A$ = lexp

$\alpha$ = (op lexp-seq)

FIRST((op lexp-seq))  =  {(}

$\therefore$              $M$[lexp, (]  =  lexp → (op lexp–seq) (*iii*) Consider,                 $OP \rightarrow +$

$\therefore$                 $M[OP, +] = OP \rightarrow +$

(*iv*) Consider                 $op \rightarrow -$

$M[op, —] = op \rightarrow -$

(*v*) Consider                 $op \rightarrow *$

$M[op, *] = op \rightarrow *$

(*vi*) Consider,         lexp-seq $\rightarrow$ lexp-seq lexp

Compare it with                 $A \rightarrow \alpha$

Here,     $A$ = lexp-seq

$\alpha$ = lexp-seq lexp

FIRST (lexp-seq lexp) = FIRST (lexp-seq)

= {number, (}

$M$[lexp-seq, number] = lexp-seq $\rightarrow$ lexp-seq lexp

$M$[lexp-seq, (] = lexp-seq $\rightarrow$ lexp-seq lexp.

(*vii*) Consider         lexp-seq $\rightarrow$ lexp

Compare with                 $A \rightarrow \alpha$

Here,     $A$ = lexp-seq

$\alpha$ = lexp

FIRST (lexp) = {number, (}

$M$[lexp-seq, number] = lexp-seq $\rightarrow$ lexp

$M$[lexp-seq, (] = lexp-seq $\rightarrow$ lexp

| Non Terminals | Inputs | | | | | | |
|---|---|---|---|---|---|---|---|
| | **number** | **+** | **−** | **\*** | **(** | **)** | **$** |
| lexp | lexp → number | | | | lexp → (op lexp seq) | | |
| op | | op → + | op → − | op → * | | | |
| lexp-seq | lexp–seq → lexp-seq lexp  lexp-seq → lexp | | | | lexp-seq → lexp-seq lexp  lexp-seq → lexp | | |

The above table shows multiple entries for $M$[lexp-seq, number] and $M$[lexp-seq, (]

Hence the given Grammar is not LL(1)

## PROBLEM 3

Consider the Grammar,

$$\text{declaration} \rightarrow \text{type var-list}$$

$$\text{type} \rightarrow \text{int|float}$$

$$\text{var-list} \rightarrow \text{identifier, var-list|identifier}$$

For the given Grammar to be LL(1) first perform left factoring and then proceed.

(*i*) Left factor the Grammar.

(*ii*) For the obtained Grammar construct FIRST and FOLLOW Set.

(*iii*) Show that the resulting Grammar is LL(1)

(*iv*) Construct the LL(1) parsing table.

(*v*) Show the action for input string int *x, y, z*.

## SOLUTION

(*i*) Consider,         Var-list → identifier, var-list|identifier

So,                Var-list → identifier var-list'

var-list' →, var-list|ε

So after left factoring we have

$$\text{declaration} \rightarrow \text{type var-list}$$

$$\text{type} \rightarrow \text{int|float}$$

$$\text{var-list} \rightarrow \text{identifier var-list'}$$

$$\text{var-list'} \rightarrow, \text{var-list|ε}$$

(*ii*) **FIRST Set:**

First (declaration) = FIRST (type) = {int, float}

FIRST (var–list) = {identifier}

FIRST (var-list') = {, ε}

**FOLLOW Set:**

FOLLOW (declaration) = {$}

**FOLLOW (type):**

Consider,    declaration → type var-list

FOLLOW(type) = FIRST (Var–list)–{ε}

FOLLOW(type) = {identifier}

**FOLLOW (Var–list)**

(*i*) Consider    declaration → type var–list

FOLLOW (var–list) = FOLLOW(declaration)

= {$}

(*ii*) Consider,    Var–list → Var–list|ε

FOLLOW (var–list) = FOLLOW (var–list)

= {$}

∴    FOLLOW (var–list) = {$}

**FOLLOW (Var–list'):**

Consider,    var list' = ε

var–list → identifier var–list' ⇒ v

∴    FOLLOW (var–list') = FOLLOW(var–list)

**FOLLOW (Var-list'):**

Consider,    var–list → identifier var–list'

put var–list' = ε

∴    var–list → identifier

∴    FOLLOW (var–list') = {$}

So, after FIRST and FOLLOW sets we can summarize as,

FIRST (declaration) = {int, float}

FIRST (type) = {int, float}

FIRST (var-list) = {identifier}

FIRST (var–list') = {, ε}

FOLLOW (declaration) = {$}

FOLLOW (type) = {identifier}

$$\text{FOLLOW (var–list)} = \{\$\}$$

$$\text{FOLLOW (var–list')} = \{\$\}$$

(*iii*) Consider, declaration → type var-list

Compare it with          $A \rightarrow \alpha$

Here,      $A$ = delcaration

$\alpha$ = type var-list

$\therefore$      FIRST (type var-list) = FIRST (type)

$= \{\text{int, float}\}$

$\therefore$      M[declaration, int] = declaration → type var-list

M[declaration, Float] = declaration → type var-list

Consider,          declaration = $D$

identifier = $id$

type = $T$

var–list = $V$

var–list' = $V'$

$\therefore$          $M[D, \text{int}] = D \rightarrow T\,V$

$M[D, \text{float}] = D \rightarrow T\,V$

(*iv*) Consider type → int

Compare with A → $\alpha$

Here,      $A$ = type

$\alpha$ = int

$M[T, \text{int}] = \text{type} \rightarrow \text{int}$

(*c*) Consider type → float

Compare with          $A \rightarrow \alpha$

Here,      $A$ = type

$\alpha$ = float

$\therefore$          $M[T, \text{float}] = T \rightarrow \text{float}$

(*d*) Var-list → identifier var–list'

Compare with          $A \rightarrow \alpha$

Here,    $A$ = var–list

$\alpha$ = identifier var–list'

FIRST (identifier var–list') = FIRST(identifier)

= {identifier}

$\therefore$    $M[V, id]$ = $V \to$ id $v'$

(e) var–list' $\to$ , var–list

Compare with    $A \to \alpha$

Here,    $A$ = var–list'

$\alpha$ = , var–list

FIRST(, var–list) = {,}

$\therefore$    $M[V'. ,]$ = $V' \to$ , $V$

(f) var–list $\to \varepsilon$

Compare    $A \to \alpha$

$A$ = var–list'

$\alpha = \varepsilon$

$\therefore$    FOLLOW (var–list') = {$\$$}

$\therefore$    $M[$var–list', $\$] $ = var–list' $\to \varepsilon$

i.e.,    $M[V', \$] $ = $V' \to \varepsilon$

**Step 2:** Construct predictive parsing table.

| Non Terminal | Inputs | | | | |
|---|---|---|---|---|---|
| | int | float | id | , | $ |
| $D$ | $D \to TV$ | $D \to TV$ | | | |
| $T$ | $T \to$ int | $T \to$ float | | | |
| $V$ | | | $V \to$ id $V'$ | | |
| $V'$ | | | | $V' \to$ , $V$ | $V' \to \varepsilon$ |

**Step 3:** To parse the string int $x, y, z$ using predective parsing table.

| Matched | Stack | Input | Action |
|---|---|---|---|
| | $D \$$ | int $x, y, z \$$ | — |
| | $TV \$$ | int $x, y, z \$$ | $D \to TV$ |

| | int $V$ \$ | int $x, y, z$ \$ | $T \rightarrow$ int |
|---|---|---|---|
| mached int | $V$\$ | $x, y, z,$ \$ | mached int |
| | $xV'$ \$ | $x, y, z$ \$ | $V \rightarrow id\ V'$ |
| int $x$ | $V'$ \$ | $, y\ z$ \$ | mached $x$ |
| | $, V$ \$ | $y, z$ \$ | $V' \rightarrow , V$ |
| int $x,$ | $V$ \$ | $y, z$ \$ | matched |
| | $y\ V'$ \$ | $y, z$ \$ | $V \rightarrow id\ V'$ |
| int $x, y$ | $V'$ \$ | $y, z$ \$ | matched $y$ |
| | $,V$\$ | $,z$\$ | $V' \rightarrow , V$ |
| int $x, y$ | $V$ \$ | $z$\$ | matched, |
| | $z\ V'$ \$ | $z$ \$ | $V \rightarrow id\ V'$ |
| int $x, y, z$ | $V'$ \$ | \$ | matched $z$ |
| int $x, y, z$ | \$ | \$ | $V' \rightarrow \varepsilon$ |

# SYNTAX ANALYSIS–II

## 4.1 BOTTOM–UP–PARSING

A bottom-up parse corresponds to the construction of a parse tree for an input string beginning at the leaves (bottom) and working up towards the root (top).

### EXAMPLE

Consider the Grammar,

$$E \rightarrow E + T|T$$
$$T \rightarrow T * F|F$$
$$F \rightarrow (E)|id$$

Given the input string $id * id$

### SOLUTION

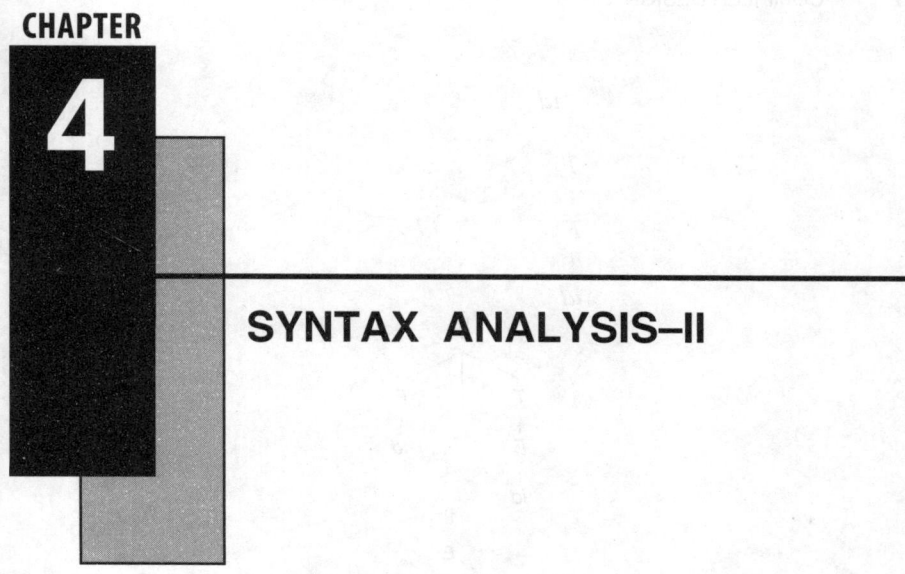

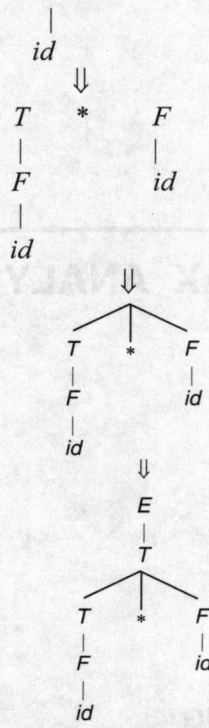

- The sequence starts with the input string *id * id* The first reduction produces *F * id*, by reducing the leftmost id to *F*. Using the production *F → id*.

- The second reduction produces *T * id*, by reducing *F* to *T* using the production *T → F*

Now we have a choice between reducing the string *T*, which is the body of *E → T* and the string consisting of second id, which is the body of *F → id*. Rather than reduce *T* to *E*, the second *id* is reduced to *F*, resulting in the string *T * F*.

This string then reduces to *T*. The parse completes with the reduction of *T* to the start symbol *E*.

By definition, a reduction is the reverse of the step in a derivation.

The goal of bottom-up parsing is to construct a derivation in reverse.

The following derivation corresponds to the parse

$$E \Rightarrow T$$
$$\Rightarrow T * F$$
$$\Rightarrow T * id$$

$$\Rightarrow F * id$$

$$\Rightarrow id * id \text{ is a rightmost derivation.}$$

## Exercise

(1) Describe the Languages denoted by the following Regular Expressions.

    (*i*) *a(a/b)\*a*

  (*ii*) *((ε|a) b\*)\**

  (*iii*) *(a + b)\*a(a/b) (a/b)*

  (*iv*) *a\* ba \* ba \* ba\**

(2) Consider the CFG

$$S \rightarrow SS + |SS*|a$$

ind a string *aa + a\**

    (*i*) Give the Leftmost derivation.

   (*ii*) Give the Rightmost derivation.

  (*iii*) Give a parse tree for the string.

  (*iv*) Is the grammar ambigous or unambigous? Justify.

   (*v*) Describe the language generated by this Grammar.

(3) Repeat the Above for each of the following grammar

    (*a*) $S \rightarrow OS1|01$ with string 000111

    (*b*) $S \rightarrow +SS| *SS|a$ with string +* *aaa*

    (*c*) $S \rightarrow S(S)S|\varepsilon$ with string (() ())

    (*d*) $S \rightarrow S + S|SS|(S)|S *|a$ with string *(a + a)\*a*

    (*e*) $S \rightarrow (L)|a, L \rightarrow L, S|S$ with strong ((*a, a*), *a(a)*)

    (*f*) $S \rightarrow aSbS|bSaS|\varepsilon$ with string *aabbab*

(4) Construct *LL*(1) parsing table for the grammar.

$$S \rightarrow iEts|iEtSeS|a$$

$$E \rightarrow b$$

and also verify the above grammar is LL(1) or not.

## 4.2 HANDLES

A **handle** is a substring that matches the body of a production and whose reduction represents one step along the reverse of a Rightmost derivation.

If there is a production $A \rightarrow \beta$, then $\beta$ is said to be handle since it can be reduced to A in the string $\alpha \beta \omega$.

Reducing $\beta$ to A in $\alpha\beta\omega$ is said to be pruning the handle.

### EXAMPLE

Consider the Grammar,

$$E \rightarrow E + E$$
$$E \rightarrow E * E$$
$$E \rightarrow (E)$$
$$E \rightarrow id$$

is Rightmost derivation is given by.

$$E \rightarrow \underline{E + E}$$
$$\Rightarrow E + \underline{E + E}$$
$$\Rightarrow E + E * \underline{id3}$$
$$\Rightarrow \underline{id2} * id3$$
$$\Rightarrow \underline{id1} + id2 * id3$$

Handles are underlined for each right sentential form $id$ is a handle of the right sentential form $id1 + id2 * id3$ because $id$ is the right side of the production $E \rightarrow id$, replacing $id1$ by $E$ produces the previous right sentential form $E + id2 * id3$.

Now, $id2$ is the handle, because replacing $id2$ by $E$ gives the previous right sentential form $E + E * id3$.

Similarly replacing all the handles by the non terminals of their production, finally yields the start symbol $E$.

### PROBLEM 1

Consider the Grammar,

$$E \rightarrow E + T | T$$
$$T \rightarrow T * F | F$$
$$F \rightarrow (E) | id$$

Indicate the handle for the following right sentential form $id1 * id2$.

## SOLUTION

| Right Sentential form | Handle | Reducing Production |
|:---:|:---:|:---:|
| id1 * id2 | $id_1$ | $F \rightarrow id$ |
| F * id2 | F | $T \rightarrow F$ |
| T * id2 | id2 | $F \rightarrow id$ |
| T * F | T * F | $T \rightarrow T * F$ |
| T | T | $E \rightarrow T$ |
| E | — | — |

$$E \rightarrow T$$
$$\Rightarrow T * F$$
$$\Rightarrow T * id2$$
$$\Rightarrow F * id2$$
$$\Rightarrow id1 * id2 \text{ is the Rightmost derivation}$$

## PROBLEM 2

Consider the Grammar,

$$E \rightarrow E + E$$
$$E \rightarrow E * E$$
$$E \rightarrow (E)$$
$$E \rightarrow id$$

indicate the handle for the following right sentential from $id1 + id2 * id3$.

## SOLUTION

$$E \rightarrow E + E$$
$$\Rightarrow E + E * E$$
$$\Rightarrow E + E * id3$$
$$\Rightarrow E + id2 * id3$$
$$\Rightarrow id1 + id2 * id3$$

is the rightmost derivation.

| Right Sentential form | Handle | Reducing Production |
|---|---|---|
| $id1 + id2 * id3$ | $id1$ | $E \to id$ |
| $E + id2 * id3$ | $id2$ | $E \to id$ |
| $E + E * id3$ | $id3$ | $E \to id$ |
| $E + E * E$ | $E * E$ | $E \to E * E$ |
| $E + E$ | $E + E$ | $E \to E + E$ |
| $E$ | — | — |

## 4.3 SHIFT REDUCE PARSER

Shift Reduce Parsing is a form of bottom up parsing in which stack holds Grammar symbol and input buffer holds the rest of the string to be parsed.

- Shift Reduce Parser requires the following data Structures.
    1. Input buffer storing the input string
    2. A stack for storing and accessing the LHS and RHS of rules.
- The initial configuration of shiftreduce parser is given below.

- The parser performs the following basic operations:
    (*i*)  **Shift:** Shift the next input symbol onto the top of the stack.
    (*ii*)  **Reduce:** The right end of the String to be reduced must be at the top of the stack. Locate the left end of the String written the stack and decide with what nonterminal to replace the String.
    (*iii*)  **Accept:** Announces successful completion of parsing.
    (*iv*)  **Error:** Discover a syntax error and call an error recovery technique.

## PROBLEM 1

Consider the Grammar.

$$E \to E + E$$
$$E \to E * E$$
$$E \to (E)$$
$$E \to id$$

Perform shift reduce parsing for the string $id1 + id2 * id3$.

## SOLUTION

The stack implementation is as shown below

$$E \rightarrow E + E$$
$$\Rightarrow E + E * E$$
$$\Rightarrow E + E * id_3$$
$$\Rightarrow E + id_2 * id_3$$
$$\Rightarrow id_1 + id_2 * id_3 \text{ is the rightmost derivation.}$$

| Stack | Input | Action |
|---|---|---|
| $ | id1 + id2 * id3 $ | Shift |
| $ id1 | + id2 * id3 $ | Reduc $E \rightarrow id$ |
| $ E | + id2 * id3 $ | Shift |
| $ E + | id2 * id3$ | Shift |
| $ E + id2 | * id3$ | Reduce $E \rightarrow id$ |
| $ E + E | * id3$ | Shift |
| $ E + E* | id3 $ | Shift |
| $ E + E * id3 | $ | Reduce $E \rightarrow id$ |
| $ E + E * E | $ | Reduce $E \rightarrow E * E$ |
| $ E + E | $ | Reduce $E \rightarrow E + E$ |
| $ E | $ | accept |

→ At the beginning stack is empty indicated by $ and the input is $id1 + id2 * id3$ $ where $ indicates the end of the string.

→ Since Shift reduce parser is a bottom up parser, a handle should be on top of the stack so that it can be reduced.

In the first step $id_1$ is shifted on stack, $id_1$ can be reduced to $E$ using $E \rightarrow id$. So the $id_1$ which is handle appearing on the top of the stack is reduced to $E$.

Now there is no handle on the top of the stack which can be reduced. So the next input is +, shifted into the stack. So the contents of stack is $ $E$ + here is no production to reduce $E+$ again the next input symbol is shifted to the stack i.e., $id_2$ $id_2$ is again reduced to $E$ using $E + id$.

Now, the stack contains $ $E + E$ even though $E + E$ can be reduced to $E$ by the production $E \rightarrow E + E$, we do not reduce, instead we shift the next input symbol * onto the stack.

This is because **shift reduce is the reverse of right most derivation.** If $E + E$ is reduced to $E$, it becomes the reverse of leftmost derivation which is not the characteristic of shift reduce parser.

Similarly by performing shift and reduce actions we can get the start symbol on the stack *i.e.* $E$ which indicates the acceptance of the string by the grammar.

## PROBLEM 2

Consider the Grammar.

$$E \rightarrow E + T | T$$
$$T \rightarrow T * F | F$$
$$F \rightarrow (E) | id$$

Perform shift reduce parsing for the string $id1 * id2$.

## SOLUTION

$$E \rightarrow T$$
$$\Rightarrow T * F$$
$$\Rightarrow T * id_2$$
$$\Rightarrow F * id_2$$
$$\Rightarrow id_1 * id_2.$$

| Stack | Input | Action |
|:---:|:---:|:---:|
| $ | $id_1 * id_2$ $ | Shift |
| $ $id_1$ | $* id_2$ $ | reduce by $F \rightarrow id$ |
| $ $F$ | $* id_2$ $ | reduce by $T \rightarrow F$ |
| $ $T$ | $* id_2$$ | Shift |
| $ $T*$ | $id_2$$ | Shift |
| $ $T * id_2$ | $ | reduce $F \rightarrow id$ |
| $ $T * F$ | $ | reduce $T \rightarrow T * F$ |
| $ $T$ | $ | reduce $E \rightarrow T$ |
| $ $E$ | $ | accept |

## PROBLEM 3

Consider the Grammar.

$$S \rightarrow TL;$$

$$T \rightarrow int|float$$

$$L \rightarrow L, id|id$$

parse the input string int *id, id*; using shift reduce parser.

## SOLUTION

$$S \rightarrow TL;$$

$$\Rightarrow TL, id;$$

$$\Rightarrow T\ id,\ id;$$

$$\Rightarrow int\ id,\ id;$$

| Stack | Input | Action |
|-------|-------|--------|
| $ | int *id, id*; $ | Shift |
| $ int | *id, id*; $ | Reduce by $T \rightarrow$ int |
| $ T | *id, id*; $ | Shift |
| $ T *id* | , *id*; $ | Reduce by $L \rightarrow id$ |
| $ TL | , *id*; $ | Shift |
| $ TL, | *id*; $ | Shift |
| $ TL, *id* | ; $ | Reduce by $L \rightarrow L, id$ |
| $ TL | ; $ | Shift |
| $ TL; | $ | Reduce by $S \rightarrow TL$; |
| $ S | $ | accept |

## 4.4  CONFLICTS DURING SHIFT–REDUCE PARSING

When the shift reduce parser is applied to some CFG, it leads to some conflicts because shift reduce parser cannot be used for CFG.

The conflicts are:

(*i*) **Shift|Reduce Conflict:** The parser even after knowing the entire stack content and the next input symbol, cannot decide whether to shift or to reduce. This is called shift|reduce conflict.

(*ii*) **Reduce|Reduce Conflict:** The parser knowing the entire stack content and the next input symbol, cannot decide which productions to use or which several reductions to make. This is called reduce|reduce conflict.

For example,

Consider a dangling else grammar.

Stmt → if expr then Stmt

      | if expr then

When Shift reduce parser is applied to this grammar, we reach the configuration.

| Stack | Input |
|-------|-------|
| If expr then stmt | else ......$ |

Under this configuration, we cannot tell whether 'if expr then stmt' is handle or not. This leaves the earser in confusion whether to shift or reduce the stack top element. There is a **Shift-reduce conflict** because it is possible to reduce "if expr then stmt" in the stack to "stmt" (or) it is also possible to shift else and then look for another stmt to complete the alternative "if expr then stmt else stmt" which can be reduce to "stmt".

Thus we cannot tell whether to shift or reduce.

## 4.5 INTRODUCTION TO LR PARSING

## Simple LR (SLR)

This is the most efficient method of bottom-up parsing which can be used to parse the large class of CFG. This method is also called LR(k) parsing here L stands for Left to Right scanning.

*R* stands for Rightmost derivation in reverse

*k* stands for number of input symbols. If *k* is omitted it is assumed to be 1.

## Model or Structure of LR Parser

A schematic diagram of LR parser is shown below

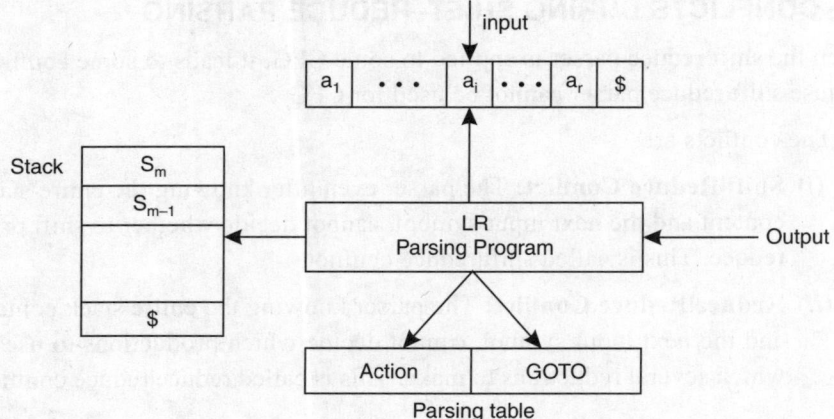

Parsing table

It consists of an input, a output, a stack a drive program and parsing table has 2 parts *i.e.*, Action and Goto.

The parsing program reads charecter from an input buffer one at a time.

The program uses a stack to store a string of the form $S_0 X_1\ S_1 X_2.... X_m\ S_m$, where $S_m$, where $S_m$ is on the top Each $X_i$ is a grammar symbol and each $S_i$ is a symbol called as state.

The combination of state symbol on the top of the stack and the current input symbol are used to index the parsing table and determine the shift reduce parsing action.

The parsing table consists of two parts–A parsing action function called ACTION and goto function called GOTO.

**1. The Action Function:** It takes as arguments a state $i$ and a terminal '$a$' (or, $, the input end marker. The value of action. Action $[i,\ a]$ can have one of the four forms.

(*i*)  **Shift:** Where $j$ is a state. The action taken by the parser effectively shifts input '$a$' to the stack but uses state $j$ to represent '$a$'.

(*ii*)  **Reduce** $A \rightarrow \beta$: The action of the parser effectively reduces $\beta$ on the top of the stack to $A$.

(*iii*)  **Accept:** The parser accepts the input and finishes parsing.

(*iv*)  **Error:** The parser discovers an error in its input and takes some corrective action (Error Recovery).

2. We extend the goto function defined on set of item to state if GOTO $[I_i,\ A] = I_j$, then goto maps a state $i$ and a nonterminal $A$ to state $j$.

## Types of Parser

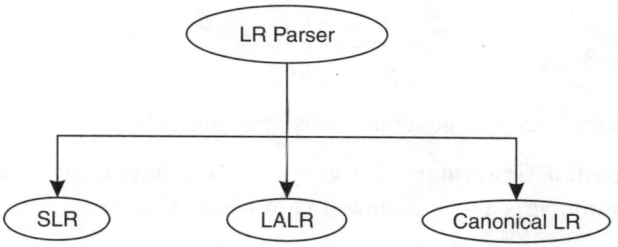

The SLR means simple LR parser, LALR means **Look ahead LR parser** and canonical LR or LR.

The overall structure of all these LR parsers are seen, all are table driven parsers.

The relative powers of these parsers is SLR (1) $\leq$ LALR(1) $\leq$ LR(1)

## Construction of Simple (SLR) Parsing

It is the weakest of the three methods but it is easy to implement

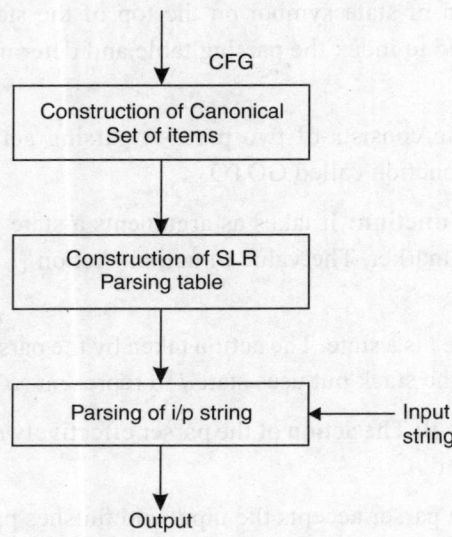

## Definitions of LR(O) Items and Related Items

**1. LR(O) Items:** LR(O) item for grammar $G$ is a production rule in which is inserted at some position in RHS on the rule.

For example.

$$S \rightarrow .ABC$$

$$S \rightarrow A.BC$$

$$S \rightarrow AB.C$$

$$S \rightarrow ABC.$$

The production $S \rightarrow \varepsilon$ generates only one item $S\rightarrow$.

**2. Augmented Grammar:** If a grammar $G$ is having start symbol $S$ then augmented grammar is a new grammar $G$ in which $S'$ is a new start symbol such that $S' \rightarrow S$.

The purpose of this grammar is to indicate the acceptance of input *i.e.* When parser is about to reduce $S' \rightarrow S$, it reaches to acceptance state.

**3. Kernel Items:** It is a collection of items $S' \rightarrow .S$ and all the items, whose dots are not at the leftmost end of RHS of the rule.

**Non-Kernel Items:** The collection of all items in which are at the left end of the RHS of the rule.

**1. Functions Closure and Goto:** These are two important functions require to create collection of canonical set of items.

**2. Viable Prefix:** It is the set of prefixes in the right sentential form of the production $A \rightarrow \alpha$. This set can appear on the stack during shift|reduce action.

## Closure Operation

For a context free grammar G if $I$ is the set of items then the function closure $(I)$ can be constructed using the following rules.

($i$) Consider $I$ is a set of canonical items and initially every item $I$ is added to closure $(I)$.

($ii$) If rule $A \rightarrow \alpha.B\beta$ is a rule in closure $(I)$ and there is another rule for $B$ such as $B \rightarrow \sqrt{}$, then

Closure $(I)$: $\qquad\qquad A \rightarrow \alpha.B\beta$

$\qquad\qquad\qquad\qquad\quad B \rightarrow .\sqrt{}$

This rule has to be applied until no more new items can be added to closure $(I)$.

## Goto Operation

The function goto can be defined as follows. If there is a production $A \rightarrow \alpha.B\beta$ then

$$\text{goto } (A \rightarrow \alpha.B\beta) = A \rightarrow \alpha B.\beta$$

that means simply shifting of dot one position ahead that means simply shifting of dot one position ahead over the grammar symbol (may be terminal or non terminal

The rule $A \rightarrow \alpha.B\beta$ is in $I$, then the same goto function can be written as, goto $(I, B)$.

## PROBLEM 1

Consider the Grammar.

$$X \rightarrow Xb|a$$

Compute closure $(I)$ and goto $(I)$.

## SOLUTION

Let $I: X \rightarrow Xb|a$

$$\text{Closure } (I) = X \rightarrow .Xb$$

$$X \rightarrow .a$$

The goto function can be computed as

$$\text{goto } (I, X) = X \rightarrow X.b$$

$$\text{goto } (I, a) = X \rightarrow a$$

## PROBLEM 2

Consider the Grammar

$$S \rightarrow Aa|bAC|Bc|bBa$$

$$A \rightarrow d$$

$$B \rightarrow d$$

Compute closure $(I)$ and goto $(I)$.

## SOLUTION

Let: $I : Aa|bAc|Bc|bBa$

Closure $(I)$

$$I_0: S \rightarrow .Aa$$

$$S \rightarrow .bAc$$

$$S \rightarrow .Bc$$

$$S \rightarrow .bBa$$

$$A \rightarrow .d$$

$$B \rightarrow .d$$

Goto$(I_0. A)$

$$I_1: S \rightarrow A.a$$

Goto$(I_0, b)$

$$I_2 : S \rightarrow b.Ac$$

$$A \rightarrow .d$$

$$S \rightarrow b.Ba$$

$$B \rightarrow .d$$

Goto$(I_0, B)$

$$I_3: S \rightarrow B.C$$

Goto($I_0$. $d$)

$$I_4: A \rightarrow d.$$
$$B \rightarrow d.$$

## PROBLEM 3

Consider the Grammar

$$S \rightarrow AS|b$$
$$A \rightarrow SA|a$$

Compute closure ($I$) and goto ($I$).

## SOLUTION

Closure ($I$)

$$I_0 : S \rightarrow \cdot AS$$
$$S \rightarrow \cdot b$$
$$A \rightarrow \cdot SA$$
$$A_1 \rightarrow \cdot a$$

goto($I_0$, $A$)

$$I_1 : S \rightarrow A \cdot S$$
$$S \rightarrow \cdot b \ ]$$
$$S \rightarrow \cdot AS$$
$$A \rightarrow \cdot SA$$
$$A \rightarrow \cdot a$$

goto ($I_0$, $b$)

$$I_2 : S \rightarrow b \cdot$$

goto ($I_0$, $a$)

$$I_3 : S \rightarrow a \cdot$$

goto($I_0$, $S$)

$$I_4 : A \rightarrow S \cdot A$$
$$A \rightarrow \cdot a$$
$$A \rightarrow \cdot SA$$
$$S \rightarrow \cdot AS$$
$$S \rightarrow \cdot b$$

## CONSTRUCTION OF CANONICAL COLLECTION OF SET OF ITEM

1. For the grammar $G$ initially add $S' \to .S$ in the set of item $C$(closure).

2. Find closure set and goto sets.

## PROBLEM 1

Consider the grammar

$$E \to E + T$$
$$E \to T$$
$$T \to T * F$$
$$T \to F$$
$$F \to (E)$$
$$F \to id$$

Obtain the SLR parser and parse the input string $id * id + id$.

## SOLUTION

In this grammar add the augmented grammar $E' \to E$ in $I$. Then apply the closure of $I$.

Closure $(I)$

$$I_0 : E' \to \cdot E$$
$$E \to \cdot E + T$$
$$E \to \cdot T$$
$$T \to \cdot T * F$$
$$T \to \cdot F$$
$$F \to \cdot (E)$$
$$F \to \cdot id$$

Goto$(I_0, E)$

$$I_1 : E' \to E\cdot$$
$$E \to E\cdot + T$$

Goto$(I_0, T)$

$$I_2 : E \to T\cdot$$

$$T \rightarrow T \cdot * F$$

Goto $(I_0, F)$

$$I_3 : T \rightarrow F \cdot$$

Goto $(I_0, C)$

$$I_4 : F \rightarrow (\cdot E)$$
$$E \rightarrow \cdot E + T$$
$$E \rightarrow \cdot T$$
$$T \rightarrow \cdot T * F$$
$$T \rightarrow \cdot F$$
$$F \rightarrow \cdot (E)$$
$$F \rightarrow \cdot id$$

Goto $(I_0, id)$

$$I_5 : F \rightarrow id \cdot$$

Goto $(I_1, +)$

$$I_6 : E \rightarrow E + \cdot T$$
$$T \rightarrow \cdot T * F$$
$$T \rightarrow \cdot F$$
$$F \rightarrow \cdot (E)$$
$$F \rightarrow \cdot id$$

Goto $(I_2, *)$

$$I_7 : T \rightarrow T * \cdot F$$
$$F \rightarrow (E)$$
$$F \rightarrow \cdot id$$

Goto $(I_4, E)$ :      $I_8 \ F \rightarrow (E \cdot)$

$$E \rightarrow E \cdot + T$$

Goto $(I_4, T)$ :      $I_2 : E \rightarrow T$          (repeated)

$$T \rightarrow T \cdot * F$$

Goto $(I_4, id)$ :      $I_5 : F \rightarrow id \cdot$          (repeated)

Goto $(I_4, F)$ :      $I_3 : T \rightarrow F \cdot$          (repeated)

Goto $(I_4, ()$ :          $I_4 : F \rightarrow (\cdot E)$          (repeated)

$\qquad\qquad\qquad\qquad\quad E \rightarrow \cdot E + T$

$\qquad\qquad\qquad\qquad\quad E \rightarrow \cdot T$

$\qquad\qquad\qquad\qquad\quad T \rightarrow \cdot T * F$

$\qquad\qquad\qquad\qquad\quad F \rightarrow \cdot (E)$

$\qquad\qquad\qquad\qquad\quad F \rightarrow \cdot id$

Goto $(I_6, T)$ :          $I_9 : E \rightarrow E + T\cdot$

$\qquad\qquad\qquad\qquad\quad T \rightarrow T \cdot * F$

Goto $(I_6, F)$ :          $I_3 : T \rightarrow F\cdot$          (repeated)

Goto $(I_6, ()$ :          $I_4 : F \rightarrow (\cdot E)$          (repeated)

$\qquad\qquad\qquad\qquad\quad E \rightarrow \cdot E + T$

$\qquad\qquad\qquad\qquad\quad E \rightarrow \cdot T * F$

$\qquad\qquad\qquad\qquad\quad F \rightarrow \cdot (E)$

$\qquad\qquad\qquad\qquad\quad F \rightarrow \cdot id$

Goto $(I_6, id)$ :          $I_5 : F \rightarrow id\cdot$          (repeated)

Goto $(I_7, F)$ :          $I_{10} : T \rightarrow T * F.$

Goto $(I_7, ()$ :          $I_4 : F \rightarrow (E)$          (repeated)

$\qquad\qquad\qquad\qquad\quad E \rightarrow \cdot E + T$

$\qquad\qquad\qquad\qquad\quad E \rightarrow \cdot T$

$\qquad\qquad\qquad\qquad\quad T \rightarrow \cdot F$

$\qquad\qquad\qquad\qquad\quad F \rightarrow \cdot (E)$

$\qquad\qquad\qquad\qquad\quad F \rightarrow \cdot id$

Goto $(I_7, id)$;          $I_5 : F \rightarrow id\cdot$          (repeated)

Goto $(I_8, ))$ :          $I_{11} : F \rightarrow (E).$

Goto $(I_8, +)$ :          $I_6 : E \rightarrow E + \cdot T$          (repeated)

$\qquad\qquad\qquad\qquad\quad T \rightarrow \cdot T * F$

$\qquad\qquad\qquad\qquad\quad T \rightarrow \cdot F$

$\qquad\qquad\qquad\qquad\quad F \rightarrow \cdot (E)$

$$F \rightarrow \cdot id$$

$\text{Goto}(I_9, *) : \qquad I_7 : T \rightarrow T * \cdot F \qquad\qquad \text{(repeated)}$

$$F \rightarrow .(E)$$

$$F \rightarrow \cdot id$$

Thus, the collection of items,

$$C = \{I_0, I_1, I_2, I_3, I_4, I_5, I_6, I_7, I_8, I_9, I_{10}, I_{11}\}$$

Considering $I_0$ to $I_{11}$ as different states, the transition diagram can be written as.

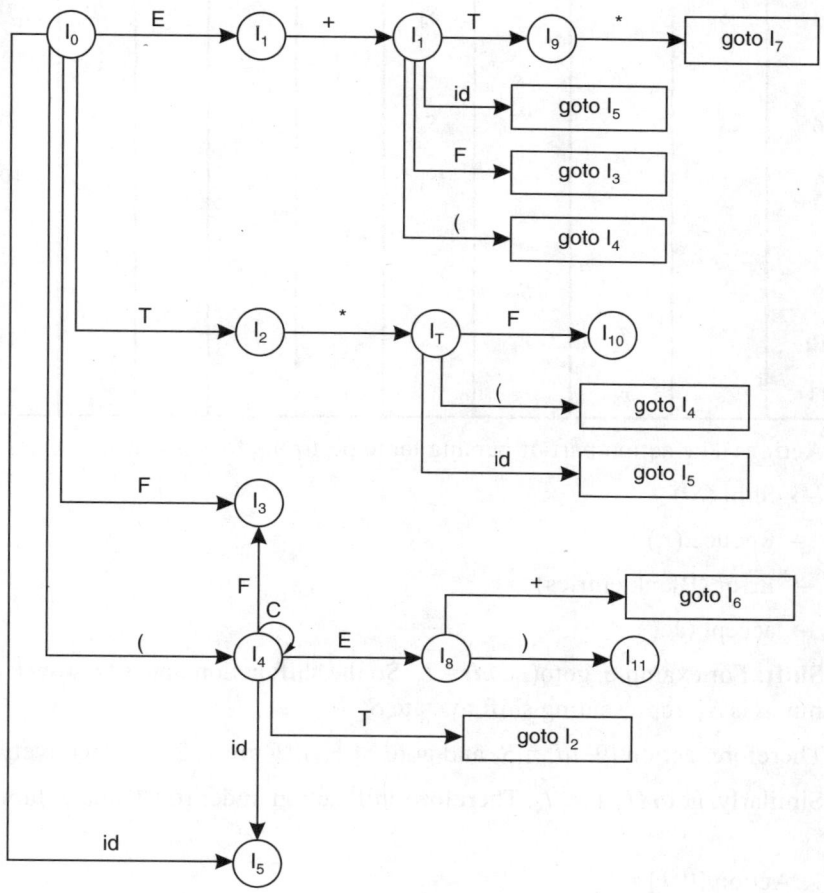

**Step 2:** Construction of parsing table.

The parsing table is constructed as shown below.

The 11 items are considered as 11 states.

| State | Action | | | | | | Goto | | |
|---|---|---|---|---|---|---|---|---|---|
| | $id$ | $+$ | $*$ | $($ | $)$ | $\$$ | $E$ | $T$ | $F$ |
| 0 | $S_5$ | | | $S_4$ | | | 1 | 2 | 3 |
| 1 | | $S_6$ | | | | $acc$ | | | |
| 2 | | $r_2$ | $S_1$ | | $r_2$ | $r_2$ | | | |
| 3 | | $r_4$ | $r_4$ | | $r_4$ | $r_4$ | | | |
| 4 | $S_5$ | | | $S_4$ | | | 8 | 2 | 3 |
| 5 | | $r_6$ | $r_6$ | | $r_6$ | $r_6$ | | | |
| 6 | $S_5$ | | | $S_4$ | | | | 9 | 3 |
| 7 | $S_5$ | | | $S_4$ | | | | | 10 |
| 8 | | $S_6$ | | | $S_{11}$ | | | | |
| 9 | | $r_1$ | $S_7$ | | $r_1$ | $r_1$ | | | |
| 10 | | $r_3$ | $r_3$ | | $r_3$ | $r_3$ | | | |
| 11 | | $r_5$ | $r_5$ | | $r_5$ | $r_5$ | | | |

**Action:** The action part of parsing table performs four actions.

→ Shfit $(Si)$

→ Reduce $(r_i)$

→ Error (Blank entries)

→ accept (ac( )

**Shift:** For example, goto$(I_0, id) = I_5$. So the shift action under the row 0 and column $id$ is $S_5$, representing shift to state $S$.

Therefore, action $[0, id] = S_5$ and goto of $E, T, F$ are 1, 2, 3 respectively.

Similarly, goto $(I_0, () = I_4$. Therefore shift action under row 0 and column is $S_4$.

∴ Action $[0, (] = S_4$

Similarly it is done for all other states.

**Reduce:** Compute the FIRST and FOLLOW sets for the grammar

$$\text{FIRST } (E) = \text{FIRST } (T) = \text{FIRST } (F) = \{(, id\}$$

$$\text{FOLLOW } (E) \ = \ \{ \ ), +, \$\}$$
$$\text{FOLLOW } (T) \ = \ \{*, +, ), \$\}$$
$$\text{FOLLOW } (F) \ = \ \{*, +, ), \$\}$$

- Select the items where • is present at the end except for the starting production, *i.e., E' → E·*

- Give the number for the productions other than the starting production (Augmented Grammar) as shown below.

  1. $E \to E + T$

  2. $E \to T$

  3. $T \to T * F$

  4. $T \to F$

  5. $F \to (E)$

  6. $F \to id$

- If the production is $A \to \alpha \cdot$, Compute FOLLOW($A$) then apply reduce $A \to \alpha$ for all grammar symbols in FOLLOW($A$).

- For example

Item $I_2$ has · at the end of production $E \to T$.

The number for this production is 2. Then Compute FOLLOW(E) = {+, ), $}.

Therefore Action (2, )) = Action (2, +) = Action (2, $) = $r_2$

The next item for which · is at the end is $I_3$. $T \to F \cdot$ the production number is 4.

Then Compute, FOLLOW($T$) = {*, +, ), $}

Therefore Action (3, *) = Action (3, +) = Action (3, )) = Action (3, $) = $r_4$

Follow the same steps for other states.

**Accept:** Find the item which contains · at the end of starting production. here the item $I_1$ consists of $E' \to E \cdot$ Then the accept action is represented on the row $I_1$ and the column $.

∴            action [1, $]  =  *acc*

**Error:** The blank represents the error message.

**Step 3:** Parse the input string $id * id + id$

| Sl. No. | Stack | Input | Action |
|:---:|:---:|:---:|:---:|
| 1 | 0 | $id * id + id$ \$ | Shift |
| 2 | 0*id*5 | $* id + id$ \$ | reduce $F \to id$ |
| 3 | 0 *F*3 | $* id + id$ \$ | reduce $T \to F$ |
| 4. | 0*T*2 | $* id + id$ \$ | Shift |
| 5 | 0*T*2*7 | $id + id$ \$ | Shift |
| 6 | 0*T*2 * 7 *id*5 | $+ id$ \$ | reduce $F \to id$ |
| 7 | 0*T*2*7*F*10 | $+ id$\$ | reduce $T \to T * F$ |
| 8 | 0*T*2 | $+ id$\$ | reduce $E \to T$ |
| 9 | 0*E*1 | $+ id$\$ | Shift |
| 10 | 0*E*1 + 6 | $id$ \$ | Shift |
| 11 | 0*E*1 + 6*id* 5 | \$ | reduce $F \to id$ |
| 12 | 0*E*1 + 6*F*3 | \$ | reduce $T \to F$ |
| 13 | 0*E*1 + 6 *T* 9 | \$ | reduce $E \to E + T$ |
| 14 | 0*E*1 | \$ | accept |

## PROBLEM 2

Consider the Grammar

$$S \to L = R | R$$

$$L \to *R | id$$

$$R \to L$$

verify the grammar is SLR(1) or not.

## SOLUTION

**Step 1:** To construct canonical set of Items

$$I_0 : S' \to \cdot S \qquad\qquad \text{[closure } (I)\text{]}$$

$$S \to \cdot L = R$$

$$S \to \cdot R$$

$$L \to \cdot *R$$

$$L \to \cdot id$$

$$R \to \cdot L$$

goto $(I_0, S)$ :                    $I_1 : S' \rightarrow S\cdot$

goto $(I_0, L)$ :                    $I_2 : S \rightarrow L\cdot = R$

                                    $R \rightarrow L\cdot$

goto $(I_0, R)$ :                    $I_3 : S \rightarrow R\cdot$

goto $(I_0, *)$ :                    $I_4 : L \rightarrow * \cdot R$

                                    $R \rightarrow \cdot L$

                                    $L \rightarrow \cdot * R$

                                    $L \rightarrow \cdot id$

goto $(I_0, id)$ :                    $I_5 : L \rightarrow id\cdot$

goto $(I_2, =)$ :                    $I_6 : S \rightarrow L = \cdot R$

                                    $R \rightarrow \cdot L$

                                    $L \rightarrow \cdot * R$

                                    $L \rightarrow \cdot id$

goto $(I_4, R)$ :                    $I_7 : L \rightarrow * R\cdot$

goto $(I_4, L)$ :                    $I_8 : R \rightarrow L\cdot$

goto $(I_4, *)$ :                    $I_4 : L \rightarrow * \cdot R$

                                    $R \rightarrow \cdot L$                         (repeated)

                                    $L \rightarrow \cdot * R$

                                    $L \rightarrow \cdot id$

goto $(I_4, id)$ :                    $I_5 : L \rightarrow id.$                   (repeated)

goto $(I_6, R)$ :                    $I_9 : S \rightarrow L = R\cdot$

goto $(I_6, L)$ :                    $I_8 : R \rightarrow L\cdot$                   (repeated)

goto $(I_6, *)$ :                    $I_4 : L \rightarrow * \cdot R$                (repeated)

                                    $R \rightarrow \cdot L$

                                    $L \rightarrow \cdot * R$

                                    $L \rightarrow \cdot id$

goto $(I_6, id)$ :                    $I_5 : L \rightarrow id.$                   (repeated)

The corresponding transition diagram is shown below.

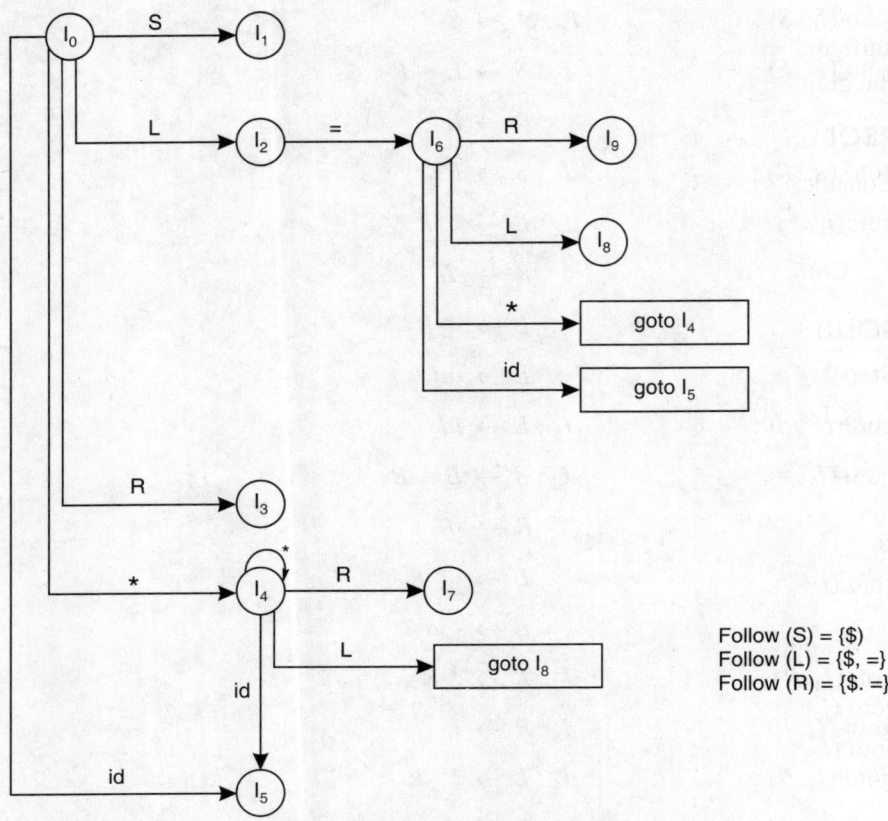

Follow (S) = {$}
Follow (L) = {$, =}
Follow (R) = {$. =}

**Step 2:** Construct the parsing table.

| State | Action | | | | Goto | | |
|---|---|---|---|---|---|---|---|
| | = | * | *id* | $ | S | L | R |
| 0 | | $S_4$ | $S_5$ | | 1 | 2 | 3 |
| 1 | | | | *acc* | | | |
| 2 | $(S_6/r_5)$ | | | $r_5$ | | | |
| 3 | | | | $r_2$ | | | |
| 4 | | $S_4$ | $S_5$ | | | 8 | 7 |
| 5 | $r_4$ | | | $r_4$ | | | |
| 6 | | $S_4$ | $S_5$ | | | 8 | 9 |
| 7 | $r_3$ | | $r_3$ | | | | |
| 8 | $r_5$ | | | $r_5$ | | | |
| 9 | | | | $r_1$ | | | |

As we are getting multiple entries in ACTION $[2, =] = S_6$ and $r_5$ that means shift and reduce *i.e.* both Shift|reduce conflict occurs on input symbol =. Hence the grammar is not SLR(1).

## PROBLEM 3

Consider the Grammar

$$S \rightarrow (S) \, S | \varepsilon$$

Construct *SLR(1)* parser and parse the input string () ().

## SOLUTION

**Step 1:** Construct Canonical set of items.

Closure (*I*):           $I_0 : S' \rightarrow \cdot S$

                  $S \rightarrow \cdot (S)S$

                  $S \rightarrow \cdot$

goto ($I_0, S$) :      $I_1 : S' \rightarrow S\cdot$

goto ($I_0, ()$) :      $I_2 : S \rightarrow (\cdot S)S$

                  $S \rightarrow \cdot (S)S$

                  $S \rightarrow \cdot$

goto ($I_2, S$) :      $I_3 : S \rightarrow (S\cdot)S$

goto ($I_2, ()$) :      $I_2 : S \rightarrow (\cdot S)S$                    (repeated)

                  $S \rightarrow \cdot (S)S$

                  $S \rightarrow \cdot$

goto ($I_3, )$) :      $I_4 : S \rightarrow (S) \cdot S$

                  $S \rightarrow \cdot (S)S$

                  $S \rightarrow \cdot$

goto ($I_4, S$) :      $I_5 : S \rightarrow (S)S\cdot$

goto ($I_4, ()$) :      $I_2 : S \rightarrow (\cdot S)S$                    (repeated)

                  $S \rightarrow \cdot (S)S$

                  $S \rightarrow \cdot$

The corresponding transition diagram is shown below

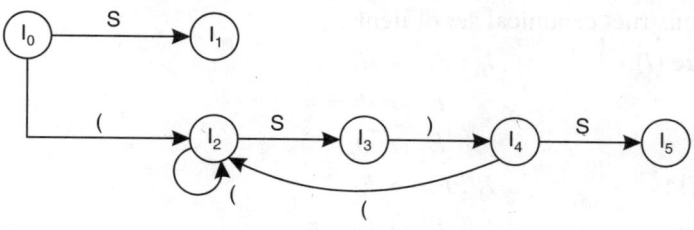

**Step 2:** Construct the parsing table.

| State | Action | | | Goto |
|---|---|---|---|---|
| | **(** | **)** | **$** | |
| 0 | $S_2$ | $r_2$ | $r_2$ | 1 |
| 1 | | | acc | |
| 2 | $S_2$ | $r_2$ | $r_2$ | 3 |
| 3 | | $S_4$ | | |
| 4 | $S_2$ | $r_2$ | $r_2$ | 5 |
| 5 | | $r_1$ | $r_1$ | |

**Step 3:** Constructing table to parse the input string.

| Sl.No. | Stack | Input | Action |
|---|---|---|---|
| 1 | $ 0 | ( ) ( ) $ | Shift |
| 2 | 0 ( 2 | ) ( ) $ | Reduce $S \rightarrow \varepsilon$ |
| 3 | 0 ( 2 S3 | ) ( ) $ | Shift |
| 4 | 0 (2S3)4 | ( ) $ | Shift |
| 5 | 0 (2S3) 4 (2 | )$ | Reduce $S \rightarrow \varepsilon$ |
| 6 | 0(2S3)4 (2S3 | ) $ | Shift |
| 7 | 0(2S3)4 (2S3)4 | $ | Reduce $S \rightarrow \varepsilon$ |
| 8 | 0(2S3)4 (2S3)4S5 | $ | Reduce $S \rightarrow (S)S$ |
| 9 | 0(2S3)4S5 | $ | Reduce $S \rightarrow (S)S$ |
| 10 | 0S1 | $ | accept |

## PROBLEM 4

Consider the Grammar.

$$E \rightarrow E + n|n$$

Construct SLR parsing table and parse the input string $n + n + n$.

## SOLUTION

**Step 1:** Construct canonical set of items.

Closure ($I$):    $I_0 : E' \rightarrow \cdot E$

$E \rightarrow \cdot E + n$

$E \rightarrow \cdot n$

goto ($I_0, E$) :    $I_1 : E' \rightarrow E\cdot$

$E \rightarrow E\cdot + n$

goto $(I_0, n)$ :              $I_2 : E \rightarrow n\cdot$

goto $(I_1, +)$ :              $I_3 : E \rightarrow E + \cdot n$

goto $(I_3, n)$ :              $I_4 : E \rightarrow E + n\cdot$

The corresponding transition diagram is shown below.

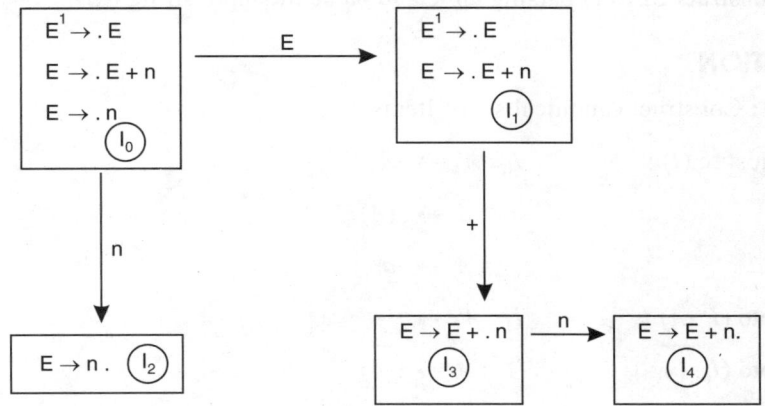

**Step 2:** To construct the parsing table.

| State | Action | | | Goto |
|---|---|---|---|---|
|  | $n$ | $+$ | $\$$ | $E$ |
| 0 | $S_2$ | | | 1 |
| 1 | | $S_3$ | accept | |
| 2 | | $r_2$ | $r_2$ | |
| 3 | $S_4$ | | | |
| 4 | | $r_1$ | $r_1$ | |

**Step 3:** To parse the input string $n + n + n$.

| Sl.No. | Stack | Input | Action |
|---|---|---|---|
| 1 | $\$ \, 0$ | $n + n + n\$$ | Shift |
| 2 | $\$ \, 0n2$ | $+ n + n\$$ | reduce $E \rightarrow n$ |
| 3 | $\$ \, 0E1$ | $+ n + n\$$ | Shift |
| 4 | $\$0E1 + 3$ | $n + n\$$ | Shift |
| 5 | $\$0E1 + 3n4$ | $+ n\$$ | reduce $E \rightarrow E + n$ |
| 6 | $\$ \, 0E1$ | $+ n\$$ | Shift |
| 7 | $\$ \, 0E1 + 3$ | $n \, \$$ | Shift |
| 8 | $\$ \, 0E1 + 3n4$ | $n\$$ | Reduce $E \rightarrow E + n$ |
| 9 | $\$ \, 0E \, 1$ | $\$$ | accept. |

## PROBLEM 5

Consider the Grammar

$$A \rightarrow (A)|a$$

Construct SLR(1) parsing table and parse the input string $((a))$.

## SOLUTION

**Step 1:** Construct canonical set of Items.

| | |
|---|---|
| Closure $(I)$ : | $I_0 : A' \rightarrow \cdot A$ |
| | $A \rightarrow \cdot(A)$ |
| | $A \rightarrow \cdot a$ |
| goto $(I_0, A)$ : | $I_1 : A' \rightarrow A\cdot$ |
| goto $(I_0, ( )$ : | $I_2 : A \rightarrow (\cdot A)$ |
| | $A \rightarrow \cdot(A)$ |
| | $A \rightarrow \cdot a$ |
| goto $(I_0, a)$ : | $I_3 : A \rightarrow a.$ |
| goto $(I_2, A)$ : | $I_4 : A \rightarrow (A\cdot)$ |
| goto $(I_2, ( )$ : | $I_2 : A \rightarrow (\cdot A)$       (repeated) |
| | $A \rightarrow \cdot(A)$ |
| | $A \rightarrow \cdot a$ |
| goto $(I_2, a)$ : | $I_3 : A \rightarrow a\cdot$       (repeated) |
| goto $(I_4, ) )$ : | $I_5 : A \rightarrow (A)\cdot$ |

The corresponding transition diagram is shown below.

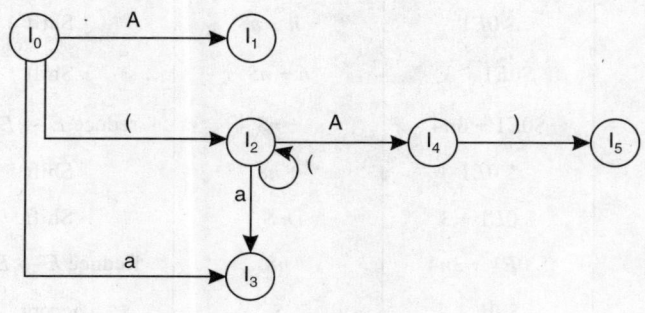

**Step 2:** Construct the parsing table

| State | Action | | | | Goto |
|---|---|---|---|---|---|
| | ( | ) | a | $ | A |
| 0 | $S_2$ | | $S_3$ | | 1 |
| 1 | | | | acc | |
| 2 | $S_2$ | | $S_3$ | | 4 |
| 3 | | $r_2$ | | $r_2$ | |
| 4 | | $S_5$ | | | |
| 5 | | $r_1$ | | $r_1$ | |

**Step 3:** To parse the input string $((a))$.

| Sl.No. | Stack | Input | Action |
|---|---|---|---|
| 1 | 0 | $((a))$$ | Shift |
| 2 | 0(2 | $(a))$$ | Shift |
| 3 | 0(2(2 | a )) $ | Shift |
| 4 | 0(2(2a3 | )) $ | reduce A → a |
| 5 | 0(2(2A4 | ))$ | Shift |
| 6 | 0(2(2A4)5 | ) $ | reduce A → (A) |
| 7 | 0(2A4 | )$ | Shift |
| 8 | 0(2A4)5 | $ | reduce A → (A) |
| 9 | 0A1 | $ | accepted |

## 4.6 VIABLE PREFIXES

Viable Prefixes are the set of prefixes of right sentential forms that can appear on the stack of **Shift|Reduce parser.**

Consider the augmented expression grammar whose set of items and goto functions shown in Problem 1. Clearly, the string $E + T*$ is a viable prefix of the Grammar.

The DFA of figure shown will be in state 7 after reading $E + T*$. State 7 contains the items.

$$T \rightarrow T * \cdot F$$

$$F \rightarrow \cdot (E)$$

$$F \rightarrow \cdot id$$

which are precisely the items valid for $E + T*$

Consider the Rightmost derivation.

$$E' \rightarrow E$$
$$\Rightarrow E + T$$
$$\Rightarrow E + T * F$$

$$E' \rightarrow E$$
$$\Rightarrow E + T$$
$$\Rightarrow E + T * F$$
$$\Rightarrow E + T * (E)$$

$$E' \rightarrow E$$
$$\Rightarrow E + T$$
$$\Rightarrow E + T * F$$
$$\Rightarrow E + T * id$$

The first derivation shows the validity of $T \rightarrow T * \cdot F$. Second the validity of $F \rightarrow \cdot (E)$ and third the validity of $F \rightarrow \cdot id$

It can be shown that there are no other valid items for $E + T*$.

# 5

# SYNTAX ANALYSIS–III

## 5.1 MORE POWERFUL LR PARSERS

## Canonical LR(1) Parsing or LR(1) Parsing or LR Parsing

In canonical LR parsing method, the general form of an item is,

$$[A \to \alpha\beta, a]$$

where, $A \to \alpha\beta$ is a production and

'$a$' is a terminal or a right end marker $.

Such an object is called LR(1) items. The 1 refers the length of second component called the **look-ahead of the item.**

### OR

The canonical set of items is a parsing technique in which look ahead symbol is generated while constructing set of items. Hence the collection of set of items is considered as LR(1). THe value 1 indicates there is no lookahead symbol in set of items.

The steps used in canonical LR parser is same as SLR parser.

**Step 1:** Construction of canonical set of items (LR(1)) along with look ahead.

**Step 2:** Constructing canonical LR parsing table.

**Step 3:** Parse the input string using canonical LR parsing table.

## Construction of Canonical Set of Items (LR(1) Along with Look Ahead

**Step 1:** For the grammar G initially add augmented grammar $S' \rightarrow \cdot S$ in the set of item $C$.

**Step 2:** For each set of items, $I_i$ in $C$ and for each grammar symbol $X$ (may be terminal or nontermal add closure $(I_i, X)$

This process should be repeated by applying goto $(I_i, X)$ is not empty and not in $C$.

**Step 3:** The closure function can be computed as follow:

For each item $[A \rightarrow \alpha \cdot x\beta, a]$ and rule $X \rightarrow \cdot \sqrt{}$ and $b \varepsilon$ FIRST $(\beta, a)$ such that.

$x \rightarrow \cdot \sqrt{}$ and $b$ is not in $I$ then add $x \rightarrow \cdot \sqrt{}, b$ to $I$

**Step 4:** Similarly the goto function can be computed as follows.

For each item, $[A \rightarrow \alpha \cdot x\beta, a]$ is in $I$ and rule

$[A \rightarrow \alpha X \cdot \beta, a]$ is not in goto item, then add

$[A \rightarrow \alpha X \cdot \beta, a]$ to go to items.

This process is repeated until no more set of items can be added to the collection of $C$.

## PROBLEM 1

Consider the Grammar

$$S \rightarrow CC$$
$$C \rightarrow aC | d$$

Construct $LR(1)$ set of items, parsing table and also parse the input string *aadd*.

## SOLUTION

**Step 1:** Construct canonical set of items add to augmented grammar $S' \rightarrow S$ to the above grammar and find closure $(I)$

$$\therefore \qquad S' \rightarrow \cdot S$$
$$S \rightarrow \cdot CC$$

$$C \rightarrow \cdot aC$$
$$C \rightarrow \cdot d$$

Initially adding $ as look ahead symbol.

$$S' \rightarrow \cdot S, \$$$
$$S \rightarrow \cdot CC, \$$$
$$C \rightarrow \cdot ac, \$$$
$$C \rightarrow \cdot d, \$$$

To find Closure ($I$):

Consider, $S' \rightarrow \cdot S, \$$

Compare with $[A \rightarrow \alpha \cdot \times \beta, a]$

$$A = S', \alpha = \varepsilon, X = S, \beta = \varepsilon, a = \$$$
$$b \in \text{FIRST} (\beta, a)$$
$$\in \text{FIRST} (\varepsilon, \$)$$
$$b \in \$$$
$$b = \$$$

$\therefore$ Add $S \rightarrow \cdot cc, \$$ to closure ($I$)

Consider, $S \rightarrow \cdot CC, \$$

Compare with $[A \rightarrow \alpha \cdot \times \beta, a]$

$$A = S,$$
$$\alpha = \varepsilon$$
$$X = C$$
$$\beta = C$$
$$a = \$$$
$$b \in \text{FIRST} (\beta, a)$$
$$\in \text{FIRST} (C, \$)$$
$$\in \text{FIRST} (C)$$
$$b \in \{a, d\}$$
$$b = \{a, d\}$$

Add $\qquad C \rightarrow \cdot ac, a|d$

$$C \rightarrow \cdot d, a/d \text{ to closure } (I)$$

$\therefore$ $\qquad$ $I_0 : S' \rightarrow \cdot S, \$$

$$S \rightarrow \cdot CC, \$$$

$$C \rightarrow \cdot ac, a|d$$

$$C \rightarrow \cdot d, a|d$$

goto on $I_0$:

goto $(I_0, S)$ : $\qquad$ $I_1 : S' \rightarrow S\cdot, \$$

goto $(I_0, C)$ : $\qquad$ $S \rightarrow C\cdot C, \$$

Compare with $[A \rightarrow \alpha \cdot \times \beta, a]$

$$b \in \text{FIRST } (\beta, a)$$

$$\in \text{FIRST } (\varepsilon, \$)$$

$$b = \$$$

$\therefore$ goto $(I_0, C)$ : $\qquad$ $I_2 : S \rightarrow C.C, \$$

$$C \rightarrow \cdot ac, \$$$

$$C \rightarrow \cdot d, \$$$

goto$(I_0, a)$ : $\qquad$ $C \rightarrow a.c, a|d$

Compare with $[A \rightarrow \alpha \cdot X \beta, a]$

$$b \in \text{FIRST } (\beta, a)$$

$$\in \text{FIRST } (\in, a/d)$$

$$b = a|d$$

goto$(I_0, a)$ : $\qquad$ $I_3 : c \rightarrow a \cdot c, a|d$

$$c \rightarrow \cdot ac, a|d$$

$$c \rightarrow \cdot d \cdot a|d$$

goto $(I_0, d)$ : $\qquad$ $I_4 : c \rightarrow d\cdot, a|d$

goto $(I_2, c)$ : $\qquad$ $I_5 : S \rightarrow cc\cdot, \$$

goto$(I_2, a)$ : $\qquad$ $c \rightarrow a.c, \$$

$$b \in \text{FIRST } (\beta, a)$$

$$\in \text{FIRST } (\in, \$)$$

$$b = \$$$

$\therefore$ goto $(I_2, a)$ :          $I_6 : c \rightarrow a \cdot c, \$$

                                                   $c \rightarrow \cdot ac, \$$

                                                   $c \rightarrow \cdot d, \$$

goto $(I_2, d)$ :               $I : c \rightarrow d \cdot, \$$

goto $(I_3, c)$ :               $I_8 : c \rightarrow ac \cdot, a|d$

goto $(I_3, a)$ :               $I_3 : c \rightarrow a \cdot c, a|d$                          (repeated)

                                                   $c \rightarrow \cdot ac, a|d$

                                                   $c \rightarrow \cdot d, a|d$

                                                   $b \in \text{FIRST} (\beta, a)$

                                                   $b \in \text{FIRST} (\in, a|c)$

                                                   $b = \{a, d\}$

goto $(I_3, d)$ :               $I_4 : c \rightarrow d \cdot, a|d$                          (repeated)

goto $(I_6, c)$ :               $I_9 : c \rightarrow ac \cdot, \$$

goto $(I_6, a)$ :               $I_6 : c \rightarrow a \cdot c, \$$                 $b \in \text{FIRST} (\beta, a)$

                                                   $c \rightarrow \cdot ac, \$$                 $\in \text{FIRST} (\varepsilon, \$) \, b = \$$

                                                   $c \rightarrow \cdot d, \$$                                (repeated)

goto $(I_6, d)$ :               $I_9 : c \rightarrow d \cdot, \$$                                (repeated)

The corresponding transition diagram is shown below:

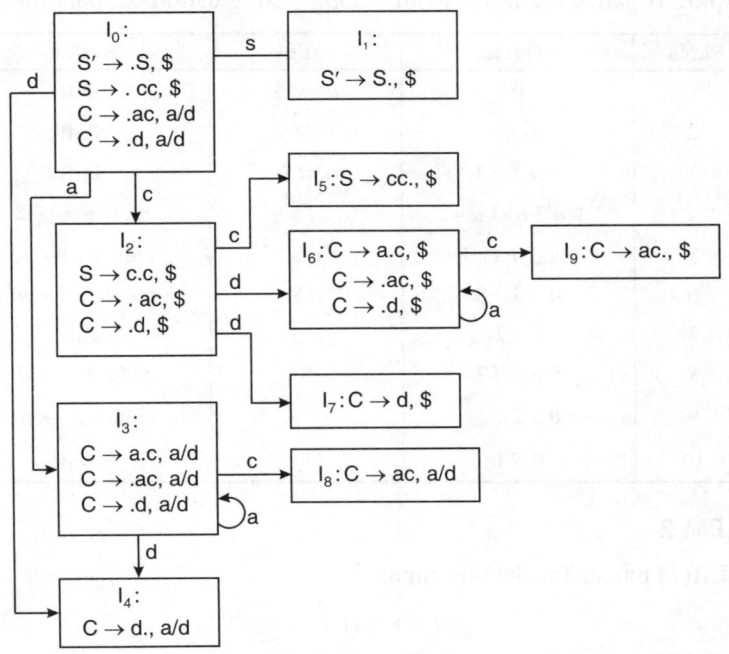

**Step 2:** To construct canonical LR parsing table.

| State | Action | | | Goto | |
|---|---|---|---|---|---|
| | $a$ | $d$ | $\$$ | $S$ | $C$ |
| 0 | $S_3$ | $S_4$ | | 1 | 2 |
| 1 | | | acc | | |
| 2 | $S_6$ | $S_7$ | | | 5 |
| 3 | $S_3$ | $S_4$ | | | 8 |
| 4 | $r_3$ | $r_3$ | $r_3$ | | |
| 5 | | | $r_1$ | | |
| 6 | $s_6$ | $s_7$ | | | 9 |
| 7 | $r_3$ | $r_3$ | $r_3$ | | |
| 8 | $r_2$ | $r_2$ | $r_2$ | | |
| 9 | $r_2$ | $r_2$ | $r_2$ | | |

- FOLLOW $(c) = \{\$, a, d\}$          (1) $S \rightarrow cc$
- FOLLOW $(S) = \{\$\}$                    (2) $c \rightarrow ac$
                                                     (3) $c \rightarrow d$

**Step 3:** To parse the input string "*aadd*" using canonical parsing table.

| Sl.No. | Stack | Input | Action |
|---|---|---|---|
| 1 | 0 | aadd $\$$ | Shift |
| 2 | 0a3 | add $\$$ | Shift |
| 3 | 0 a 3 a 3 | d d $\$$ | Shift |
| 4 | 0 a 3 a 3 d 4 | d $\$$ | reduce $c \rightarrow d$ |
| 5 | 0 a 3 a 3 c 8 | d $\$$ | reduce $c \rightarrow ac$ |
| 6 | 0 a 3 c 8 | d $\$$ | reduce $c \rightarrow ac$ |
| 7 | 0 c 2 | d $\$$ | Shift |
| 8 | 0 c 2 d 7 | $\$$ | reduce $c \rightarrow d$ |
| 9 | 0 c 2 c 5 | $\$$ | reduce $S \rightarrow cc$ |
| 10 | 0 S 1 | $\$$ | accept |

## PROBLEM 2

Obtain LR(1) parser for the Grammar

$$A \rightarrow (A)|a$$

## SOLUTION

**Step 1:** To construct canonical set of items.

Add augmented grammar,

$$A' \rightarrow \cdot A$$
$$A \rightarrow \cdot (A)$$
$$A \rightarrow \cdot a$$

Initially add $ as look ahead symbol

$$A' \rightarrow \cdot A, \$$$
$$A \rightarrow \cdot (A), \$$$
$$A \rightarrow \cdot a, \$$$

| | | |
|---|---|---|
| Closure $(I)$ : | $I_0 : A' \rightarrow \cdot A, \$$ | $b = \text{FIRST } (\beta, a)$ |
| | $A \rightarrow \cdot (A), \$$ | $b = \$$ |
| | $A \rightarrow \cdot a, \$$ | |
| goto $(I_0, A)$ : | $I_1 : A' \rightarrow A \cdot, \$$ | |
| goto $(I_0, ()$ : | $I_2 : A \rightarrow (\cdot A), \$$ | $b = \text{FIRST } (\beta, a)$ |
| | $A \rightarrow \cdot (A), )$ | $= \{), \$\}$ |
| | $A \rightarrow \cdot a, )$ | |
| goto $(I_0, a)$ : | $I_3 : A \rightarrow a \cdot, \$$ | |
| goto $(I_2, A)$ : | $I_4 : A \rightarrow (A \cdot), \$$ | |
| goto $(I_2, ()$ : | $I_5 : A \rightarrow (\cdot A), )$ | $b = \text{FIRST } (\beta, a)$ |
| | $A \rightarrow \cdot (A), )$ | $= \text{FIRST } (), x)$ |
| | $A \rightarrow \cdot a, )$ | $b = \{)\}$ |
| goto $(I_2, a)$ : | $I_6 : A \rightarrow a \cdot, )$ | |
| goto $(I_4, ))$ : | $I_7 : A \rightarrow (A) \cdot, \$$ | |
| goto $(I_5, A)$ : | $I_8 : A \rightarrow (A \cdot), )$ | |
| goto $(I_5, ()$ : | $I_5 : A \rightarrow (\cdot A), )$ | (repeated) |
| | $A \rightarrow \cdot (A), )$ | |
| | $A \rightarrow \cdot a, )$ | |
| goto $(I_5, a)$ : | $I_6 : A \rightarrow a \cdot, )$ | (repeated) |
| goto $(I_6, ))$ : | $I_9 : A \rightarrow (A) \cdot, )$ | |

The corresponding transition diagram is shown below:

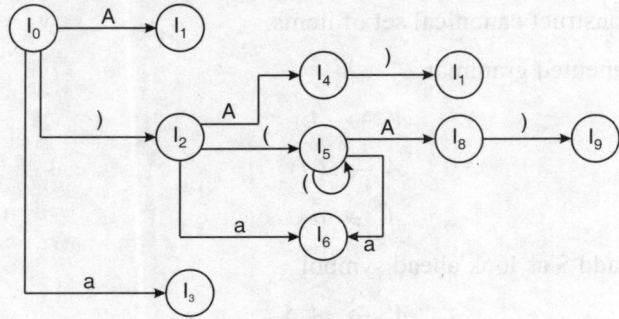

**Step 2:** To construct canonical parsing table.

| State | Action | | | | Goto |
|---|---|---|---|---|---|
| | **(** | **)** | **a** | **$** | **A** |
| 0 | | $S_2$ | $S_3$ | | 1 |
| 1 | | | | *acc* | |
| 2 | $S_5$ | | $S_6$ | | 4 |
| 3 | | $r_2$ | | $r_2$ | |
| 4 | | $S_7$ | | | |
| 5 | $S_5$ | | $S_6$ | | 8 |
| 6 | | $r_2$ | | $r_2$ | |
| 7 | | $r_1$ | | $r_1$ | |
| 8 | | $S_9$ | | | |
| 9 | | $r_1$ | | $r_1$ | |

FOLLOW $(A) = \{(, \$\}$     (1) $A \rightarrow (A)$

(2) $A \rightarrow a$

## 5.2  LALR PARSER (LOOKAHEAD LR PARSER)

Construction of LALR parser is same as LR parser, but the only difference is that in construction of LR(1) items for LR parser, we have defered the two states the second component is different. But in this case we will merge two states by merging offirst and second component from both states.

For example in Problem 1 of LR paser we have $I_3$ and $I_6$ because of different in second component, but for LALR parser we will consider these two states as same by merging these states.

*i.e.,*    $$I_3 + I_6 = I_{36}$$

Hence

$I_{36}$ : goto $(I_0, a)$

$$c \rightarrow a \cdot c, a|d|\$$$

$$c \rightarrow \cdot ac, a|d|\$$$

$$c \rightarrow \cdot d, a|d|\$$$

## PROBLEM 1

Consider the Grammar,

$$S \rightarrow cc$$

$$c \rightarrow ac$$

$$c \rightarrow d$$

Construct set of LR(1) items and also parsing table using LALR parser.

## SOLUTION

**Step 1:** Construct set of LR(1) items. We obtain

$$I_0 : S' \rightarrow \cdot S, \$$$

$$S \rightarrow \cdot cc, \$$$

$$c \rightarrow \cdot ac, a|d$$

$$c \rightarrow \cdot d, a|d$$

goto $(I_0, S)$ :    $I_1 : S' \rightarrow S\cdot, \$$

goto $(I_0, c)$ :    $I_2 : S \rightarrow c \cdot c, \$$

$$c \rightarrow \cdot ac, \$$$

$$c \rightarrow \cdot d, \$$$

goto $(I_0, a)$ :    $I_3 : c \rightarrow a \cdot c, a|d$

$$c \rightarrow \cdot ac, a|d$$

goto $(I_0, d)$ :    $I_4 : c \rightarrow d \cdot, a|d$

goto $(I_2, c)$ :    $I_5 : S \rightarrow cc \cdot, \$$

goto $(I_2, a)$ :    $I_6 : c \rightarrow a \cdot c, \$$

$$c \rightarrow \cdot ac, \$$$

$$c \to \cdot d, \$$$

goto $(I_2, d)$ :    $I_7 : c \to d \cdot, \$$

goto $(I_3, c)$ :    $I_8 : c \to ac \cdot, a|d$

goto $(I_3, a)$ :    $I_3 : c \to a \cdot c, a|d$

$$c \to \cdot ac, a|d$$

$$c \to \cdot d, a|d$$

goto $(I_3, d)$ :    $I_4 : c \to d \cdot, a|d$

goto $(I_6, c)$ :    $I_9 : c \to ac \cdot, \$$

goto $(I_6, a)$ :    $I_6 : c \to a \cdot c, \$$

$$c \to \cdot ac, \$$$

$$c \to \cdot d, \$$$

goto $(I_6, d)$ :    $I_7 : c \to d \cdot, \$$

Now in $I_3$, $I_6$ and $I_4$, $I_7$ and $I_8$, $I_9$ only second component differs. So we merge these states in order to get $I_{36}$. $I_{47}$, $I_{89}$ as states.

So we obtain,

$$I_0 : S' \to \cdot S, \$$$

$$S \to \cdot cc, \$$$

$$c \to \cdot ac, a|d$$

$$c \to \cdot d, a|d$$

goto $(I_0, S)$ :    $I_1 : S' \to S \cdot, \$$

goto $(I_0, c)$ :    $I_2 : S \to c \cdot c, \$$

$$c \to \cdot ac, \$$$

$$c \to \cdot d, \$$$

goto $(I_0, a)$ :    $I_{36} : c \to a \cdot c, a|d|\$$

$$c \to \cdot ac, a|d|\$$$

$$c \to \cdot d, a|d|\$$$

goto $(I_0, d)$ :    $I_{47} : c \to d \cdot, a|d|\$$

goto $(I_2, c)$ :    $I_5 : S \to cc \cdot \$$

goto $(I_3, c)$ :    $I_{89} : c \to ac \cdot, a|d|\$$

So the states $i.e.$, set of LR(1) items are

$$c = \{I_0, I_1, I_2, I_{36}, I_{47}, I_5, I_{89}\}$$

**Step 2:** To construct passing table of LALR parsing table.

| State | $a$ | $d$ | $ | S | $c$ |
|-------|------|------|------|---|-----|
| 0 | $S_{36}$ | $S_{47}$ | | 1 | 2 |
| 1 | | | $acc$ | | |
| 2 | $S_{36}$ | $S_{47}$ | | | 5 |
| 36 | $S_{36}$ | $S_{47}$ | | | 89 |
| 47 | $r_3$ | $r_3$ | $r_3$ | | |
| 5 | | | $r_1$ | | |
| 89 | $r_2$ | $r_2$ | $r_2$ | | |

The corresponding transistion diagram is shown below.

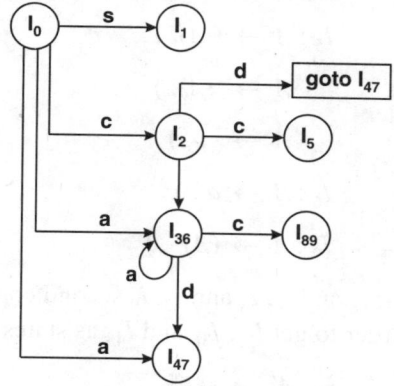

## PROBLEM 2

Obtain LALR parser for the Grammar,

$$A \rightarrow (A)|a$$

## SOLUTION

**Step 1:** Construct Set of LR(1) items, we obtain

$$I_0 : A' \rightarrow \cdot A, \$$$

$$A \rightarrow \cdot(A), \$$$

$$A \rightarrow \cdot a, \$$$

goto $(I_0, A)$ :          $I_1 : A' \rightarrow A \cdot, \$$

goto $(I_0, c)$ :          $I_2 : A \rightarrow (\cdot A), \$$

$$A \to \cdot (A), )$$

$$A \to \cdot a, )$$

goto $(I_0, a)$:          $I_3 : A \to a \cdot, \$$

goto $(I_2, A)$ :         $I_4 : A \to (A \cdot), \$$

goto $(I_2, ( )$ :        $I_5 : A \to (\cdot A), )$

$$A \to \cdot (A), )$$

$$A \to \cdot a, )$$

goto $(I_2, a)$ :         $I_6 : A \to a \cdot, )$

goto $(I_4, )$ :          $I_7 : A \to (A) \cdot, \$$

goto $(I_5, A)$ :         $I_8 : A \to (A \cdot), )$

goto $(I_5, ( )$ :        $I_5 : A \to (\cdot A), )$

$$A \to \cdot (A), )$$

$$A \to \cdot a, )$$

goto $(I_5, a)$ :         $I_6 : A \to a \cdot, )$

goto $(I_8, )$ :          $I_9 : A \to (A) \cdot, )$

Now in $I_2$, $I_5$ and $I_3$, $I_6$ and $I_4$, $I_8$ and $I_7$, $I_9$ second component differs. So we merge these states in order to get $I_{25}$. $I_{36}$ and $I_{48}$ as states.

$$I_0 : A' \to \cdot A, \$$$

$$A \to \cdot (A) \cdot \$$$

$$A \to \cdot a, \$$$

goto $(I_0, A)$ :         $I_1 : A' \to A \cdot, \$$

goto $(I_0, ( )$ :        $I_{25} : A \to (\cdot A), \$|)$

$$A \to \cdot (A),)$$

$$A \to \cdot a, )$$

goto $(I_0, a)$ :         $I_{36} : A \to a \cdot, \$|)$

goto $(I_2, A)$ :         $I_{48} : A \to (A \cdot), \$|)$

goto $(I_4, )$ :          $I_{79} : A \to (A) \cdot, \$|)$

The corresponding transition diagram is shown on next page.

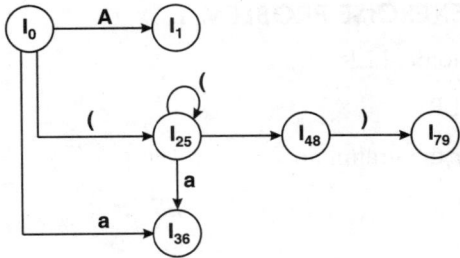

**Step 2:** Construction of parsing table.

| State | ( | a | ) | $ | A |
|-------|-----|-----|-----|-----|-----|
| 0 | $S_{25}$ | $S_{36}$ | | | 1 |
| 1 | | | | acc | |
| 25 | $S_{25}$ | $S_{36}$ | | | 48 |
| 36 | | | $r_2$ | $r_2$ | |
| 48 | | | $S_{79}$ | | |
| 79 | | | $r_1$ | $r_1$ | |

**Note:** SLR and LALR tables for a grammar always have a same number of states whereas canonical LR have several states for the same language.

**Exercise Problems:**

1. Construct

    (a) Canonical LR

    (b) LALR Set of items for the Grammar

    $S \rightarrow SS + |SS *|a$

2. Show that the following Grammar

    $$S \rightarrow Aa|bAc|dc|bda$$

    $$A \rightarrow d$$

    is LALR (1) but not SLR(1).

3. Show that the following Grammar

    $$S \rightarrow Aa|bAc|Bc|bBa$$

    $$A \rightarrow d$$

    $$B \rightarrow d$$

    is LR (1) but not LALR (1).

## SOLUTION FOR EXERCISE PROBLEM 1

Construct  (a)  Canonical LR

  (b)  LALR

Set of items for the grammar

$$S \rightarrow SS + |SS*|a$$

## SOLUTION

(a) To construct canonical LR(1) items.

Add augmented grammar

$$S' \rightarrow \cdot S$$
$$S \rightarrow \cdot SS +$$
$$S \rightarrow \cdot SS*$$
$$S \rightarrow \cdot a$$

Initially add $ as look ahead symbol

$$S' \rightarrow \cdot S, \$$$
$$S \rightarrow \cdot SS +, \$$$
$$S \rightarrow \cdot SS *, \$$$
$$S \rightarrow \cdot a, \$$$

To find $I_0$:

$$I_0 : S' \rightarrow \cdot S, \$$$
$$S \rightarrow \cdot SS +, \$$$
$$S \rightarrow \cdot SS *, \$$$
$$S \rightarrow \cdot a, \$$$

goto $(I_0, S)$ :

$$I_1 : S' \rightarrow S \cdot, \$$$
$$S \rightarrow S \cdot S +, \$$$
$$S \rightarrow \cdot SS +, +$$
$$S \rightarrow \cdot SS *, +$$
$$S \rightarrow \cdot a, +$$
$$S \rightarrow S \cdot S *, \$$$
$$S \rightarrow \cdot SS +, *$$
$$S \rightarrow \cdot SS *, *$$

$$S \rightarrow \cdot a, *$$

goto $(I_0, a)$ :                 $I_2 : S \rightarrow a \cdot, \$$

goto $(I_1, S)$ :                 $I_3 : S \rightarrow SS \cdot +, \$$

$$S \rightarrow S \cdot S +, +$$

$$S \rightarrow \cdot SS +, +$$

$$S \rightarrow \cdot SS *, +$$

$$S \rightarrow \cdot a, +$$

$$S \rightarrow S \cdot S *, +$$

$$S \rightarrow \cdot SS +, * \mid +$$

$$S \rightarrow \cdot SS *, *|+$$

$$S \rightarrow \cdot a, *|+$$

$$S \rightarrow SS \cdot *, \$$

$$S \rightarrow S \cdot S +, *$$

$$S \rightarrow S \cdot S *, *$$

$$S \rightarrow \cdot SS +, *$$

$$S \rightarrow \cdot SS *, *$$

$$S \rightarrow \cdot a, *$$

goto $(I, a)$ :                 $I_4 : S \rightarrow a \cdot, +$

$$S \rightarrow a \cdot, *$$

goto $(I_3, +)$ :                 $I_5 : S \rightarrow SS + \cdot, \$$

goto $(I_3, S)$ :                 $I_6 : S \rightarrow SS \cdot +, +$

$$S \rightarrow S \cdot S +, +$$

$$S \rightarrow \cdot SS +, +$$

$$S \rightarrow \cdot SS *, +$$

$$S \rightarrow \cdot a, +$$

$$S \rightarrow S \cdot S *, +$$

$$S \rightarrow \cdot SS +, *|+$$

$$S \rightarrow \cdot SS *, *|+$$

$$S \rightarrow \cdot a, * |+$$

$$S \rightarrow SS \cdot *, +$$

$$S \rightarrow S \cdot S+, *|+$$
$$S \rightarrow S \cdot S*, *|+$$
$$S \rightarrow SS \cdot +, *$$
$$S \rightarrow SS \cdot *, *$$
$$S \rightarrow S \cdot S+, *$$
$$S \rightarrow S \cdot S*, *$$
$$S \rightarrow \cdot SS+, *$$
$$S \rightarrow \cdot SS*, *$$
$$S \rightarrow \cdot a, *$$

goto $(I_3, a)$ :     $I_7 : S \rightarrow a \cdot, +$
$$S \rightarrow a \cdot, *|+$$
$$S \rightarrow a \cdot, *$$

goto $(I_3, *)$ :     $I_8 : S \rightarrow SS * \cdot, \$$

goto $(I_6, +)$ :     $I_9 : S \rightarrow SS + \cdot, +$
$$S \rightarrow SS + \cdot, *$$

goto $(I_6, S)$ :     $I_{10} : S \rightarrow SS \cdot +, +$
$$S \rightarrow S \cdot S+, +$$
$$S \rightarrow \cdot SS+, +$$
$$S \rightarrow \cdot SS*, +$$
$$S \rightarrow \cdot a, +$$
$$S \rightarrow S \cdot S*, +$$
$$S \rightarrow \cdot SS+, *|+$$
$$S \rightarrow \cdot SS*, *|+$$
$$S \rightarrow \cdot a, *|+$$
$$S \rightarrow SS \cdot *, +$$
$$S \rightarrow S \cdot S+, *|+$$
$$S \rightarrow S \cdot S*, *|+$$
$$S \rightarrow SS \cdot +, *|+$$
$$S \rightarrow SS \cdot *, *|+$$
$$S \rightarrow SS \cdot +, *$$

$$S \rightarrow SS \cdot +, *$$
$$S \rightarrow SS \cdot *, *$$
$$S \rightarrow S \cdot S +, *$$
$$S \rightarrow SS \cdot *, *$$
$$S \rightarrow S \cdot S +, *$$
$$S \rightarrow S \cdot S + , *$$
$$S \rightarrow S \cdot S *, *$$
$$S \rightarrow \cdot SS +, *$$
$$S \rightarrow \cdot SS *, *$$
$$S \rightarrow \cdot a, *$$

goto $(I_6, *)$ :    $I_{11} : S \rightarrow SS * \cdot, +$
$$S \rightarrow SS* \cdot, *$$

goto $(I_6, a)$ :    $I_7 : S \rightarrow a \cdot, +$
$$S \rightarrow a \cdot, *|+$$
$$S \rightarrow a \cdot, *$$

goto $(I_{10}, +)$:    $I_{12} : S \rightarrow SS + \cdot, +$
$$S \rightarrow SS + \cdot, *|+$$
$$S \rightarrow SS + \cdot, *$$

goto $(I_{10}, S)$  :    $I_{10} : S \rightarrow SS \cdot +, +$
$$S \rightarrow S \cdot S +, +$$
$$S \rightarrow \cdot SS +, +$$
$$S \rightarrow \cdot SS *, +$$
$$S \rightarrow \cdot a, +$$
$$S \rightarrow S \cdot S *, +$$
$$S \rightarrow S \cdot S +, *|+$$
$$S \rightarrow \cdot SS +, *|+$$
$$S \rightarrow \cdot SS *, *|+$$
$$S \rightarrow \cdot a, *|+$$
$$S \rightarrow S \cdot S *, *|+$$
$$S \rightarrow SS \cdot +, *|+$$

$$S \to SS \cdot *, *|+$$
$$S \to SS \cdot +, *$$
$$S \to SS \cdot *, *$$
$$S \to \cdot SS +, *$$
$$S \to \cdot SS *, *$$
$$S \to \cdot a, *$$

goto $(I_{10}, *)$ :          $I_{13} : S \to SS* \cdot, +$
$$S \to SS* \cdot, *|+$$
$$S \to SS * \cdot, *$$

goto $(I_{10}, a)$ :          $I_{17} : S \to a \cdot, +$
$$S \to a \cdot, *|+$$
$$S \to a \cdot, *$$

goto $(I_{10}, *)$ :          $I_{13} : S \to SS* \cdot, +$
$$S \to SS *|+$$
$$S \to SS * \cdot, *$$

goto $(I_{10}, a)$ :          $I_7 : S \to a \cdot, +$
$$S \to a \cdot, *|+$$
$$S \to a \cdot, *$$

$\therefore$ The canonical set of items for LR(1) parser is

$$C = \{I_0, I_1, I_2, I_3, I_4, I_5, I_6, I_7, I_8, I_9, I_{10}, I_{11}, I_{12}, I_{13}\}$$

(*b*) To construct canonical set of items for LALR parser

$$I_0 : S' \to \cdot S, \$$$
$$S \to \cdot SS +, \$$$
$$S \to \cdot SS *, \$$$
$$S \to \cdot a, \$$$

goto $(I_0, S)$ :          $I_1 : S' \to S \cdot, \$$
$$S \to S \cdot S +, \$$$
$$S \to \cdot SS +, +$$
$$S \to \cdot SS *, +$$
$$S \to \cdot SS *, +$$
$$S \to \cdot a, +$$
$$S \to S \cdot S *, \$$$

$$S \rightarrow \cdot SS +, *$$

$$S \rightarrow \cdot SS *, *$$

$$S \rightarrow \cdot a, *$$

## 5.3 USING AMBIGUOUS GRAMMAR TO (REDUCE) RESOLVE SHIFT|REDUCE CONFLICT

The various parsing methods can be used if at all the grammar is ambiguous. Then it creates then conflicts and we cannot parse the input string with such ambiguous grammar.

While using ambiguous grammar for parsing the input string we use all the disambiguity rules such that each time only one parse tree will be generated for that specific input. Thus ambiguous grammar can be used in controlled manner for parsing the input.

Using **precedence** and **associativity** we can resolve the parsing action conflicts.

### PROBLEM 1

Consider an ambigous grammar for arithmetic expression

$$E \rightarrow E + E$$

$$E \rightarrow E * E$$

$$E \rightarrow (E)$$

$$E \rightarrow id$$

### SOLUTION

Construct LR(0) items for this Grammar.

$$I_0 : E' \rightarrow \cdot E$$

$$E \rightarrow \cdot E + E$$

$$E \rightarrow \cdot E \times E$$

$$E \rightarrow \cdot (E)$$

$$E \rightarrow \cdot id$$

goto $(I_0, E)$ :  $\quad I_1 : E' \rightarrow E\cdot$

$$E \rightarrow E \cdot + E$$

$$E \rightarrow E \cdot * E$$

goto $(I_0 \, ())$ :  $\quad I_2 : E \rightarrow (\cdot E)$

$$E \rightarrow \cdot E + E$$
$$E \rightarrow \cdot E * \text{E}$$
$$E \rightarrow \cdot (E)$$
$$E \rightarrow \cdot id$$

goto $(I_0, id)$ :          $I_3 : E \rightarrow id \cdot$

goto $(I_1 , +)$ :          $I_4 : E \rightarrow E + \cdot E$
$$E \rightarrow \cdot E + E$$
$$E \rightarrow \cdot E * E$$
$$E \rightarrow \cdot (E)$$
$$E \rightarrow \cdot id$$

goto $(I_1, *)$ :          $I_5 : E \rightarrow E * \cdot E$
$$E \rightarrow \cdot E + E$$
$$E \rightarrow \cdot E * E$$
$$E \rightarrow \cdot (E)$$
$$E \rightarrow \cdot id$$

goto $(I_2, E)$ :          $I_6 : E \rightarrow (E \cdot)$
$$E \rightarrow E \cdot + E$$
$$E \rightarrow E \cdot * E$$

goto $(I_2, ()$ :          $I_2 : E \rightarrow (\cdot E)$
$$E \rightarrow \cdot E + E$$
$$E \rightarrow \cdot E * E$$
$$E \rightarrow \cdot (E)$$
$$E \rightarrow \cdot id$$

goto $(I_2, id)$ :          $I_3 : E \rightarrow id \cdot$

goto $(I_4, E)$ :          $I_7 : E \rightarrow E + E \cdot$
$$E \rightarrow E \cdot + E$$
$$E \rightarrow E \cdot * E$$

goto $(I_4 , ()$ :          $I_2 : E \rightarrow (\cdot E)$
$$E \rightarrow \cdot E + E$$
$$E \rightarrow \cdot E * E$$
$$E \rightarrow \cdot (E)$$
$$E \rightarrow \cdot id$$

| State | id | + | * | ( | ) | $ | E |
|---|---|---|---|---|---|---|---|
| 0 | $S_3$ | | | $S_2$ | | | 1 |
| 1 | | $S_4$ | $S_5$ | | | acc | — |
| 2 | $S_3$ | | | $S_2$ | | | 6 |
| 3 | | $r_4$ | $r_4$ | | $r_4$ | $r_4$ | |
| 4 | $S_3$ | | | $S_2$ | | | 7 |
| 5 | $S_3$ | | | $S_2$ | | | 8 |
| 6 | | $S_4$ | $S_5$ | | $S_9$ | | |
| 7 | | $S_4|r_1$ | $S_5|r_1$ | | $r_1$ | $r_1$ | |
| 8 | | $S_4|r_2$ | $S_5|r_2$ | | $r_2$ | $r_2$ | |
| 9 | | $r_3$ | $r_3$ | | $r_3$ | $r_3$ | |

As we see in the parsing table, the Shift|reduce conflict occurs at state 7 and 8 and we try to resolue it.

Consider the string $id + id + id$

| Stact | Input | Action with Conflict Resolution |
|---|---|---|
| $0 | $id + id * id \$$ | Shift |
| $0 id 3 | $+ id * id \$$ | reduce $E \rightarrow id$ |
| $ 0 E 1 | $+ id * id \$$ | Shift |
| $0 E 1 + 4 | $id + id \$$ | Shift |
| $ 0E1 + 4 id3 | $* id \$$ | reduce $E \rightarrow id$ |
| $ 0E1 + 4E7 | $* id \$$ | Conflict can be resolved by shifting |
| $ 0E1 + 4E7*5 | $id \$$ | Shift |
| $ 0E1 + 4 E 7* 5 id 3 | $\$$ | reduce $E \rightarrow id$ |
| $ 0E 1 + 4 E 7 * 5 E 8 | $\$$ | reduce $E \rightarrow E * E$ |
| $ 0E1 + 4 E 7 | $\$$ | reduce $E \rightarrow E + E$ |
| $ 0E1 | $\$$ | accept |

As * has precedence over +, we have to perform multiplication operation first and for that it is necessary to push * an top of the stack. The stack portion will be

| * |
|---|
| + |

By this we can perform $E * E$ first and then $E + E$. So parsing conflict can be resolved by shifting as shown above.

*i.e.,* action $[7, *] = S_5$

Similarly, if we consider the input *id * id + id* the conflict in action $[8, +]$ = $S_4$ or $r_2$ can be resolved by allowing $r_2$ action as we have to perform $E * E$ operation first. So the conflicts for action $[7, +]$ and action $[8, *]$ = $r_1$ and $r_2$ respectively.

Finally the ambiguous grammar without any conflict has the following SLR parsing table.

| State | id | + | * | ( | ) | $ | E |
|-------|-----|-----|-----|-----|-----|-----|-----|
| 0 | $S_3$ | | | $S_2$ | | | 1 |
| 1 | | $S_4$ | $S_5$ | | | acc | |
| 2 | $S_3$ | | | $S_2$ | | | 6 |
| 3 | | $r_4$ | $r_4$ | | $r_4$ | $r_4$ | |
| 4 | $S_3$ | | | $S_2$ | | | 7 |
| 5 | $S_3$ | | | $S_2$ | | | 8 |
| 6 | | $S_4$ | $S_5$ | | | $S_7$ | |
| 7 | | $r_1$ | $S_5$ | | $r_1$ | $r_1$ | |
| 8 | | $r_2$ | $r_2$ | | $r_2$ | $r_2$ | |
| 9 | | | $r_3$ | | $r_3$ | $r_3$ | |

## PROBLEM 2

Using danging else ambiguity consider the Grammar

$$S \rightarrow i\, SeS | iS | a$$

## SOLUTION

Similarly, we can show for this without having any shift|reduce conflict.

*i.e.*, First find the LR(0) items and then construct SLR parsing table. The parsing table constructed contains shift|reduce conflict *i.e.*, in the parsing table for action $[4, e] = S_5|r_2$.

Now consider the input *iiaea$* for processing.

## SOLUTION

Construct LR(0) items for this Grammar.

$$I_0 : S' \rightarrow \cdot S$$

$$S \rightarrow \cdot iSeS$$

$$S \rightarrow \cdot is$$

$$S \rightarrow \cdot a$$

goto $(I_0, S)$ :  $\quad I_1 : S' \rightarrow S \cdot$

goto $(I_0, i)$ :  $\quad I_2 : S \rightarrow i \cdot SeS$

$$S \rightarrow i \cdot S$$

$$S \rightarrow \cdot i SeS$$

$$S \rightarrow \cdot iS$$

$$S \rightarrow a$$

goto $(I_0, a)$ :  $\quad I_3 : S \rightarrow a \cdot$

goto $(I_2, S)$ :  $\quad I_4 : S \rightarrow i S \cdot e S$

$$S \rightarrow i S \cdot$$

goto $(I_2, i)$ :  $\quad I_2 : S \rightarrow i \cdot SeS$

$$S \rightarrow i \cdot S$$

$$S \rightarrow \cdot i SeS$$

$$S \rightarrow \cdot iS$$

$$S \rightarrow \cdot a$$

goto $(I_2, a)$ :  $\quad I_3 : S \rightarrow a \cdot$

goto $(I_4, e)$ :  $\quad I_5 : S \rightarrow iSe \cdot S$

$$S \rightarrow \cdot iSeS$$

$$S \rightarrow \cdot iS$$

$$S \rightarrow \cdot a$$

goto $(I_5, S)$ :  $\quad I_6 : S \rightarrow iSeS \cdot$

goto $(I_5, i)$ :  $\quad I_2 : S \rightarrow i \cdot SeS$

$$S \rightarrow i \cdot S$$

$$S \rightarrow \cdot i SeS$$

$$S \rightarrow \cdot iS$$

$$S \rightarrow \cdot a$$

goto $(I_5, a)$ :  $\quad I_3 : S \rightarrow a.$

The corresponding parsing table is shown below

| State | $i$ | $e$ | $a$ | $ | $S$ |
|-------|-----|-----|-----|-----|-----|
| 0 | $S_2$ | | $S_3$ | | 1 |
| 1 | | | | $Acc$ | |
| 2 | $S_2$ | | $S_3$ | | 4 |
| 3 | | $r_3$ | | $r_3$ | |
| 4 | | $S_5\|r_5$ | | $r_2$ | |
| 5 | $S_2$ | | $S_3$ | | 6 |
| 6 | | $r_1$ | | $r_2$ | |

| Stack | Input | Action with Conflict Resolution |
|-------|-------|--------------------------------|
| 0 | $ii\ aea\ \$$ | Shift |
| $0\ i2$ | $iaea\$$ | Shift |
| $0i2i2$ | $aea\$$ | Shift |
| $0i2i2a3$ | $ea\$$ | reduce $S \rightarrow a$ |
| $0i2i2S4$ | $ea\$$ | Conflict can be resolved by Shifting |
| $0i2i2S4e5$ | $a\$$ | Shift |
| $0i2i2S4e5a3$ | $\$$ | reduce $S \rightarrow a$ |
| $0i2i2S4e5S6$ | $\$$ | reduce $S \rightarrow iSeS$ |
| $0i2S4$ | $\$$ | reduce $S \rightarrow iS$ |
| $0S1$ | $\$$ | Accept |

Finally the ambiguous grammar without any conflict has the following parsing table.

| State | $i$ | $e$ | $a$ | $ | $S$ |
|-------|-----|-----|-----|-----|-----|
| 0 | $S_2$ | | $S_3$ | | 1 |
| 1 | | | | $Acc$ | |
| 2 | $S_2$ | | $S_3$ | | 4 |
| 3 | | $r_3$ | | $r_3$ | |
| 4 | | $r_5$ | | $r_2$ | |
| 5 | $S_2$ | | $S_3$ | | 6 |
| 6 | | $r_1$ | | $r_2$ | |

# 6

# SYNTAX DIRECTED TRANSLATION

## 6.1 SYNTAX DIRECTED DEFINITION (SDD)

- To translate a programing language construct compiler has to keep track of many quantites such as the type of the construct, location of first instruction in target code or the number of instructions generated.

- A formalist called as syntax directed definitions is used for specifying translations for programming language constructs.

- A syntax directed definition is a generalization of a context free grammar in which each grammar symbol has associated set of attributes and each production is associated. With a set of semantic rules.

## Definition of Syntax Directed Definition (SDD)

SDD is a generalization of CFG in which each grammar production $X \rightarrow \alpha$ is associated with it a set of semantic rules of the form

$$a : = f(b_1..., b_2 ....b_k)$$

where a is an attribute obtained from the function $f$.

The two attributes for non-terminals are.

**1. Synthesized Attribute (S-attribute): ($\uparrow$):** An attribute is said to be synthesized attribute if its value of a parse tree node is determined from attribute values at the children of the node.

**2. Inherited Attribute: ($\rightarrow$, $\uparrow$):** An inherited attribute is one whose value at parse tree node is determined in terms of attributes at the parent and|or siblings or that node.

- The attribute can be string, a number, a type, a memory location or anything else.

- The parse tree showing the value of attributes at each node is called an annotated parse tree.

The process of computing the attribute values at the node is called annotating or decorating the parse tree.

**1. Synthesized Attributes**

Consider the CFG

$$S \rightarrow EN$$
$$E \rightarrow E + T$$
$$E \rightarrow E - T$$
$$E \rightarrow T$$
$$T \rightarrow T * F$$
$$T \rightarrow T|F$$
$$T \rightarrow F$$
$$F \rightarrow (E)$$
$$F \rightarrow \text{digit}$$
$$N \rightarrow ;$$

**Solution:** The syntax directed definition can be written for the above grammar by writing semantic actions for each production.

| Production rule | Semantic actions |
|---|---|
| $S \rightarrow EN$ | Print $(E \cdot \text{val})$ |
| $E \rightarrow E_1 + T$ | $E \cdot \text{val} = E_1 \cdot \text{val} + T \cdot \text{val}$ |
| $E \rightarrow E_1 - T$ | $E \cdot \text{val} = E_1 \cdot \text{val} - T \cdot \text{val}$ |
| $E \rightarrow T$ | $E \cdot \text{val} = T \cdot \text{val}$ |
| $T \rightarrow T * F$ | $T \cdot \text{val} = T \cdot \text{val} * F \cdot \text{val}$ |
| $T \rightarrow T|F$ | $T \cdot \text{val} = T \cdot \text{val}| F \cdot \text{val}$ |
| $F \rightarrow (E)$ | $F \cdot \text{val} = E \cdot \text{val}$ |
| $T \rightarrow F$ | $T \cdot \text{val} = F \cdot \text{val}$ |
| $F \rightarrow \text{digit}$ | $F \cdot \text{val} = \text{digit} \cdot \text{lexval}$ |
| $N \rightarrow ;$ | can be ignored by lexical analyzer as ; is terminating symbol. |

For the non-terminals $E$, $T$ and $F$ the values can be obtained using the attribute "val".

The token digit has synthesizedattribute "lexval".

In $S \rightarrow EN$, symbol $S$ is the start symbol. This rule is to print the final answer of the expression.

Following steps are followed to compute $S$ attributed definition.

1. Write the SDD using the appropriate semantic actions for corresponding production rule of the given grammar.

2. The annotated parse tree is generated and attribute values are computed. The computation is done in bottom up manner.

3. The value obtained at the node is supposed to be final output.

## PROBLEM 1

Consider the string 5 * 6 + 7; Construct syntax free, parse tree and annotated tree.

## SOLUTION

**Syntax tree:**

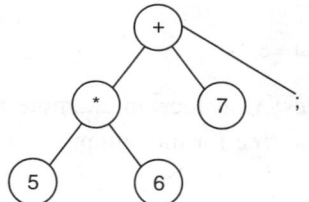

**Parse Tree:**

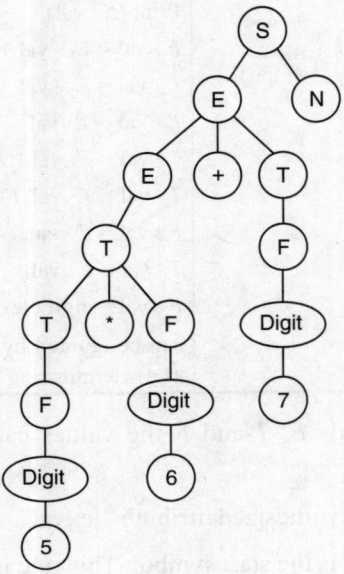

The corresponding annotated parse tree is shown below for the string
5 * 6 + 7;

**Annoted Parse Tree:**

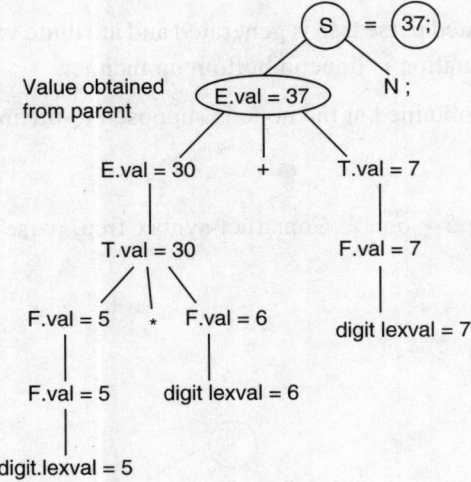

**2. Inherited Attributes:** Consider an example and compute the inherited attributes annotate the parse tree for the computation of inherited attributes for the given string int *a, b, c.*

$$S \rightarrow TL$$
$$T \rightarrow \text{int}$$
$$T \rightarrow \text{float}$$
$$T \rightarrow \text{char}$$
$$T \rightarrow \text{double}$$
$$L \rightarrow L, id$$
$$L \rightarrow id$$

The steps are to be followed are:

1. Construct the syntax directed definition using semantic action.

2. Annotate the parse tree with inherited attributes by processing in top down fashion.

The SDD is given below:

| Production rule | Semantic actions |
|---|---|
| $S \rightarrow TL$ | $L \cdot in\ h = T \cdot type$ |
| $T \rightarrow \text{int}$ | $T \cdot type = \text{int}$ |
| $T \rightarrow \text{Float}$ | $T \cdot type = \text{Float}$ |
| $T \rightarrow \text{Char}$ | $T \cdot type = \text{Char}$ |
| $T \rightarrow \text{double}$ | $T \cdot type = \text{double}$ |
| $L \rightarrow L, id$ | $L \cdot in\ h = L \cdot in\ h$ Enter–type ($id \cdot$ entry, $L$ in $h$) |
| $L \rightarrow id$ | Enter_type ($id \cdot$ entry , $L \cdot in\ h$) |

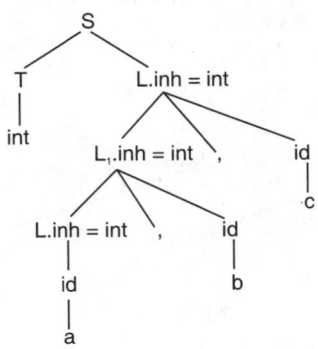

**Figure:** Annotated parse tree

## PROBLEMS

# PROBLEM 1

Consider the grammar that is used for simple desk calculator. Obtain the semantic action and also the annotated parse tree for the string $3 * 5 + 4n$.

$$L \rightarrow En$$
$$E \rightarrow E_1 + T$$
$$E \rightarrow T$$
$$T \rightarrow T_1 * F$$
$$T \rightarrow F$$
$$F \rightarrow (E)$$
$$F \rightarrow \text{digit}$$

## SOLUTION

| Production rule | Semantic actions |
|---|---|
| $L \rightarrow En$ | $L \cdot \text{val} = E \cdot \text{val}$ |
| $E \rightarrow E_1 + T$ | $E \cdot \text{val} = E_1 \cdot \text{val} + T \cdot \text{val}$ |
| $E \rightarrow T$ | $E \cdot \text{val} = T \cdot \text{val}$ |
| $T \rightarrow T_1 * F$ | $T \cdot \text{val} = T_1 \cdot \text{val} * F \cdot \text{val}$ |
| $T \rightarrow F$ | $T \cdot \text{val} = F \cdot \text{val}$ |
| $F \rightarrow E$ | $F \cdot \text{val} = E \cdot \text{val}$ |
| $F \rightarrow \text{digit}$ | $F \cdot \text{val} = \text{digit} \cdot \text{lexal}$ |

The corresponding annotated parse tree is shown below, for the string
$3 * 5 + 4n$

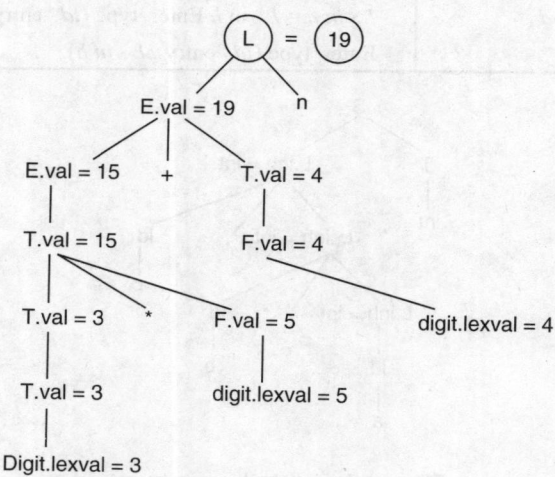

**Figure:** Annotated parse tree

## PROBLEM 2

For the SDD of the problem 1 give annotated parse tree for the following expressions.

(a) $(3 + 4) * (5 + 6)n$

(b) $1 * 2 * 3 * (4 + 5)n$

(c) $(9 + 8 * (7 + 6) + 5) * 4n$

## SOLUTIONS

(a)

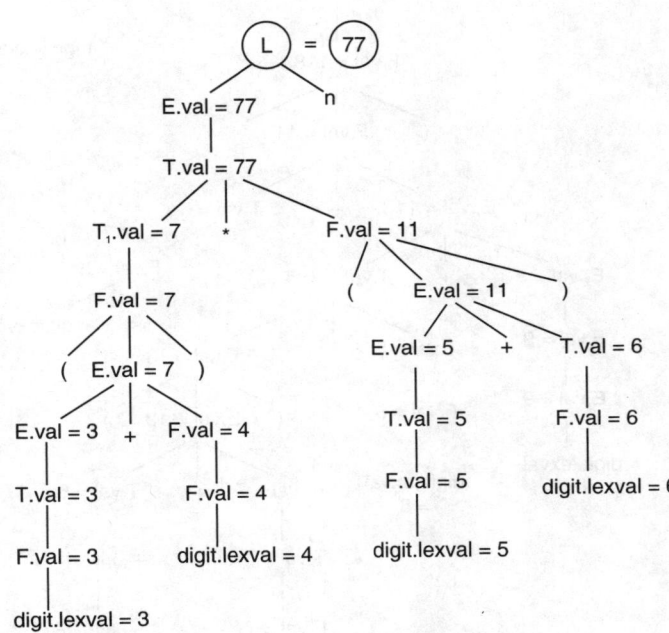

(b)

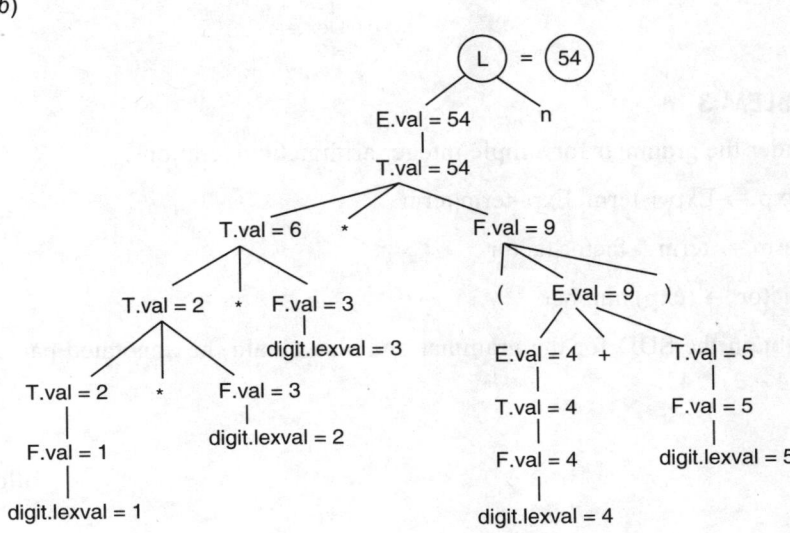

(c)

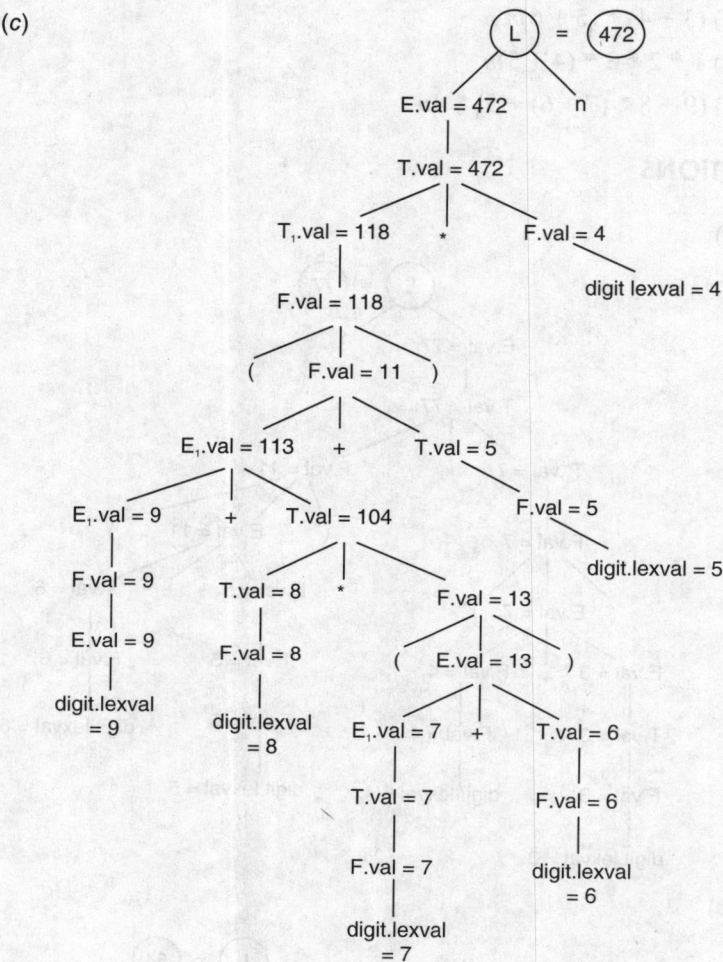

## PROBLEM 3

Consider the grammar for simple integer arithmetic operations.

Exp → Exp + term| Exp–term|term

term → term * factor|factor

factor → (exp)|number

Obtain the SDD for the grammar and also obtain the annotated parse free for (34 – 3) * 42.

## SOLUTION

| Production rule | Semantic actions |
|---|---|
| $exp_1 \rightarrow exp_2 + term_1$ | $expival = exp_2 \cdot val + term_1\ val$ |
| $exp_1 \rightarrow exp_2 - term_1$ | $exp_1 \cdot val = exp_2 \cdot val - term_1 \cdot val$ |
| $exp_1 \rightarrow term_1$ | $exp_1 \cdot val = term_1 \cdot val$ |
| $term_1 \rightarrow term_2 * Factor$ | $term_1 \cdot val = term_2 \cdot val * factor \cdot va$ |
| $term_1 \rightarrow factor$ | $term \cdot val = factor \cdot val$ |
| $factor \rightarrow (exp_1)$ | $factor \cdot val = exp \cdot val$ |
| $factor \rightarrow number$ | $factor \cdot val = number \cdot val$ |

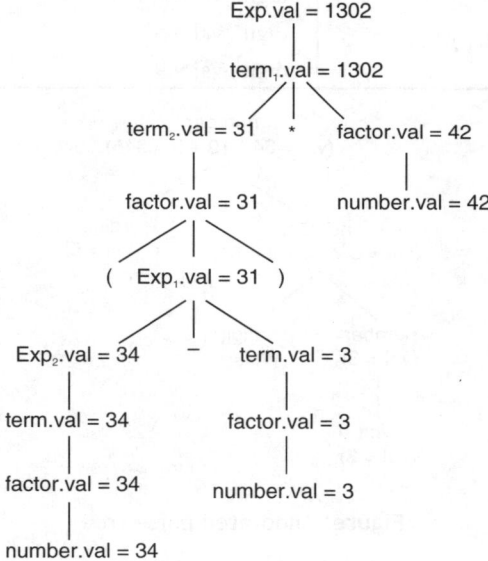

## PROBLEM 4

Consider the following simple grammar for unsigned numbers:

number $\rightarrow$ number digit|digit

digit $\rightarrow$ 0|1|2|3|4|5|6|7|8|9

Obtain the SDD for the grammar and annoted parse tree for 345.

## SOLUTION

**Note:**                     $34 = 3 * 10 + 4$

number $\cdot$ val = number $\cdot$ val $* 10 +$ digit $\cdot$ val

| Production rule | Semantic actions |
|---|---|
| number → number digit | number₁· val = number 2 · val digit · val |
| number → digit | number · val = digit · val |
| digit → 0 | digit · val = 0 |
| digit → 1 | digit · val = 1 |
| digit → 2 | digit · val = 2 |
| digit → 3 | digit · val = 3 |
| digit → 4 | digit · val = 4 |
| digit → 5 | digit · val = 5 |
| digit → 6 | digit · val = 6 |
| digit → 7 | digit · val = 7 |
| digit → 8 | digit · val = 8 |
| digit → 9 | digit · val = 9 |

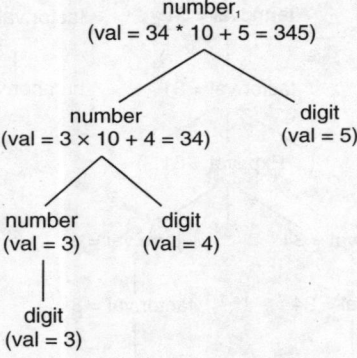

**Figure:** Annotated parse tree

## PROBLEM ON INHERITED ATTRIBUTE

## PROBLEM 1

For the grammar construct the SDD and the annotated parse tree for the string
3 * 5.

$$T \to FT'$$

$$T' \to * FT'$$

$$T' \to \varepsilon$$

$$F \to \text{digit}$$

## SOLUTION

| Production rule | Semantic actions |
|---|---|
| $T \rightarrow FT'$ | $T' \cdot \text{in } h = F \cdot \text{val}$ |
| | $T \cdot \text{val} = T' \cdot Syn$ |
| $T' \rightarrow * FT'$ | $T'_1 \cdot \text{in } h = T' \cdot \text{in } h * F. \text{val}$ |
| | $T' \cdot \text{Syn} = T'_1 \cdot \text{Syn}$ |
| $T' \rightarrow \varepsilon$ | $T'_1 \cdot \text{Syn} = T'_1 \cdot \text{in } h$ |
| $F \rightarrow \text{digit}$ | $F \cdot \text{val} = \text{digit} \cdot \text{lexval}$ |

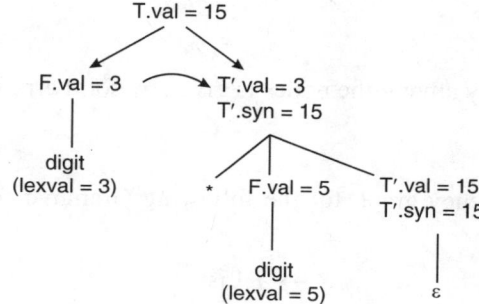

## 6.2  EVALUATION ORDERS FOR SDDS

Dependency graphs are a useful tool for determining an evaluation order for the attribute instance in a given parse tree.

The directed graph that represents interdependent between synthesized and inherited attributes at the nodes in the parse tree is called dependency graph.

For the rule $X \rightarrow yz$, the semantic action is given by, $x \cdot x \rightarrow F(y \cdot y, z \cdot z)$

Then synthesized attribute is $x \cdot x$ and $x \cdot x$ depends upon attributes $y. y$ and $z \cdot z$.

## PROBLEM 1

Design the dependency graph for the following Grammar.

$$E \rightarrow E_1 + E_2$$
$$E \rightarrow E_1 * E_2$$

## SOLUTION

The semantic rule is given on next page.

| Production rule | Semantic actions |
|---|---|
| $E \rightarrow E_1 + E_2$ | $E \cdot val = E_1 \cdot val + E_2 \cdot val$ |
| $E \rightarrow E_1 * E_2$ | $E \cdot val = E_1 \cdot val * E_2 \cdot val$ |

The dependency graph is given below:

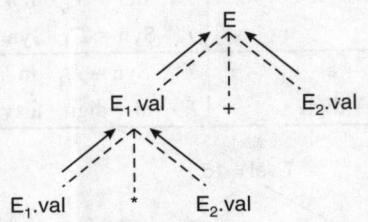

The dependency among the nodes is given by solid arrows.

## PROBLEM 2

Design the dependency graph for the following Grammar for the input string int $a, b, c$.

$$S \rightarrow T \text{ List}$$
$$T \rightarrow \text{int}$$
$$T \rightarrow \text{float}$$
$$T \rightarrow \text{char}$$
$$T \rightarrow \text{double}$$
$$\text{List} \rightarrow \text{List}, id$$
$$\text{List} \rightarrow id$$

## SOLUTION

The dependency graph is shown below:

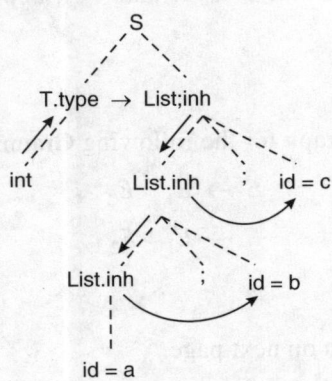

The semantic rule is given below:

| Production rule | Semantic actions |
|---|---|
| $S \rightarrow T$ List | List $\cdot$ in $h = T \cdot$ type |
| $T \rightarrow$ int | $T_1 \cdot$ type = int |
| $T \rightarrow$ Float | $T \cdot$ type = float |
| $T \rightarrow$ Char | $T \cdot$ type = char |
| $T \rightarrow$ double | $T \cdot$ type = double |
| List $\rightarrow$ List, $id$ | List $\cdot$ in $h$ = List $\cdot$ in $h$ |
|  | Enter–type ($id \cdot$ entry, List $\cdot$ inh) |
| $\overline{\text{List}} \cdot id$ | Enter–type ($id \cdot$ entry, List $\cdot$ inh) |

**Evaluation Order:** The **topological sort** of the dependency graph decides the evaluation order in a parse tree. In deciding evaluation order, the semantic rule in SDD are used. Thus the translation is specified by **Syntax Directed Definitions.**

## PROBLEM 1

Obtain the dependency graph and order of execution for the Grammar.

$$T \rightarrow FT'$$

$$T \rightarrow *FT'$$

$$T' \rightarrow \varepsilon$$

$$F \rightarrow \text{digit}$$

and for the input string 3 * 5.

## SOLUTION

The semantic rule is given below.

| Production rule | Semantic actions |
|---|---|
| $T \rightarrow FT'$ | $T' \cdot$ in $h = F \cdot$ val |
|  | $T \cdot$ val $= T' \cdot$ syn |
| $T' \rightarrow * FT_1'$ | $T_1' \cdot$ in $h = T' \cdot$ in $h * F \cdot$ val |
|  | $T \cdot$ syn $= T_1' \cdot$ syn |
| $T' \rightarrow \epsilon$ | $T' \cdot$ syn $= T_1' \cdot$ in$h$ |
| $F \rightarrow$ digit | $F \cdot$ val $=$ digit$\cdot$lexval |

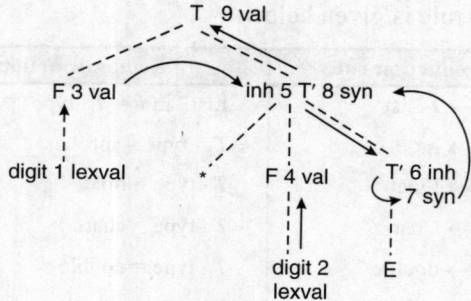

For the above example obtain the dependency graph and order of evaluation for the input String 3 * 5 * 4.

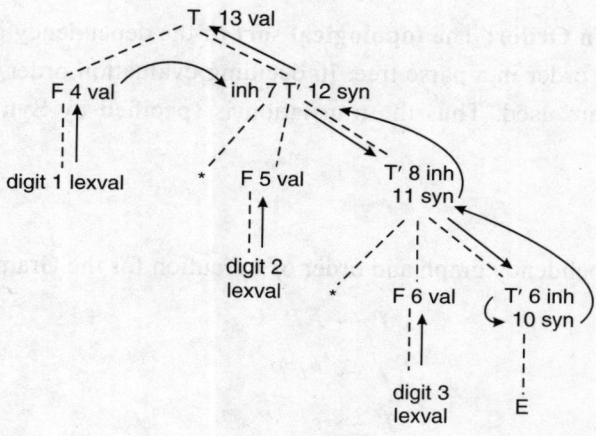

**Figure:** Dependency graph

## PROBLEM 2

Obtain SDD, annotated pars, tree and The dependency graph for the Grammar.

$$D \rightarrow TL$$

$$T \rightarrow int$$

$$T \rightarrow float$$

$$L \rightarrow L_1, id$$

$$L \rightarrow id$$

For the input string float $id_1, id_2, id_3$.

## SOLUTION

| Production rule | Semantic actions |
|---|---|
| $D \to TL$ | $L \cdot$ in $h = T \cdot$ type |
| $T \to$ int | $T \cdot$ type = int |
| $T \to$ float | $T \cdot$ type = float |
| $L \to L_1$ , $id$ | $L_i \cdot$ in $h = L \cdot$ in $h$ |
|  | enter-type ($id \cdot$ entry, $L \cdot$ in $h$) |
| $L \to id$ | enter –type ($id \cdot$ entry, $L \cdot$ in $h$) |

**Figure:** Semantic actions

**Annotated Parse Tree:**

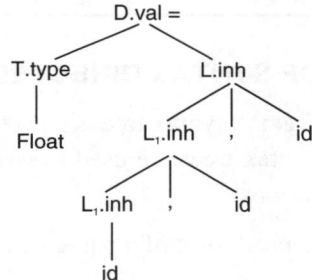

**Dependency Graph:**

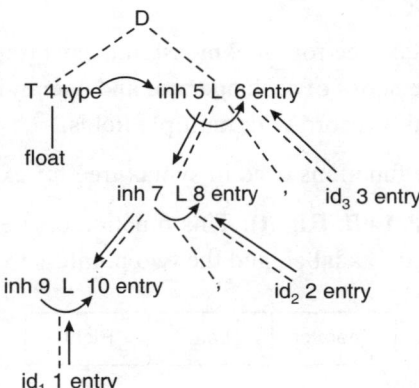

**S-attributed Definitions:** A syntax directed definition that uses synthesized attributes is said to be an S-attributed definition.

Synthesized attributes can be evaluated by a bottom-up parser as the input is parsed.

The parser keeps the values of synthesized attributes with the Grammar symbol on its stack. Whenever a reduction is made, the values of the new synthesized attributes are computed from the attributes appearing on the stack for the Grammar symbols on the right side of the reducing Production.

**L-attributed Definitions:** A syntax directed definitions which we inherited attributes is said to be L-attributed definitions.

If L-attributed definitions, the attributes are always evaluated in **Depth First Order.** The L is for left because the attribute information flow from left to right.

| Production rule | Semantic actions |
|---|---|
| $T \rightarrow FT'$ | $T'.\text{in } h = \text{F.val}$ |
| $T \rightarrow *FT$ | $T_1' \cdot \text{inh} = T'.\text{in } h* \text{ Fval}$ |

## 6.3  APPLICATIONS OF SYNTAX DIRECTED TRANSLATION

**Construction of Syntax Tree:** A syntax tree is an abstract representation of the language constructs. The syntax trees are used to write the translation routines using syntax directed definitions.

A syntax tree is a condensed form of a parse tree.

In a syntax tree, **Operators and keywords donot appear as leaves,** but rather they are associated with the interior node that would be parent of those leaves in the parse tree.

Constructing syntax tree for an expression means translation of expression into **postfix form.** The nodes of each operator and operand is created. Each node can be implemented as a record with multiple fields.

Following are the functions used in syntax tree for expressions.

**1. New Node (OP, Left, Right):** This function creates a node into the field operator having operator as label, and the two pointers to left and right.

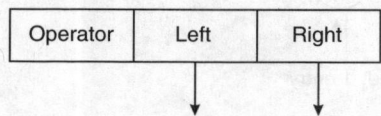

**2 New Leaf (*id*, entry):** The function creates an identifier node with label *id* and a pointer to the symbol table is given by **entry**.

**3. New Leaf (num, val):** This function creates node for numbers with label num and val is for value of that number.

| num | |
|---|---|

## EXAMPLE

Construct the Syntax Tree for the the expression $x * y - 5 + z$.

## SOLUTION

**Step 1:** Convert the expression from infix to post fix $xy * 5 - z +$

**Step 2:** Make use of the functions new node (), new leaf ($id$, ptr), new leaf (num, val).

**Step 3:** The sequence of function calls is given below:

| Symbol | Operation/Semantic rules |
|---|---|
| $x$ | $P_1$ = new leaf ($id$, $id \cdot$ entry of $x$) |
| $y$ | $P_2$ = new leaf ($id$, $id$, entry of $y$) |
| * | $P_3$ = new node (*, $P_1$, $P_2$) |
| 5 | $P_4$ = new leaf (num, 5) |
| – | $P_5$ = new node ($-p_3$, $p_4$) |
| 2 | $P_6$ = new leaf ($id$, $id \cdot$ entry of $z$) |
| + | $P_7$ = new node (+, $P_5$, $P_6$) |

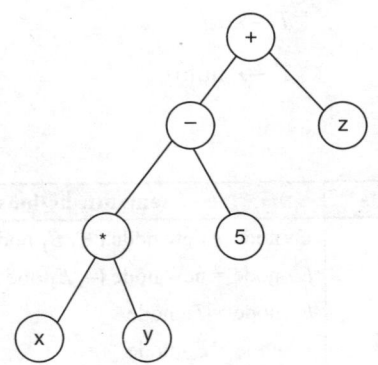

**Figure:** Syntax tree

For the input string, the syntax tree is as shown on next page.

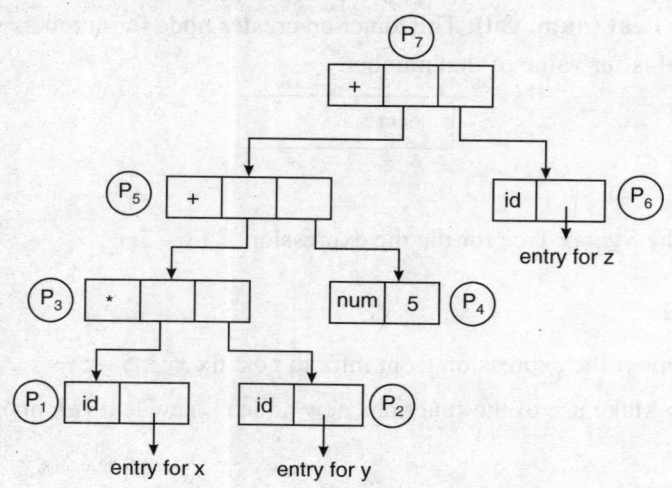

## PROBLEM 1

Obtain the SDD for the following expression and also obtain syntax tree/ annotated syntax tree for the expression $a - 4 + c$ for the Grammar

$$E \to E_1 + T$$
$$E \to E_1 - T$$
$$E \to T$$
$$T \to (E)$$
$$T \to id$$
$$T \to num$$

## SOLUTION

| Production rule | Semantic actions |
|---|---|
| $E \to E_1 + T$ | $E \cdot node = new\ node\ (+, E_1\ node, T \cdot node)$ |
| $E \to E_1 - T$ | $E \cdot node = new\ node\ (-, E_1\ node, T \cdot node)$ |
| $E \to T$ | $E \cdot node = T \cdot node$ |
| $T \to (E)$ | $T \cdot node = E \cdot node$ |
| $T \to id$ | $T \cdot node = new\ leaf\ (id \cdot id \cdot entry)$ |
| $T \to num$ | $T \cdot node = new\ leaf\ (num, num \cdot val)$ |

The annotated syntax tree for the expression $a - 4 + c$ is given below.

**Step 1:** Convert the infix expression to post fix expression $a\ 4 - c+$.

**Step 2:** Make use of functions new node (), new leaf (*id*, ptr), new leaf (num · val).

**Step 3:**

| Symbol | Operation/Semantic rules |
|--------|--------------------------|
| *a*    | $P_1$ = new leaf (*id*, *id* · entry of *a*) |
| 4      | $P_2$ = new leaf (num, 4) |
| −      | $P_3$ = new node (−, P1, P2) |
| c      | $P_4$ = new leaf (id, id · entry of c) |
| +      | $P_5$ = new node (+, $P_3$, $P_4$) |

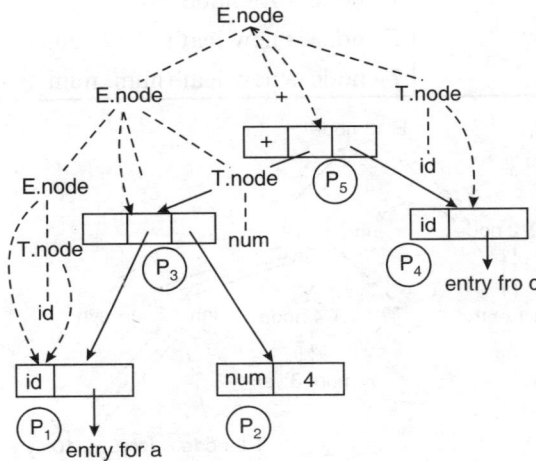

## PROBLEM 2

Construct the syntax tree for the Grammar

$$E \rightarrow TE'$$

$$E' \rightarrow + TE'$$

$$E' \rightarrow -TE'$$

$$E' \rightarrow \varepsilon$$

$$T \rightarrow (E)$$

$$T \rightarrow id$$

$$T \rightarrow num$$

Obtain the SDD for the above grammar and also the dependency graph for the input string $a - 4 + c$.

## SOLUTION

| Production rule | Semantic actions |
|---|---|
| 1. $E \rightarrow TE'$ | $E \cdot node = E^1.syn$ |
| | $E^1 \cdot in\ h = T.node$ |
| 2. $E^1 \rightarrow +TE_1'$ | $E_1' \cdot in\ h = new\ node\ (+, E_1' \cdot in\ h, T \cdot node)$ |
| | $E^1 \cdot syn = E_1' \cdot syn$ |
| 3. $E^1 \rightarrow -TE'$ | $E_1' \cdot in\ h = new\ node\ (-, E' \cdot in\ h, T \cdot node)$ |
| | $E^1 \cdot syn = E_1' \cdot syn$ |
| 4. $E^1 \rightarrow \in$ | $E' \cdot syn = E' \cdot in\ h$ |
| 5. $T \rightarrow (E)$ | $T \cdot node = E \cdot node$ |
| 6. $T \rightarrow (id)$ | $T \cdot node = new\ leaf\ (id, id \cdot entry)$ |
| 7. $T \rightarrow num$ | $T \cdot node = new\ leaf\ (num, num \cdot val)$ |

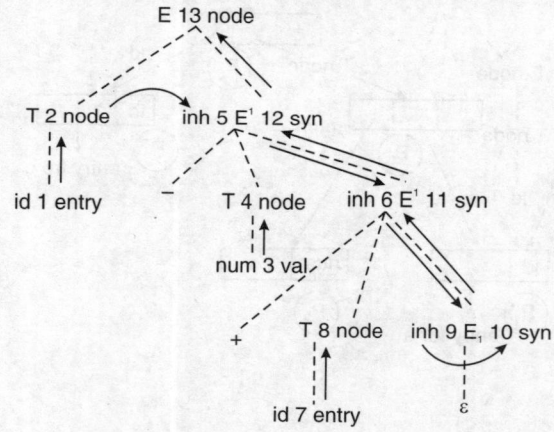

## PROBLEM 3

Construct SDD for the given productions

$$T \rightarrow BC$$
$$B \rightarrow int$$
$$B \rightarrow float$$
$$C \rightarrow [num]\ C_1$$
$$C \rightarrow \varepsilon$$

for the expression int [2] [3].

## SOLUTION:

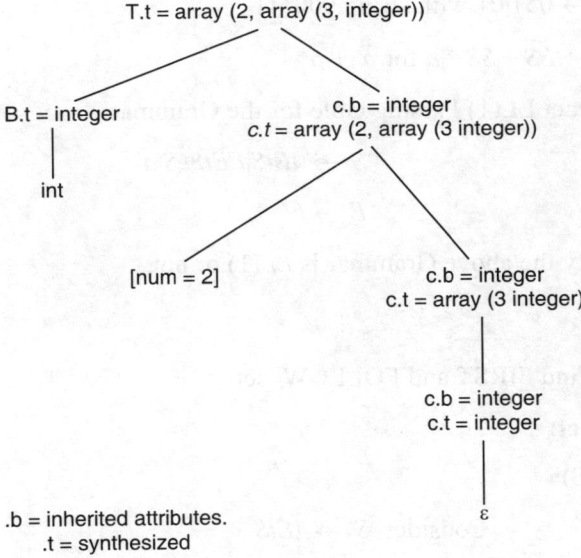

T.t = array (2, array (3, integer))

B.t = integer

int

c.b = integer
c.t = array (2, array (3 integer))

[num = 2]

c.b = integer
c.t = array (3 integer)

c.b = integer
c.t = integer

ε

.b = inherited attributes.
.t = synthesized

## EXERCISES

**1.** Consider the Grammar

$$S \rightarrow (L)|a$$

$$L \rightarrow L, S|a$$

Parse the input string $(a, (a, a))$ using shift reduce

**2.** For the Grammar

$$S \rightarrow 0S1|01 \text{ with the string } 000111$$

Indicate the handle in each of the following right sentential form.

(a) 000111 (b) 00S11

**3.** Consider the Grammar:

$$S \rightarrow SS + | \: SS * |a \text{ and string is } aa + a*$$

Indicate the handle in each of the following right sentential form.

(a) $SSS + a * +$

(b) $SS + a * a +$

(c) $aaa * a ++$

**4.** Describe all the viable prefixes of the Grammar

(a) $S \rightarrow 0S1|01$ with string 000111

(b) $S \rightarrow SS +|SS *|a$ for $a + a*$

**5.** Construct LL(1) Parsing table for the Grammar.

$$S \rightarrow iEtS|i\ EtSeS|a$$

$$E \rightarrow b$$

and also verify the above Grammar is $LL(1)$ or not.

## SOLUTION

**Step 1:** Find FIRST and FOLLOW  sets

**FIRST Set:**

**FIRST (S):**

> Consider $S \rightarrow iEtS$

$\therefore$    FIRST $(S)$ = $i$

> Consider $S \rightarrow iEtSeS$

> FIRST $(S)$ = $i$

> Consider $S \rightarrow a$

> FIRST $(S)$ = $a$

$\therefore$    FIRST $(S)$ = $\{i, a\}$

**FIRST (E):**

> Consider $E \rightarrow b$

> FIRST $(E)$ = $\{b\}$

**FOLLOW Set:**

**FOLLOW (S):**

> Consider $S \rightarrow iEtSeS$

> FOLLOW $(S)$ = $\{e\}$

> Consider $S \rightarrow iEtS$

> FOLLOW $(S)$ = FOLLOW $(S)$ = $\{e\}$

$$\therefore \qquad \text{FOLLOW } (S) = \{e, \$\}$$

[Since $S$ is start production]

**FOLLOW($E$)**

$$\text{Consider } S \rightarrow iEtS$$
$$\text{FOLLOW } (E) = \{t\}$$
$$\text{Consider } S \rightarrow iEtSeS$$
$$\text{FOLLOW } (E) = \{t\}$$

To Summarize the above we write

$$\text{FIRST } (S) = \{i, a\}$$
$$\text{FIRST } (E) = \{b\}$$
$$\text{FOLLOW } (S) = \{e, \$\}$$
$$\text{FOLLOW } (E) = \{t\}$$

**Step 2:** To construct Predictive Parsing table from FIRST and FOLLOW Set.

(*i*)  $S \rightarrow iEtS$

Compare it with $A \rightarrow \alpha$

Here,    $A = S$

$\qquad \alpha = iEtS$

$$\text{FIRST } (iEtS) = \{i\}$$
$$\therefore \qquad\qquad M[S, i] = S \rightarrow iETS$$

(*ii*)  $S \rightarrow iEtSeS$

Compare it with $A \rightarrow \alpha$

Here,    $A = S$

$\qquad \alpha = iEtSeS$

$$\text{FIRST } [iE + SeS] = \{i\}$$
$$\therefore \qquad\qquad M[S, i] = S \rightarrow iEtSeS$$

(*iii*)  $S \rightarrow a$

$\qquad$ Compare it with $A \rightarrow \alpha$

Here,    $A = S$

$\qquad \alpha = a$

$$\therefore \qquad\qquad \text{FIRST } (a) = \{a\}$$

$\therefore$ $\qquad\qquad\qquad M[S, a] = S \rightarrow a$

(iv) $E \rightarrow b$

Compare it with $\qquad\qquad A \rightarrow \alpha$

Here, $\qquad A = E$

$\qquad\qquad \alpha = b$

$\qquad\qquad$ FIRST $(b) = \{b\}$

$\therefore$ $\qquad\qquad M[E, b] = E \rightarrow b$

LL(1) Parsing Table :

| Non terminals | Inputs | | | | |
|---|---|---|---|---|---|
| | i | + | e | a | b |
| S | $S \rightarrow iEtS$ $S \rightarrow iEtSeS$ | | | $S \rightarrow a$ | |
| E | | | | | $E \rightarrow b$ |

The above table shows multiple entries for $M[S, i]$. This shows that given Grammer is not $LL(1)$.

**6.** Consider the Grammar,

$$S \rightarrow (L)|a$$

$$L \rightarrow L, S|a$$

Parse the input string $(a, (a, a))$ using shift reduce.

## SOLUTION

Consider the rightmost derivation for the string $(a, (a, a))$

$$S \rightarrow (L)$$

$$\Rightarrow (L, S)$$

$$\Rightarrow (L, (L))$$

$$\Rightarrow (L, (L, S))$$

$$\Rightarrow (L, (L, a))$$

$$\Rightarrow (L, (a, a))$$

$$\Rightarrow (a, (a, a))$$

Parsing the input string $(a, (a, a))$ using shift–Reduce. Parser is shown below.

| Stack | Input | Action |
|-------|-------|--------|
| $ | $(a, (a, a)) \$$ | Shift |
| $ ( | $a, (a, a)) \$$ | Shift |
| $ ( a | $, (a, a)) \$$ | Reduce $L \to a$ |
| $ ( L | $, (a, a)) \$$ | Shift |
| # ( L, | $(a, a)) \$$ | Shift |
| $ ( L, ( | $a, a)) \$$ | Shift |
| $(L, (a | $, a)) \$$ | Reduce $L \to a$ |
| $ (L, (L | $,a)) \$$ | Shift |
| $ (L, (L, | $a)) \$$ | Shift |
| $ (L, (L, a | $)) \$$ | Reduce $S \to a$ |
| $ (L, (L, S | $)) \$$ | Reduce $L \to L, S$ |
| $ (L, (L | $)) \$$ | Shift |
| $ (L, (L) | $) \$$ | Reduce $S \to (L)$ |
| $ (L, S | $) \$$ | Reduce $L \to L, S$ |
| $ (L | $) \$$ | Shift |
| $ (L) | $\$$ | Reduce $S \to (L)$ |
| $ S | $\$$ | accepted. |

7. For the Grammar $S \to 0S1|01$ with string $000111$ indicate Handle in each of the following right Sentential forms.

(a) $000111$          (b) $00S11$

## SOLUTION

(a) Rightmost derivation for the string $000111$.

$$S \to 0S1$$

$$\Rightarrow 00S11$$

$$\Rightarrow 000111$$

| Right Sentential form | Handle | Reducing Production |
|----------------------|--------|---------------------|
| $000111$ | $01$ | $S \to 01$ |
| $00S11$ | $0S1$ | $S \to 0S1$ |
| $0S1$ | $0S1$ | $S \to 0S1$ |
| $S$ | — | — |

8. Consider the Grammar $S \rightarrow SS + | \; SS*|a$ and string is $aa + a*$ Indicate Handle in each of the following sentential forms

(a) $SSS + a * +$

(b) $SS + a * a +$

(c) $aaa * a + +$

## SOLUTION

Consider the Rightmost derivations for the given strings.

(a) For the string $SSS + a * +$

$$S \rightarrow SS +$$
$$\Rightarrow SSS * +$$
$$\Rightarrow SS \, a * +$$
$$\Rightarrow SSS + a * +$$

(b) For the string $SS + a * a +$

$$S \rightarrow SS +$$
$$\Rightarrow S \, a +$$
$$\Rightarrow SS * a +$$
$$\Rightarrow S \, a * a +$$
$$\Rightarrow SS + a * a +$$

(c) For the String $aaa * a ++$

$$S \rightarrow SS +$$
$$\Rightarrow SSS ++$$
$$\Rightarrow SSa ++$$
$$\Rightarrow SSS * a + +$$
$$\Rightarrow SS \, a * a + +$$
$$\Rightarrow S \, a \, a * a + +$$
$$\Rightarrow a \, a \, a * a + +$$

| Right Sentential From | Handle | Reducing production |
|---|---|---|
| $SSS + a * +$ | $SS+$ | $S \rightarrow SS +$ |
| $SS + a * a +$ | $SS +$ | $S \rightarrow SS +$ |
| $aaa * a ++$ | $a$ | $S \rightarrow a$ |

# 7

# INTERMEDIATE—CODE GENERATION

## 7.1 INTRODUCTION

The task of compiler is to convert the source program into machine program. This activity can be done directly, but it is not always possible to generate such a machine code directly in one pass. Then, typically compilers generate an easy to represent form of source language called **Intermediate language.** The generation of an intermediate language leads to efficient code generation.

**Benefits of Intermediate Code Generation:** There are some benefitsof generating machine independent intermediate code.

1. A compiler for different machine's can be created by attaching different back end to the existing front ends of each machine.

2. A compiler for different source language (on the same machine) can be created by proving different front ends for corresponding source language to existing back end.

3. A machine independent code optimizer can be applied to intermediate code in order to optimize the code generation.

The logical structure of compiler front end is given below.

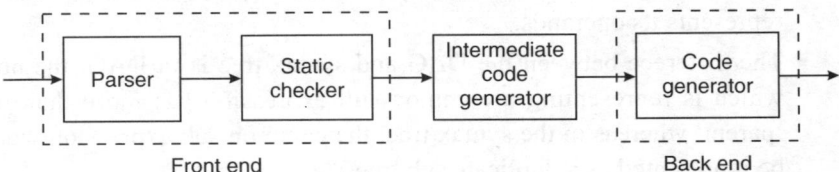

Front end                                                    Back end

**Type checking,** which ensures that operators are compiled to Compatible Operands. It also finds any syntactic checks that remain after parsing.

For example, static checking assures that a break statement in C is enclosed within a while, or switch statement, an error is reported if such an Enclosing Statement does not Exist.

## Variants of Syntax Trees

- A Syntax tree is used as the intermediate representation.
- A dag (directed acyclic graph) is another intermediate representation which is the same as the Syntax tree but it identifies the common sub expressions.

The syntax tree and DAG for assignment statement $a := b* - c + b * - c$ is given below.

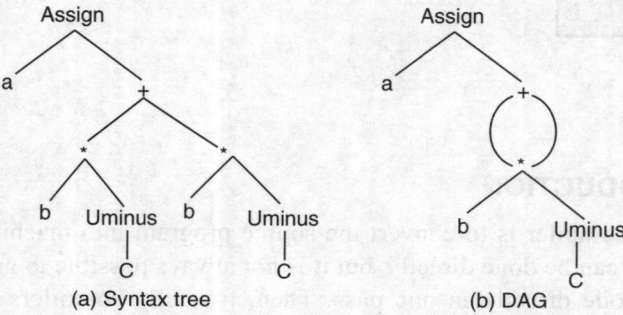

(a) Syntax tree    (b) DAG

## 7.2 DIRECTED ACYLIC GRAPHS FOR EXPRESSIONS (DAG)

- A DAG is a directed graph with no cycles which gives a picture of how the value computed by each statement in a basic block is used in subsequent statements in the block.
- A DAG for an expression identifies the common sub expression in the expression.

For example, in $(a + b) \times c + (a + b)$ the Sub Expression $(a + b)$ is repeated. This can be easily identified using DAG.

- Like a syntax tree, a dag has a node for every sub expression of the expression. An interior node represents an operator and its children represents its operands.
- The differece between the DAG and syntax tree is in DAG, the node which is representing a common sub expression has more than one 'parent' whereas in the syntax tree, the common sub expression would be represented as a duplicate sub tree.

## EXAMPLE

Construct a DAG for the expression $a + a * (b - c) + (b - c) *c$

## SOLUTION

The syntax tree a given by.

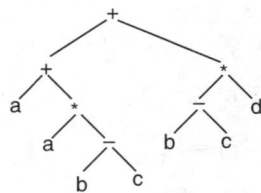

The DAG is given by

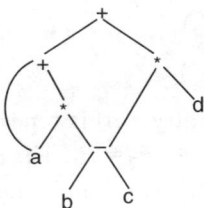

This shows that the common sub expressions $a$ and $(b - c)$ are repeated in the expression are retained only once in the DAG. The nodes which were representing the duplicate of these are eliminated in DAG. Thus the node for '$a$' has two parents nodes *i.e.,* '+' and '*'.

Similarly, the common subexpression $(b - c)$ has node * and * as its parents. It should be taken care that $b$ and $c$ are not repeated but the sub expression $(b - c)$ is repeated.

The syntax–directed defination (SDD) to produce syntax tree or DAG's a given below.

| Production | Semantic rules |
|---|---|
| 1. $E \rightarrow E_1 + T$ | E.node = new node ('+', $E_1$.node, T.node) |
| 2. $E \rightarrow E_1 - T$ | E.node = new node ('–' $E_1$.node, T.node) |
| 3. $E \rightarrow T$ | E.node = T.node |
| 4. $T \rightarrow (E)$ | T.node = E.node |
| 5. $T \rightarrow id$ | T.node = new leaf (*id*, *id*. Entry) |
| 6. $T \rightarrow$ num | T.node = new leaf (num, num · val) |

The steps for constructing the DAG is given below.

1.  $P_1$ = Leaf (*id*, Entry–*a*)

2. $P_2 = \text{Leaf } (id, \text{Entry} - a) = P_1$

3. $P_3 = \text{Leaf } (id, \text{Entry} - b)$

4. $P_4 = \text{Leaf } (id, \text{Entry} - c)$

5. $P_5 = \text{Node } ('-', P_3, P_4)$

6. $P_6 = \text{Node } ('*', P_1, P_5)$

7. $P_7 = \text{Node } ('+', P_1, P_6)$

8. $P_8 = \text{Leaf } (id, \text{Entry} - b) = P_3$

9. $P_9 = \text{Leaf } (id, \text{Entry} - c) = P_4$

10. $P_{10} = \text{Node } ('-', P_3, P_4) = P_5$

11. $P_{11} = \text{Leaf } (id, \text{Entry} - d)$

12. $P_{12} = \text{Node } ('*', P_5, P_{11})$

13. $P_{13} = \text{Node } ('+', P_7, P_{12})$

When the call to leaf $(id, \text{Entry} - a)$ is repeated at step 2, the node created by the previous call is returned, So $P_2 = P_1$. The nodes returned at steps 8 and 9 are the same as those returned at steps 3 and 4 i.e., $P_8 = P_3$ and $P_9 = P_4$. Hence, the node returned at step 10 must be same at that returned at step 5 i.e., $P_{10} = P_5$.

## EXERCISE

1. Construct the DAG for the expression.

$$((x + y) = ((x + y) * (x - y))) + ((x + y) * (x - y))$$

**Three Address Code:** In three address code form at the most three addreses are used to represent any statement. The general from of the three address code representation is

$$a : = b \; opc.$$

For the expression $a = b + c + d$ the three address code will be

$$t_1 : = b + c$$
$$t_2 = t_1 + d$$
$$a = t_2$$

Here $t_i$ and $t_2$ are the temporary names generated by the compiler. There are atmost three addresses are allowed (two for operads and one for result). Hence the name of their representation is 3 addresses three address code for the syntax tree and the DAG represented for the expression $a + a * (b - c) + (b - c)$.

$$t_1 = b - c$$
$$t_2 = a * t_1$$
$$t_3 = a + t_2$$
$$t_4 = t_1 * d$$
$$t_5 = t_3 + t_4$$

Three address code

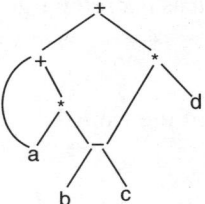

2. The three address code for expression $a := b * -c + b * -c$

| | | |
|---|---|---|
| $t_1 = -c$ | or | $t_1 = $ minus $c$ |
| $t_2 = b * t_1$ | | $t_2 = b * t_1$ |
| $t_3 = t_2 + t_2$ | | $t_3 = $ minus $c$ |
| $a = t_3$ | | $t_4 = b * t_3$ |
| | | $t_5 = t_2 + t_4$ |
| | | $a = t_5;$ |

## Address and Instructions

Three address code is built from two concepts address and instructions. An address can be one of the following.

(*i*) **A Name:** We allow source program names to appear as addresses in 3–address code. In an implementation, a source name is replaced by a pointer to its symbol table entry, where all information about the name is kept.

(*ii*) **A Constant:** A compiler must deal with many different types of constant and variables. Type conversion within expressions are considered.

(*iii*) **A Compiles-generated Temporary:** It is useful especially in optimizing compilers, to create a distinct name each time a temporary is needed. These temporary can be combined, if possible, when register are allocated to variables.

Some of the common three address statement used are:

1. Assignment statements of the from $x := y\ opz$, where $op$ is a binary arthmetic or logical operation.

2. Assignment instructions of the from $x := opy$, where $op$ is binary operator.

3. Copy statements of the form $x := y$ where the value of $y$ is assigned to $x$.

4. The unconditional Jumps goto $L$.

5. Conditional jumps such as if $x$ relop $y$ go to $L$. This instructions applies a relational operator $(<, >, <=, >=, =)$ to $x$ and $y$ and execute the statement with label $L$.

6. Indexed assignments of the from $X := Y[i]$ and $X[i] = y$

## EXAMPLE

Consider the statement

do $i = i + 1$; while $(a[i] < v)$;

## SOLUTION

Two possible translations of this statement is given below.

| | |
|---|---|
| $L : t_1\ =\ i + 1$ | $100 : t_1\ =\ i + 1$ |
| $i\ =\ t_1$ | $101 : i\ =\ t_1$ |
| $t_2\ =\ i * 8$ | $102 : t_2\ =\ i * 8$ |
| $t_3\ =\ a[t_2]$ | $103 : t_3\ =\ a[t_2]$ |
| if $t_3\ <\ v$ goto $L$ | $104 :$ if $t_3\ <\ v$ goto $100$ |
| $(a)$ Symbolic labels | |

Here $i * 8$ is appropriate for an array of element that each take 8 units of space.

## 7.3   IMPLEMENTS OF THREE–ADDRESS CODES

A three address statement is an abstract form of intermediate code. In a compiler these statements can be implemented as records with fields for the operator and the operands. Three such representations are quadruples, triples and indirect triples.

**1. Quadruples:** A quadruple has four fields which we call **OP, argl, arg$_2$ and result**. The OP field contains an internal code for the operator. For eg the 3–address instruction $x = y + z$ is represented by placing $+$ in OP, $y$ in arg 1, $z$ in arg$_2$ and $x$ in result.

The following are some exceptions

(*i*) Instructions with unary operators like $x = $ minus $y$ or $x = y$ do not use $arg_2$.

(*ii*) Operators like paranthesis use neither $arg_2$ nor result.

(*iii*) Conditional and uncondition jumps put the larget label in result.

The quadruple for the assignment statement $a : = b * - c + b * c$ is given below.

$t_1 = $ minus C

$t_2 = b * t_1$

$t_3 = $ minus C

$t_4 = b * t_3$

$t_5 = t_2 + t_4$

$a = t_5$

(a) Three-address code

| | op | are1 | are2 | result |
|---|---|---|---|---|
| 0 | minus | c | | $t_1$ |
| 1 | * | b | $t_1$ | $t_2$ |
| 2 | minus | c | | $t_3$ |
| 3 | * | b | $t_3$ | $t_4$ |
| 4 | + | $t_2$ | $t_4$ | $t_5$ |
| 5 | = | $t_5$ | | a |

(b) Quadruples

**2. Triples:** A triples has only three fields which we call OP, arg and arg2. The result fields in the quadruples is used primarily for temporary name using triples, we can refer to the results of an operation $x$ opy by its **position,** rather than by an explicit temporary name.

Thus instead of the temporary $t_1$ in quadruples, a triple represents word refer to position (0). Parenthesized numbers represent pointer into the triple structure itself.

The triple for the Expression $a: = b* - c + b* - c$, along with syntax tree is given below.

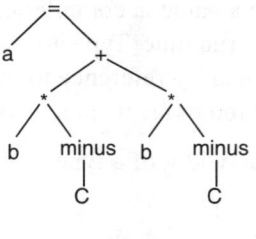

(a) Syntax tree

| | op | are1 | are2 |
|---|---|---|---|
| 0 | minus | c | |
| 1 | × | b | (0) |
| 2 | minus | c | |
| 3 | * | b | (2) |
| 4 | + | (1) | (3) |
| 5 | = | a | (4) |

(b) Triples

**3. Indirect Triples:** A indirect triples consist of a listing of Pointers to triples, rather than a listing of triples themselves, for example, use an array instruction to list pointer to triples in the desired order.

This implementation is called an indirect triples since is indirectly points to the triples with the help of the pointer to the list of triples.

| Instruction | | | op | are1 | are2 |
|---|---|---|---|---|---|
| 35 | (0) | 0 | minus | c | . |
| 36 | (1) | 1 | * | b | (0) |
| 37 | (2) | 2 | minus | c | |
| 38 | (3) | 3 | * | b | (2) |
| 39 | (4) | 4 | + | (1) | (3) |
| 40 | (5) | 5 | = | a | (4) |

**Figure:** Indirect triples represention of 3-address code

# Exercise

Translate the arthematic Expression $a + - (b + c)$ into (a) syntax tree (b) Quadruples (c) Triples (d) Indirect triplus.

**Types and Declarations:** The applications of types can be grouped under Checking and Translation.

**Type Checking:** Uses logical rules to reason about the behaviour of a program at runtime. Specifically it ensures that the types of the operads match the type expected by an operator.

**Translation Application:** From the type a name, a compiler can determine the storage that will be needed for that name at run time. Type information is also needed to calculate the address denoted by an array reference to insert explicit, type conversions and to choose the right version of an arithmetic operator.

**Computing Types and their Width:** The width of a type of the number of storage units needed for objects of that type.

Compute the types and width of the following grammar and also draw the pase tree showing the syntax–directed Translation of array types.

for int[2] [3]

| | |
|---|---|
| $T \rightarrow BC$ | $\{t = B \cdot \text{type}; \omega = \beta \cdot \text{width};\}$ |
| $B \rightarrow \text{int}$ | $\{\beta \cdot \text{type} = \text{integer}; B. \text{width} = 4;\}$ |
| $B \rightarrow \text{float}$ | $\{B. \text{type} = \text{float}; B. \text{width} = 8;\}$ |
| $C \rightarrow \varepsilon$ | $\{C. \text{type} = t; C. \text{width} = \omega;\}$ |
| $C \rightarrow [\text{num}] \, C_1$ | $\{\text{array (num. val}, C_1 . \text{type});$ |
| | $C \cdot \text{width} = \text{num} \cdot \text{val} \times C_1 \cdot \text{width};\}$ |

Parse tree for the [2] [3]

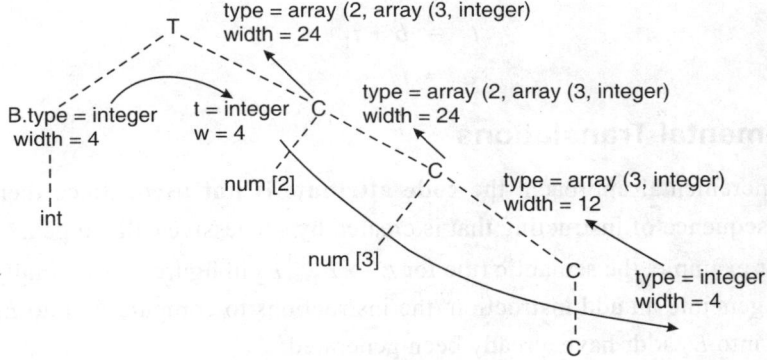

**Figure:** SDT for array types

## Translation of Expressions

1. Obtain the translation scheme for obtaining the three address code for the grammar.

$$S \rightarrow id = E;$$
$$E \rightarrow E_1 + E_2$$
$$E \rightarrow E_1 * E_2$$
$$E \rightarrow -E_1$$
$$E \rightarrow (E_1)$$
$$E \rightarrow id$$

## SOLUTION

| Production | Semantic rule |
|---|---|
| 1. $S \rightarrow id = E_1$ | $S \cdot \text{code} = E \cdot \text{code} \parallel \text{gen (top} \cdot \text{get (id.lexeme) '=' } E \cdot \text{addr}$ |
| 2. $E \rightarrow E_1 + E_2$ | $E \cdot \text{addr} = \text{new Temp( )}$ |
| | $E \cdot \text{code} = E_1 \cdot \text{code} \parallel E_2 \cdot \text{code} \parallel$ |
| | $\text{gen (Eiads '=' } E_1 \cdot \text{addr '+' } E_2 \cdot \text{addr)}$ |

| | |
|---|---|
| 3. $E \rightarrow -E_1$ | $E \cdot$ addr = new temp( ) |
| | $E \cdot$ code = $E_1 \cdot$ code \|\| gen ($E \cdot$ addr '=' minus' $E \cdot$ addr) |
| 4. $E \rightarrow (E_1)$ | $E \cdot$ addr = $E_1 \cdot$ addr |
| | $E \cdot$ code = $E_1 \cdot$ code |
| 5. $E \rightarrow id$ | $E \cdot$ addr = top $\cdot$ get ($id$, lexme) |
| | $E \cdot$ code = '' |

The SDD shown above translate the assignment statement

$$a \;=\; b + - c \text{ into the three address code}$$

$$t_1 \;=\; \text{minus } c$$

$$t_2 \;=\; b + t_1$$

$$a \;=\; t_2$$

## Incremental Translations

With incremental approach, the **code attribute is not used**. Since there is a single sequence of instructing that is created by successive calls to gen.

For example, the semantic rule for $E \rightarrow E_1 + E_2$ in figure below simply calls gen to generate an add instruction, the instructions to compute $E_1$ into $E_1$ addr and $E_2$ into $E_2$ addr have already been generated.

| Production | Semantic alling |
|---|---|
| 1. $S \rightarrow id = E$; | {gen (top $\cdot$ get ($id \cdot$ lexene) '=' $E \cdot$ addr} |
| 2. $E \rightarrow E_1 + E_2$ | {$E \cdot$ addr = new Temp( ); |
| | gen ($E \cdot$ addr '=' $E_1 \cdot$ addr '+' $E_2$.addr) ;} |
| 3. $E \rightarrow - E_1$ | {$E \cdot$ addr = new Temp. ( ); |
| | gen ($E \cdot$ addr '=' minus $E_1 \cdot$ addr);} |
| 4. $E \rightarrow (E_1)$ | {$E \cdot$ addr = $E_1 \cdot$ addr $\cdot$;} |
| 5. $E \rightarrow id$ | {$E \cdot$ addr = top $\cdot$ get ($id \cdot$ lexeme);} |

**Figure:** Generating 3-address code for expressions incrementally

## 7.4  TYPE CHECKING

Type checking is the methodology to check whether the source program follows both the syntatic and sematic conversions of the, source language. Type checking is also called of Static checking.

Type checking ensures that the errors will be detected and reported.

Type checking can take on two forms, synthesis and inference. Type synthesis builds up the type of an expression from the types of its sub expressions. It requires names to be declared before they are used. The type of $E_1 + E_2$ is defined in terms of the types of $E_1$ and $E_2$. A typical rule for type synthesis has the forms.

if $f$ has type $S \to t$ and $x$ has type $S$. Then expression $f(x)$ has type $t$.

Here $f$ and $x$ denote expressions and $S \to t$ denote a function from $S$ to $t$.

**Type Inference** determine the type of a language **construct** from the way it is used.

A typical rule for type influence has the from if $f(x)$ is an expression.

Then for same $\alpha$ and $\beta$ and has type $\alpha \to \beta$ and $x$ has type $\alpha$. This influence is needed for languages which checks types but do not require names to be declared.

**Type Conversions:** Consider expressions like $x + i$, where $x$ is of type float and $i$ is of type integer.

Suppose that integers are converted to float when necessary using a unary operator (float) for example, the integer 2 is converted a float $n$ the code for the expression. $2 * 3.14$.

$$t_1 = (\text{float})2$$
$$t_2 = t_1 * 3.14$$

**Type Synthesis** can be shown by introducing attribute $E \cdot$ type whose value is Either integer or float. The rule associated with $E_1 + E_2$ builts on the **Pseudo code**.

if $(E_1 \cdot \text{type} = \text{integer}$ and $E_2 \cdot \text{type} = \text{integer})$ $E \cdot \text{type} = \text{integer}$

else if $(E_1 \cdot \text{type} = \text{float}$ and $E_2 \cdot \text{type} = \text{integer})$...

Type conversion rules vary from language to language. Two types of conversion *i.e.,* widening conversions which are intended to preserve information and narrowing conversions which can lose information.

**Type widening rules** are given by the hierarchy in figure (*a*) any type lower in the hierarchy can be widened to a higher type. Thus a char can be widened to an int or to a float, but a char cannot be widened to a short.

**Type narrowing rules** is given in figure (b) a type $S$ can be narrowed to a type $t$ if there is a path from $S$ to $t$.

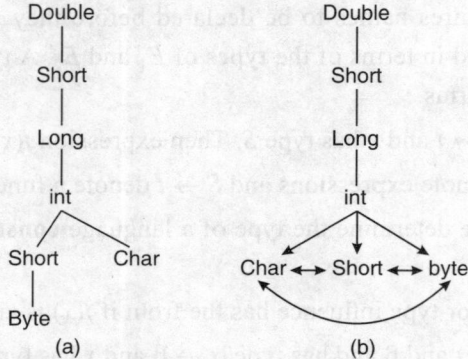

**Figure:** Conversing b/w primitive types

The semantic action for $E \rightarrow E_1 + E_2$ a given below.

$$E \rightarrow E_1 + E_2 \{E \rightarrow type = max (E_1 \cdot type, E_2 \cdot type)$$
$$a_1 = widen (E_1 \cdot addr, E_1 \cdot type, E \cdot type)$$
$$a_2 = widen (E_2 \cdot addr, E_2 \cdot type, E \cdot type);$$
$$E \cdot addr = new \ temp ();$$
$$gen (E \cdot addr \ '=' \ a_1 \ '+' \ a_2); \}$$

**Figure:** Introducing type conversion into expression evaluation

**Note:** 1. Conversions from one type to anothers is said to be **implicit** if it is done automatically by the compiler. Implicit type conversions also called **coercions**.

2. Conversions is said to be **explicit** if the programmer must write something to cause the conversion. Explicit conversions are also called **casts**.

## 7.5  UNIFICATION

Unification is the problem of determining whether two, expressions $S$ and $t$ can be made identical by substituting expressions for the variables in $S$ and $t$.

Testing equality of expressions is a special case of unification if $S$ and to have constante but no variables, then $S$ and $t$ unify if and only if they are identical.

### EXAMPLE

For the following two type expressions, obtain the equivalence classes using unification.

$$((\alpha_1 \rightarrow \alpha_2) \times list (\alpha_3)) \rightarrow list (\alpha_2)$$
$$((\alpha_3 \rightarrow \alpha_4) \times list (\alpha_3)) \rightarrow \alpha_5.$$

### SOLUTION

The following substition $S$ is the most general unifier for these expression

| $x$ | $S(x)$ |
|-----|--------|
| $\alpha_1$ | $\alpha_1$ |
| $\alpha_2$ | $\alpha_2$ |
| $\alpha_3$ | $\alpha_1$ |
| $\alpha_4$ | $\alpha_2$ |
| $\alpha_5$ | list $(\alpha_1)$ |

The substitution maps the two type Expressions to the following expressions

$$((\alpha_1 \rightarrow \alpha_2) \times \text{list }(\alpha_1) \rightarrow \text{list }(\alpha_2)$$

The two expressions are represented by the two nodes labeled $\rightarrow$ : 1 shown below. The integers at the nodes indicate the equivalence classes that the nodes belong to after the nodes numbered 1 are unified.

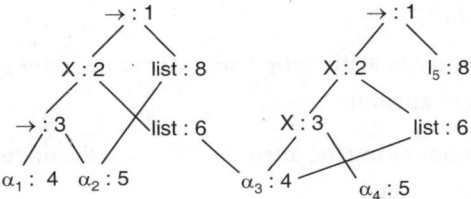

**Figure:** Equivalence closers after unification

## 7.6  SYNTAX DIRECTED TRANSLATION

## Syntax Directed Definition (SDD)

- To translate a programing language construct compiler has to keep track of many quantites such as the type of the construct, location of first instruction in target code or the number of instructions generated.

- A formalist called as syntax directed definitions is used for specifying translations for programming language constructs.

- A syntax directed definition is a generalization of a context free Grammar in which each grammar symbol has associated set of attributes and each production is associated with a set of semantic rules.

## Definition of Syntax Directed Definition (SDD)

SDD is a generalization of CFG in which each grammar production $X \rightarrow \alpha$ is associated with it a set of semantic rules of the form

$$a := f(b_1..., b_2 ....b_k)$$

where $a$ is an attribute obtained from the function $f$.

The two attributes for non-terminals are.

**1. Synthesized Attribute (S–attribute): (↑):** An attribute is said to be synthesized attribute if its value to a parse tree node is determined from attribute values at the children of the node.

**2. Inherited Attribute: (→, ↓):** An inherited attribute is one whose value at parse tree node is determined in terms of attributes at the parent and|or siblings of that node.

- The attribute can be string, a number, a type, a memory location or anything else.

- The parse tree showing the value of attributes at each node is called an annotated parse tree.

**Note:** If the grammar is arithmetic use S-attribute, data type and declaration use-Inherited attribute.

The process of computing the attribute values at the node is called annotating or decorating the parse tree.

**1. Synthesized Attributes:**

Consider the CFG

$$S \rightarrow EN$$

$$E \rightarrow E + T$$

$$E \rightarrow E - T$$

$$E \rightarrow T$$

$$T \rightarrow T * F$$

$$T \rightarrow T|F$$

$$T \rightarrow F$$

$$F \rightarrow (E)$$

$$F \rightarrow digit$$

$$N \rightarrow ;$$

# SOLUTION:

The syntax directed definition can be written for the above grammar by writing semantic actions for each production.

| Production rule | Semantic actions |
|---|---|
| $S \rightarrow EN$ | Print $(E \cdot \text{val})$ |
| $E \rightarrow E_1 + T$ | $E \cdot \text{val} = E_1 \cdot \text{val} + T \cdot \text{val}$ |
| $E \rightarrow E_1 - T$ | $E \cdot \text{val} = E_1 \cdot \text{val} - T \cdot \text{val}$ |
| $E \rightarrow T$ | $E \cdot \text{val} = T \cdot \text{val}$ |
| $T \rightarrow T * F$ | $T \cdot \text{val} = T \cdot \text{val} * F \cdot \text{val}$ |
| $T \rightarrow T|F$ | $T \cdot \text{val} = T \cdot \text{val}| F \cdot \text{val}$ |
| $F \rightarrow (E)$ | $F \cdot \text{val} = E \cdot \text{val}$ |
| $T \rightarrow F$ | $T \cdot \text{val} = F \cdot \text{val}$ |
| $F \rightarrow \text{digit}$ | $F \cdot \text{val} = \text{digit} \cdot \text{lexval}$ |
| $N \rightarrow ;$ | can be ignored by lexical analyzer as ; is terminating symbol. |

For the Non-terminals $E$, $T$ and $F$ the values can be obtained using the attribute "val".

The token digit has synthesized attribute "lexval".

In $S \rightarrow EN$, symbol $S$ is the start symbol. This rule is to print the final answer of the expression.

Following steps are followed to compute $S$ attributed definition.

1. Write the SDD using the appropriate semantic actions for corresponding production rule of the given grammar.

2. The annotated parse tree is generated and attribute values are computed. The computation is done in bottom up mannar.

3. The value obtained at the node is supposed to be final output.

## PROBLEM 1

Consider the string 5 * 6 + 7; construct syntax tree, parse tree and annotated tree.

## SOLUTION

**Syntax tree:**

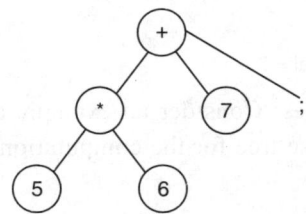

**Parse Tree:**

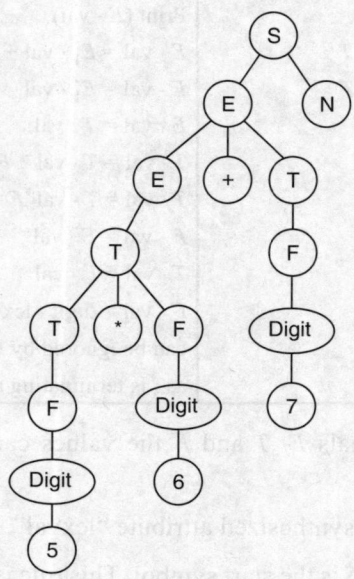

The corresponding annotated parse tree is shown below for the string $5 * 6 + 7$;

**Annotated Prese Tree:**

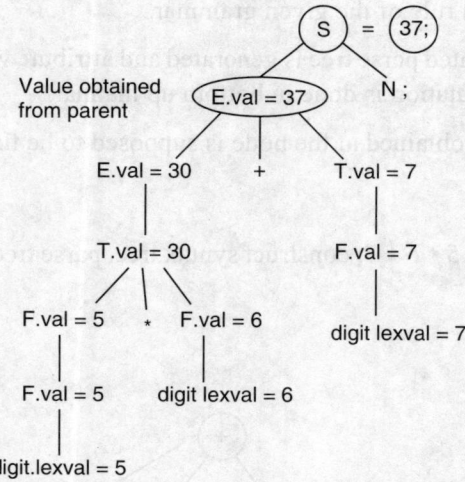

**2. Inherited Attributes:** Consider an example and compute the inherited attributes annotate the parse tree for the computation of inherited attributes for the given string int *a, b, c.*

$$S \rightarrow TL$$
$$T \rightarrow \text{int}$$
$$T \rightarrow \text{float}$$
$$T \rightarrow \text{char}$$
$$T \rightarrow \text{double}$$
$$L \rightarrow L, id$$
$$L \rightarrow id$$

The steps are to be followed are:

1. Construct the syntax directed definition using semantic action.

2. Annotate the parse tree with inherited attributes by processing in top down fashion.

The SDD is given below:

| Production rule | Semantic actions |
|---|---|
| $S \rightarrow TL$ | $L \cdot$ in $h = T \cdot$ type |
| $T \rightarrow$ int | $T \cdot$ type = int |
| $T \rightarrow$ Float | $T \cdot$ type = Float |
| $T \rightarrow$ Char | $T \cdot$ type = Char |
| $T \rightarrow$ double | $T \cdot$ type = double |
| $L \rightarrow L, id$ | $L \cdot$ in $h = L \cdot$ in $h$ ; Enter–type ($id \cdot$ entry, $L \cdot$ in $h$) |
| $L \rightarrow id$ | Enter_type ($id \cdot$ entry $\cdot$ $L \cdot$ in $h$) |

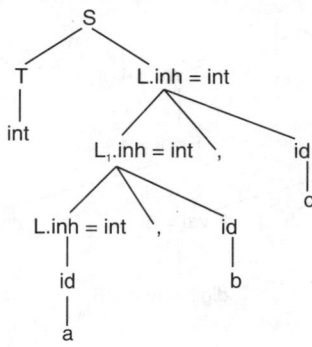

**Figure:** Annotated parse tree

## PROBLEMS

## PROBLEM 1

Consider the grammar that is used for simple desk calculator. Obtain the semantic action and also the annotated parse tree for the string $3 * 5 + 4n$.

$$L \rightarrow En$$
$$E \rightarrow E_1 + T$$
$$E \rightarrow T$$
$$T \rightarrow T_1 * F$$
$$T \rightarrow F$$
$$F \rightarrow (E)$$
$$F \rightarrow \text{digit}$$

## SOLUTION

| Production rule | Semantic actions |
|---|---|
| $L \rightarrow En$ | $L \cdot val = E \cdot val$ |
| $E \rightarrow E_1 + T$ | $E \cdot val = E_1 \cdot val + T \cdot val$ |
| $E \rightarrow T$ | $E \cdot val = T \cdot val$ |
| $T \rightarrow T_1 * F$ | $T \cdot val = T_1 \cdot val * F \cdot val$ |
| $T \rightarrow F$ | $T \cdot val = F \cdot val$ |
| $F \rightarrow E$ | $F \cdot val = E \cdot val$ |
| $F \rightarrow \text{digit}$ | $F \cdot val = \text{digit} \cdot lexval$ |

The corresponding annotated parse tree is shown below, for the string
$3 * 5 + 4n$

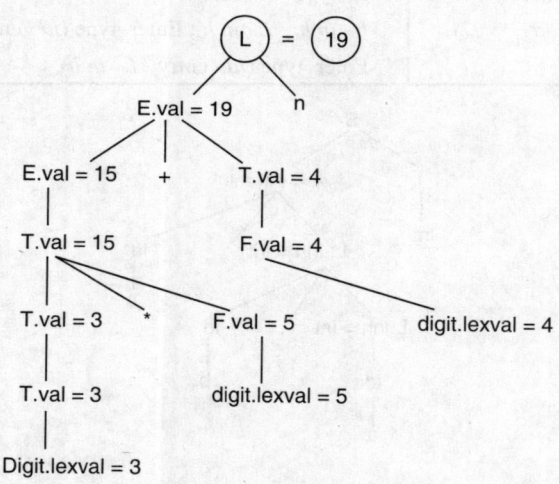

**Figure:** Annotated Parse tree

## EXERCISE

For the SDD of the problem 1 give annotated parse tree for the following expressions.

(a) $(3 + 4) * (5 + 6)n$

(b) $1 * 2 * 3 * (4 + 5)n$

(c) $(9 + 8 * (7 + 6) + 5) * 4n$

## SOLUTION

(a)

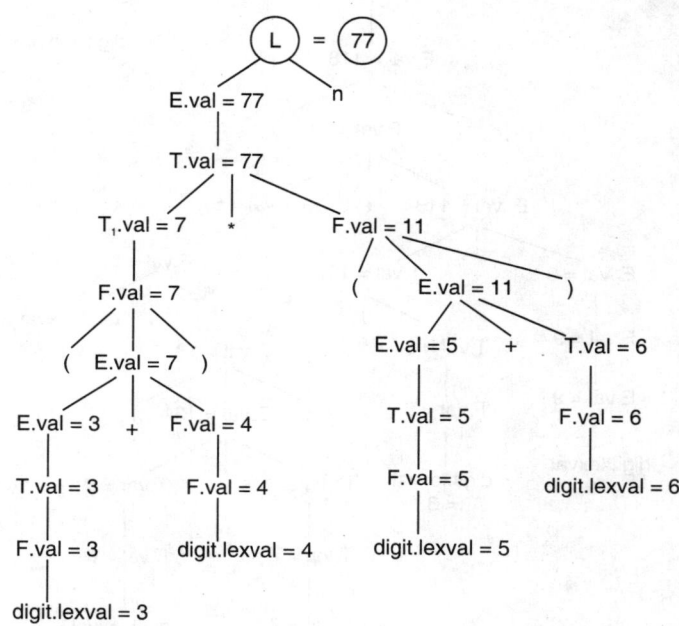

(b)

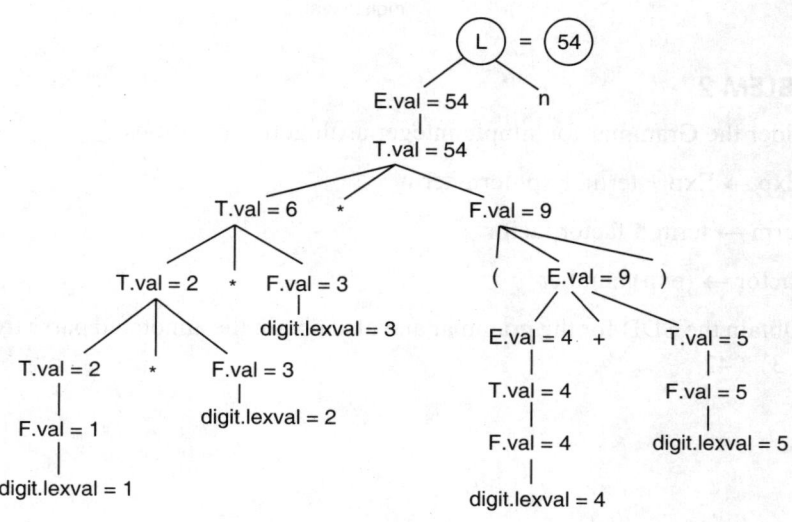

(c)

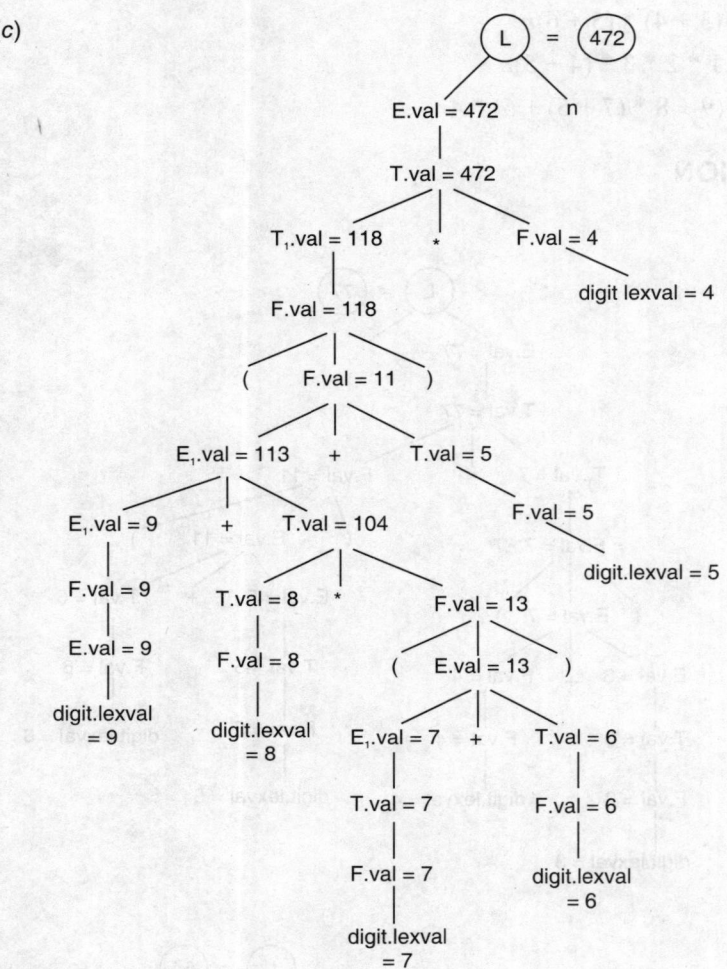

## PROBLEM 2

Consider the Grammar for simple integer arithmetic operations.

Exp → Exp + term| Exp–term|term

term → term * factor|factor

factor → (exp)|number

Obtain the SDD for the grammar and also obtain the annotated parse tree for $(34 - 3) * 42$.

## SOLUTION

| Production rule | Semantic actions |
|---|---|
| $exp_1 \rightarrow exp_2 + term_1$ | $expival = exp_2 \cdot val + term_1\ val$ |
| $exp_1 \rightarrow exp_2 - term_1$ | $exp_1 \cdot val = exp_2 \cdot val - term_1 \cdot val$ |
| $exp_1 \rightarrow term_1$ | $exp_1 \cdot val = term_1 \cdot val$ |
| $term_1 \rightarrow term_2 * Factor$ | $term_1 \cdot val = term_2 \cdot val * factor \cdot va$ |
| $term_1 \rightarrow factor$ | $term \cdot val = factor \cdot val$ |
| $factor \rightarrow (exp_1)$ | $factor \cdot val = exp \cdot val$ |
| $factor \rightarrow number$ | $factor \cdot val = number \cdot val$ |

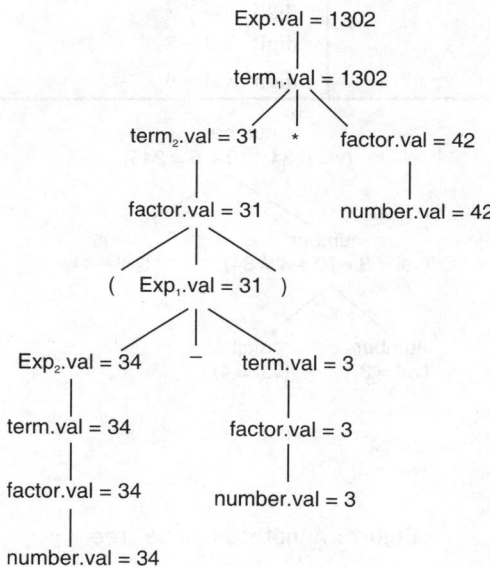

## PROBLEM 3

Consider the following simple grammar for unsigned numbers:

number → number digit|digit

digit → 0|1|2|3|4|5|6|7|8|9

Obtain the SDD for the grammar and annotated parse tree for 345.

## SOLUTION

**Note:**                     $34 = 3 * 10 + 4$

number · val = number · val * 10 + digit · val

| Production rule | Semantic actions |
|---|---|
| number → number digit | number$_1 \cdot$ val = number 2 · val digit · val |
| number → digit | number · val = digit · val |
| digit → 0 | digit · val = 0 |
| digit → 1 | digit · val = 1 |
| digit → 2 | digit · val = 2 |
| digit → 3 | digit · val = 3 |
| digit → 4 | digit · val = 4 |
| digit → 5 | digit · val = 5 |
| digit → 6 | digit · val = 6 |
| digit → 7 | digit · val = 7 |
| digit → 8 | digit · val = 8 |
| digit → 9 | digit · val = 9 |

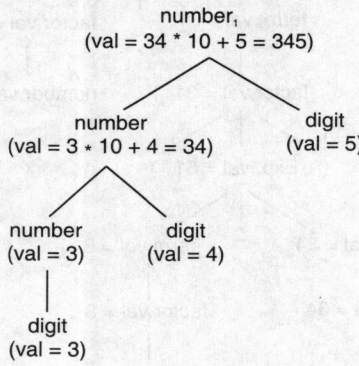

**Figure:** Annotated parse tree

## PROBLEM ON INHERITED ATTRIBUTE

## PROBLEM 1

For the grammar construct the SDD and the annotated parse tree for the string 3 * 5.

$$T \rightarrow FT'$$
$$T' \rightarrow * FT'$$
$$T' \rightarrow \varepsilon$$
$$F \rightarrow digit$$

## SOLUTION

| Production rule | Semantic actions |
|---|---|
| $T \to FT'$ | $T' \cdot in\ h = F \cdot val$ |
| | $T \cdot val = T' \cdot Syn$ |
| $T' \to * FT'$ | $T'_1 \cdot in\ h = T' \cdot in\ h * F. val$ |
| | $T' \cdot Syn = T'_1 \cdot Syn$ |
| $T' \to \varepsilon$ | $T'_1 \cdot Syn = T'_1 \cdot in\ h$ |
| $F \to digit$ | $F \cdot val = digit \cdot lexval$ |

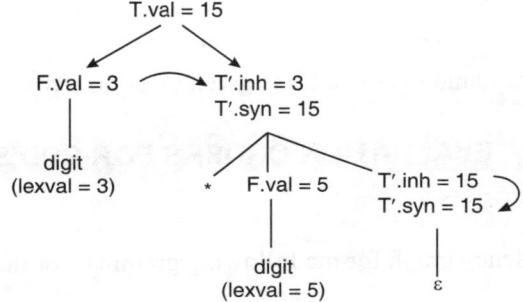

## 7.7 EVALUATION ORDERS FOR SDDS

Dependency graphs are a useful tool for determining an evaluation order for the attribute instance in a given parse tree.

The directed graph that represents interdependent between synthesized and inherited attributes at the nodes in the parse tree is called dependency graph.

For the rule $X \to yz$, the semantic action is given by, $x \cdot x \to F(y \cdot y, z \cdot z)$

Then Synthesized attribute is $x \cdot x$ and $x \cdot x$ depends upon attributes $y \cdot y$ and $z \cdot z$.

## PROBLEM 1

Design the dependency graph for the following grammar.

$$E \to E_1 + E_2$$
$$E \to E_1 * E_2$$

## SOLUTION

The semantic rule is given on next page.

| Production rule | Semantic actions |
|---|---|
| $E \rightarrow E_1 + E_2$ | $E \cdot val = E_1 \cdot val + E_2 \cdot val$ |
| $E \rightarrow E_1 * E_2$ | $E \cdot val = E_1 \cdot val * E_2 \cdot val$ |

The dependency graph is given below:

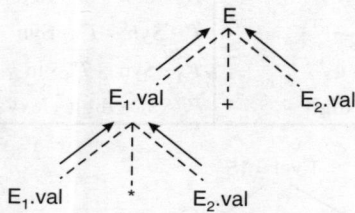

The dependency among the nodes is given by solid arrows.

## EVALUATION ORDERS FOR SDD'S

### PROBLEM 2

Design the dependency graph for the following grammar for the input string int $a, b, c$.

$$S \rightarrow T \text{ List}$$
$$T \rightarrow \text{int}$$
$$T \rightarrow \text{float}$$
$$T \rightarrow \text{char}$$
$$T \rightarrow \text{double}$$
$$\text{List} \rightarrow \text{List}, id$$
$$\text{List} \rightarrow id$$

### SOLUTION

The dependency graph is shown below:

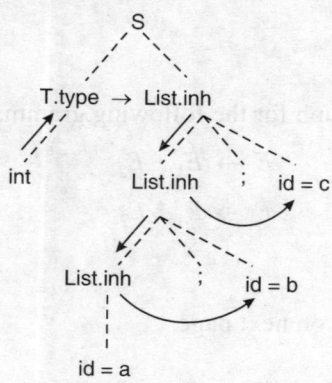

The semantic rule is given below:

| Production rule | Semantic actions |
|---|---|
| $S \rightarrow T$ List | List $\cdot$ in $h = T \cdot$ type |
| $T \rightarrow$ int | $T_1 \cdot$ type = int |
| $T \rightarrow$ Float | $T \cdot$ type = float |
| $T \rightarrow$ Char | $T \cdot$ type = char |
| $T \rightarrow$ double | $T \cdot$ type = double |
| List $\rightarrow$ List, $id$ | List $\cdot$ in $h$ = List $\cdot$ in $h$ |
| | Enter–type ($id \cdot$ entry, List $\cdot$ in $h$) |
| List $\cdot$ $id$ | Enter–type ($id \cdot$ entry, List $\cdot$ in $h$) |

**Evaluation Order:** The **topological sort** of the dependency graph decides the evaluation order in a parse tree. In deciding evaluation order, the semantic rule in SDD are used. Thus the translation is specified by **Syntax Directed Definitions.**

## PROBLEM 1

Obtain the dependency graph and order of execution for the grammar.

$$T \rightarrow FT'$$

$$T \rightarrow *FT'$$

$$T' \rightarrow \varepsilon$$

$$F \rightarrow \text{digit}$$

and for the input string 3 * 5.

## SOLUTION

The semantic rule is given below.

| Production rule | Semantic actions |
|---|---|
| $T \rightarrow FT'$ | $T' \cdot$in $h = F \cdot$val |
| | $T \cdot$val = $T' \cdot$syn |
| $T' \rightarrow * FT_1'$ | $T_1' \cdot$in $h = T \cdot$in $h * F \cdot$val |
| | $T \cdot$syn = $T_1' \cdot$syn |
| $T' \rightarrow \varepsilon$ | $T' \cdot$ syn = $T_1' \cdot$in$h$ |
| $F \rightarrow$ digit | $F \cdot$val = digit$\cdot$lexval |

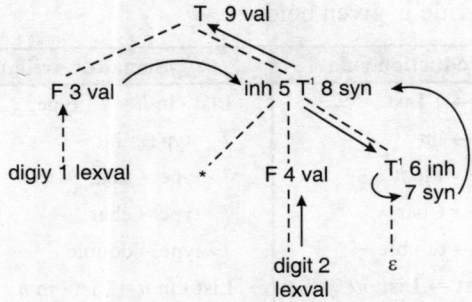

For the above example obtain the dependency graph and order of evaluation for the input string 3 * 5 * 4.

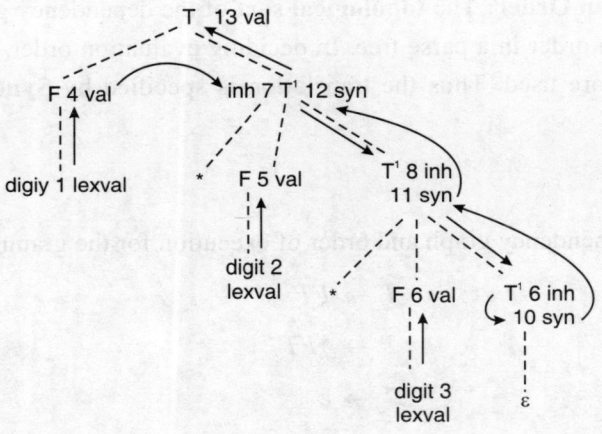

**Figure:** Dependency graph

## PROBLEM 2

Obtain SDD, annotated pars, tree and the dependency graph for the grammar.

$$D \rightarrow TL$$

$$T \rightarrow int$$

$$T \rightarrow Float$$

$$L \rightarrow L_1, id$$

$$L \rightarrow id$$

For the input string float $id_1$, $id_2$, $id_3$.

## SOLUTION

| Production rule | Semantic actions |
|---|---|
| $D \to TL$ | $L \cdot \text{in } h = T \cdot \text{type}$ |
| $T \to \text{int}$ | $T \cdot \text{type} = \text{int}$ |
| $T \to \text{Float}$ | $T \cdot \text{type} = \text{float}$ |
| $L \to L_1 , id$ | $L_i \cdot \text{in } h = L \cdot \text{in } h$ |
| | enter-type $(id \cdot \text{entry}, L \cdot \text{in } h)$ |
| $L \to id$ | enter –type $(id \cdot \text{entry}, L \cdot \text{in } h)$ |

**Figure:** Semantic actions

**Annotated Parse Tree:**

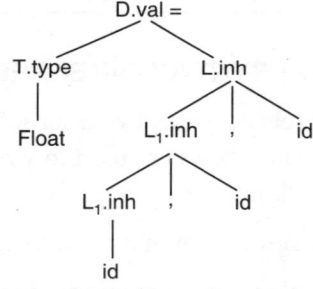

**Dependency Graph:**

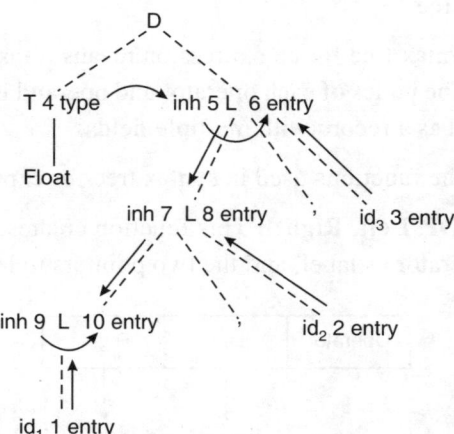

**S-attributed Definitions:** A syntax directed definition that uses synthesized attributes is said to be an S-attributed definition.

Synthesized attributes can be evaluated by a bottom–up parser as the input is parsed.

The parser keeps the values of synthesized attributes with the grammar symbol on its stack. Whenever a reduction is made, the values of the new synthesized attributes are computed from the attributes appearing on the stack for the Grammar symbols on the right side of the reducing production.

**L-attributed Definitions:** A syntax directed definitions which we inherited attributes is said to be L-attributed definitions.

If L-attributed definitions, the attributes are always evaluated in **Depth First Order:** The L is for left because the attribute information flow from left to right.

| Production rule | Semantic actions |
|---|---|
| $T \rightarrow FT'$ | $T' \cdot$ in $h = F \cdot$ val |
| $T \rightarrow *FT$ | $T_1' \cdot$ inh $= T' \cdot$ in $h^*$ Fval |

## 7.8 APPLICATIONS OF SYNTAX DIRECTED TRANSLATION

**Construction of Syntax Tree:** A syntax tree is an abstract representation of the language constructs. The syntax trees are used to write the translation routines using syntax directed definitions.

A syntax tree is a condensed from of a parse tree.

In a syntax tree, **operators and keywords donot appear as leaves,** but rather they are associated with the interior node that would be parent of those leaves in the parse tree.

Constructing syntax tree for an expression means translation of expression into **postfix form**. The nodes of each operator and operand is created. Each node can be implemented as a record with multiple fields.

Following are the functions used in syntax tree for expressions.

**1. New Node (OP, Left, Right):** This function creates a node into the field operator having operator as label, and the two pointers to left and right.

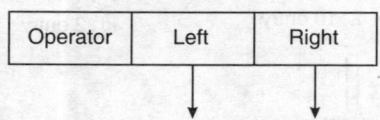

**2 New Leaf (*id*, entry):** The function creates an identifier node with label *id* and a pointer to the symbol table is given by **entry**.

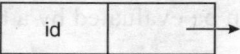

**3. New Leaf (num, val):** This function creates node for numbers with lable num and val is for value of that number.

| num | |
|-----|---|

## EXAMPLE

Construct the syntax tree for the the expression $x * y - 5 + z$.

## SOLUTION

**Step 1:** Convert the expression from infix to post fix $xy * 5 - z +$

**Step 2:** Make use of the functions new node (), new leaf ($id$, ptr), new leaf (num, val)

**Step 3:** The sequence of function calls is given below:

| Symbol | Operation/Semantic rules |
|:------:|--------------------------|
| $x$ | $P_1$ = new leaf ($id$, $id \cdot$ entry) |
| $y$ | $P_2$ = new leaf ($id$, $id$, entry of $y$) |
| * | $P_3$ = new node (*, $P_1$, $P_2$) |
| 5 | $P_4$ = new leaf (num, 5) |
| – | $P_5$ = new node ($-p_3$, $p_4$) |
| 2 | $P_6$ = new leaf ($id$, $id \cdot$ entry of $z$) |
| + | $P_7$ = new node (+, $P_5$, $P_6$) |

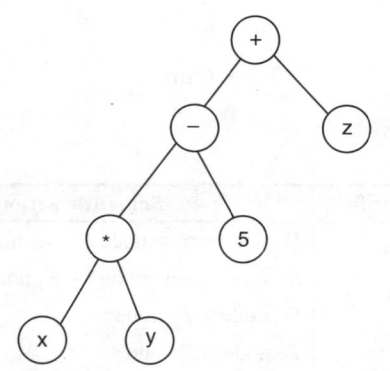

**Figure:** Syntax tree

For the input string, the syntax tree is as shown on next page.

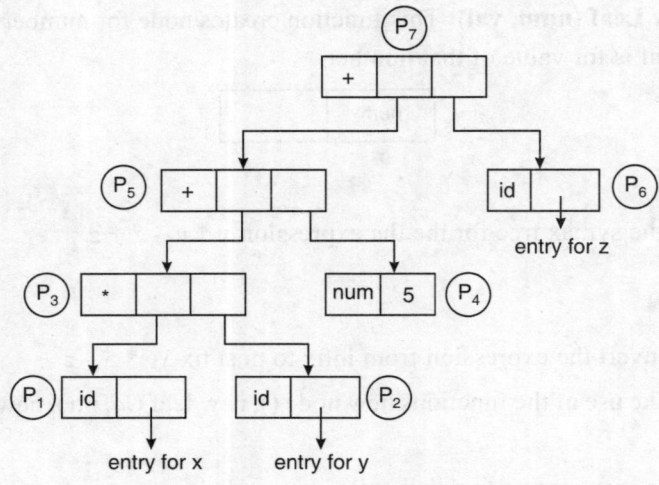

## PROBLEM 1

Obtain the SDD for the following expression and also obtain syntax tree/ annotated syntax tree for the expression $a - 4 + c$ for the grammar.

$$E \rightarrow E_1 + T$$

$$E \rightarrow E_1 - T$$

$$E \rightarrow T$$

$$T \rightarrow (E)$$

$$T \rightarrow id$$

$$T \rightarrow num$$

## SOLUTION

| Production rule | Semantic actions |
|---|---|
| $E \rightarrow E_1 + T$ | $E \cdot$ node = new node $(+, E_1$ node $, T \cdot$ node$)$ |
| $E \rightarrow E_1 - T$ | $E \cdot$ node = new node $(-, E_1$ node$, T \cdot$ node$)$ |
| $E \rightarrow T$ | $E \cdot$ node = $T \cdot$ node |
| $T \rightarrow (E)$ | $T \cdot$ node = $E \cdot$ node |
| $T \rightarrow id$ | $T \cdot$ node = new leaf $(id \cdot id \cdot$ entry$)$ |
| $T \rightarrow num$ | $T \cdot$ node = new leaf (num, num $\cdot$ val) |

The annotated syntax tree for the expression $a - 4 + c$ is given below.

**Step 1:** Convert the infix expression to post fix expression $a\, 4 - c+$.

**Step 2:** Make use of functions new node (), new leaf (*id*, ptr), new leaf (num · val).

**Step 3:**

| Symbol | Operation/Semantic rules |
|--------|--------------------------|
| *a* | $P_1$ = new leaf (*id*, *id* · entry of *a*) |
| 4 | $P_2$ = new leaf (num, 4) |
| – | $P_3$ = new node (–, P1, P2) |
| c | $P_4$ = new leaf (*id*, *id* · entry of c) |
| + | $P_5$ = new node (+, $P_3$, $P_4$) |

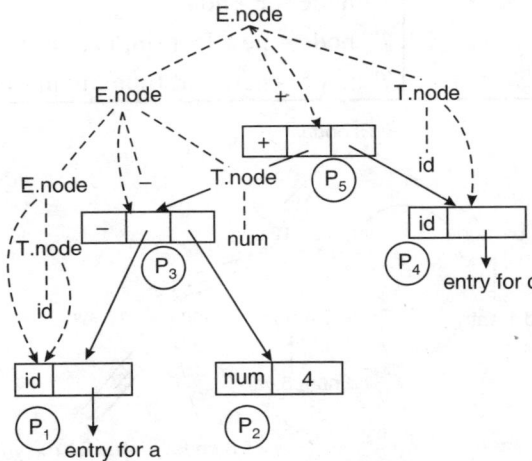

## PROBLEM 2

Construct the syntax tree for the grammar

$$E \rightarrow TE'$$

$$E' \rightarrow + TE'$$

$$E' \rightarrow -TE'$$

$$E' \rightarrow \varepsilon$$

$$T \rightarrow (E)$$

$$T \rightarrow id$$

$$T \rightarrow num$$

Obtain the SDD for the above grammar and also the dependency graph for the input string $a - 4 + c$.

## SOLUTION

| Production rule | Semantic actions |
|---|---|
| 1. $E \rightarrow TE'$ | $E \cdot node = E^1.syn$ |
| | $E^1 \cdot in\ h = T.node$ |
| 2. $E^1 \rightarrow +TE_1'$ | $E_1' \cdot in\ h = new\ node\ (+, E_1' \cdot in\ h\ T\text{-node})$ |
| | $E^1 \cdot syn = E_1' \cdot syn$ |
| 3. $E^1 \rightarrow -TE'$ | $E_1' \cdot in\ h = new\ node\ (-, E' \cdot in\ h\ T\text{-node})$ |
| | $E^1 \cdot syn = E_1' \cdot syn$ |
| 4. $E^1 \rightarrow \epsilon$ | $E' \cdot syn = E' \cdot in\ h$ |
| 5. $T \rightarrow (E)$ | $T \cdot node = E \cdot node$ |
| 6. $T \rightarrow id$ | $T \cdot node = new\ leaf\ (id, id \cdot entry)$ |
| 7. $T \rightarrow num$ | $T \cdot node = new\ leaf\ (num, num \cdot val)$ |

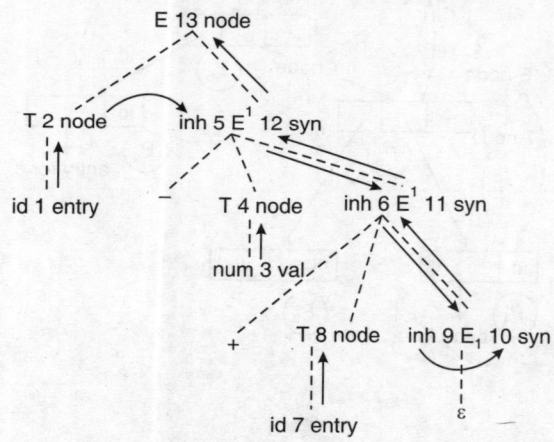

## PROBLEM 3

Construct SDD for the given productions

$$T \rightarrow BC$$

$$B \rightarrow int$$

$$B \rightarrow float$$

$$C \rightarrow [num]\ C_1$$

$$C \rightarrow \epsilon$$

for the expression int [2] [3].

## SOLUTION:

| Production | Semantic rules |
|---|---|
| $T \to BC$ | $T \cdot t = C \cdot t$ |
| | $C \cdot b = B \cdot t$ |
| $B \to$ int | $B \cdot t =$ integer |
| $B \to$ float | $B \cdot t =$ float |
| $C \to [num]C_1$ | $C \cdot t =$ array (num, val, $C_1 \cdot t$] |
| | $C_1 \cdot b = C \cdot b$ |
| $C \to \varepsilon$ | $C \cdot t = C \cdot b$ |

**Note:** Here $b$ = inherited; $t$ = synthesis attribute

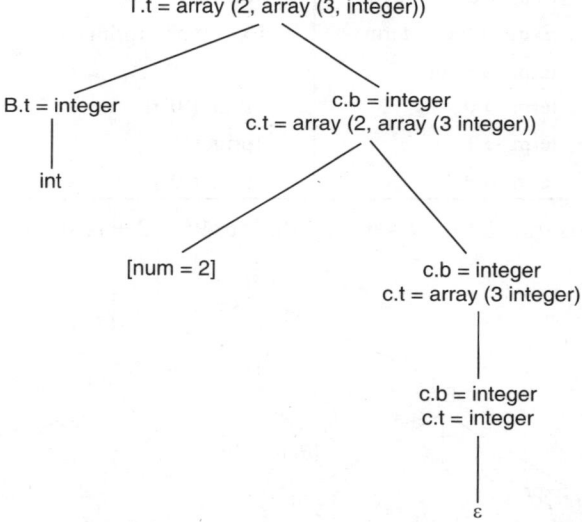

**Figure:** SDT for int [2] [3]

## 7.9 SYNTAX–DIRECTED TRANSLATION SCHEMES (SDT'S)

During the process of passing the evaluation of attribute takes place of consulting the semantic action enclosed in {} at the right of the grammar symbol. This process of Execution of code fragment. Semantic actions from the SDD is called **Syntax-directed translation.**

Thus the exectuion of syntax–directed definition can be done by syntax–directed translation scheme.

A translation scheme generates the output by executing the semantic actions in an **ordered manner.** This processing is using **depth first transversal.**

It give the translation scheme that converts infix to postfix from for the following grammar. Also generate the annotated parse tree for input string 9 – 5 + 2.

$$Exp \rightarrow Exp + temp$$
$$Exp \rightarrow Expr - term$$
$$Expr \rightarrow term$$
$$term \rightarrow 0|1|...|9$$

## SOLUTION

| Production | Expr+term Semantic rules |
|---|---|
| Exp → Expr + term | {Print ('+')} |
| Expr → Exp – term | Exp + term {print ('–')} |
| Expr → term | |
| term → 0 | {Print ('0')} |
| term → 1 | {print ('1')} |
| term → 9 | {Print ('9')} |

The actions translating 9 – 5 + 2 into into 95 – 2 + is shown below.

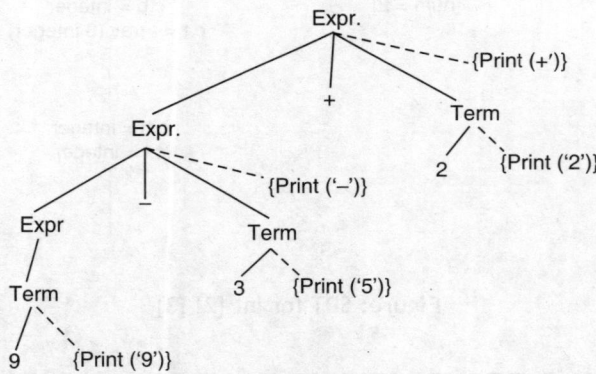

The postfix SDT given below that implements desk calculator.

$$L \rightarrow En \ \{print \ (E \cdot val);\}$$
$$E \rightarrow E_1 + T \ \{E \cdot val = E_1 \cdot val + T \cdot val;\}$$
$$E \rightarrow T \ \{E \cdot val = T \cdot val\}$$
$$T \rightarrow T_1 * F\{T_1 \ val = T_1 \cdot val \times F \cdot val\}$$
$$T \rightarrow F \ \{T_1 \ val = F \cdot val\}$$
$$T \rightarrow (E) \ \{F \cdot val = E \cdot val\}$$
$$F \rightarrow digit \ \{F \cdot val = digit \cdot lexval;\}$$

The desk calculator on a bottom up parsing stack is given below.

| Production | Actions |
|---|---|
| $L \rightarrow En$ | {Print (stack [top −1] . val); top = top − 1;} |
| $E \rightarrow E_1 + T$ | {Stack [top −2] . val = Stack [top − 2] · val + stack [top] · val top = top −2;} |
| $E \rightarrow T$ | — |
| $T_1 \rightarrow T_1 *F$ | {Stack [top − 2] · val = stack [top − 2] · val × stack [top] · val top = top − 2;} |
| $T \rightarrow F$ | — |
| $F \rightarrow (E)$ | {Stack [top − 2] · val = Stack [top − 1] · val; top = top −2 ;} |
| $F \rightarrow$ digit | — |

The following figure shows the parse tree for expression 3 * 5 + 4 with actions inserted. If we traverse we get the prefix from of the expression + *354

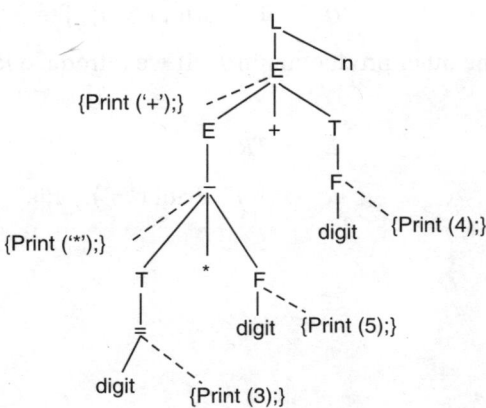

**Figure:** Parse tree with actions embedded

The SDT for infix – to Prefix translation during parsing

$$L \rightarrow En$$
$$E \rightarrow \{Print ('+');\} \ E_1 + T$$
$$E \rightarrow T$$
$$T \rightarrow \{Print \ '*');\} \ T_1 * F$$
$$T \rightarrow F$$
$$F \rightarrow (E)$$

## 7.10   ELIMINATING LEFT RECURSION FROM SDT'S

To eliminate left recursion is to take two productions.

$$A \rightarrow A\ \alpha|\beta \qquad\qquad ...(1)$$

After eliminating

$$A \rightarrow \beta R$$

$$R \rightarrow \alpha\ R|\varepsilon$$

If $\beta$ does not begin with $A$, then $A$ no longer has a left recursion.

## PROBLEM 1

Consider $E$–productions from an SDT translating infix to postfix

$$E \rightarrow E_1 + T\ \{\text{Print ('+');}\}$$

$$E \rightarrow T$$

## SOLUTION

Here, apply the standard rule to $E$, we have (compare with Equation (1))

Here,                    $\alpha\ =\ +\ T\{\text{print ('+')}\},\ \beta = T$

and $\beta$ the body of the other production in $T$ · If we introduce $R$ for the remainder of $E$ · we get.

$$E \rightarrow TR$$

$$R \rightarrow +\ T\ \{\text{Print ('+');}\}\ R|\varepsilon$$

# 8

# RUN-TIME ENVIRONMENTS

## 8.1 STORAGE ORGANIZATION

The executing target program runs on its own logical address space which is managed and organized by the compiler, operating system, and target machine.

The operating system maps the logical address into physical addresses, which are usually spread throughout memory.

The run-time representation of an object program will be as shown below:

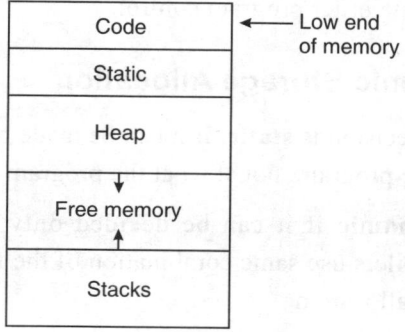

**Run-Time Storage** comes in blocks of contiguous bytes where a byte is the smallest unit of addressable memory.

The storage layout for data objects is strongly influenced by the addressing constraints of the target machine.

For example, on many machines instructions to add integers may expect integers to be aligned at an address divisible by +.

As an another example array of ten characters needs only 10 bytes to hold ten characters, compiler may allocate 12 bytes to get the proper alignment, leaving 2 bytes unused. This unused space is refered as **padding.**

When the space is at a premium a compiler may packs data so that no padding is left.

- The size of the generated code is fixed at compile time. So the compiler can place the executable target code in a statically determined area **code** usually in the low end of memory.

- The size of same program data objects such as global constants, data generated by the compiler such as information to support garbage collection are placed in another statically determined area called **static.**

- To maximize the utilization of space at run time the other two areas. **Stacks and Heap** are at the apposite ends of the remainder of the address space.

- The **stack grows towards lower addresses, the heap towards higher.** Stack is used to store data structures called **activation records** that get generated during procedure calls.

- Many programming languages allow the programmer to allocate and deallocate data order program control.

## Static Vs. Dynamic Storage Allocation

Storage–allocation decision is **static**, if it can be made by the compiler looking only at the text of the program, not at what the program does when it executes.

Decision is **dynamic** if it can be decided only while the program is running. Many compilers use same combination of the following two stategies for dynamic storage allocation.

1. **Stack Storage:** Names local to a procedure are allocated space on a stack.

2. **Heap Storage:** Data that may out live the call to the procedure that created it is usually allocated on a heap of reusable storage.

## 8.2 STACK ALLOCATION OF SPACE

Each time a procedure is called, space for its local variable is pushed onto a stack, and when the procedure terminates that space is poped out off the stack.

1. **Activation Trees:** Stack allocation would not be feasible if procedure calls, or activation of procedures, did not nest it time.

2. The **activation of $q$ terminate abnormally.** In that case $P$ ends simulltaneously with $q$.

3. The **activiation of $q$ terminates because of an exception that $q$ cannot handle.**

Procedure '$p$' may handle the exception in this case the activation of $q$ has terminated while the activation of $P$ continues.

If $P$ cannot handle the exception then this activation of $p$ terminates at the same time as the activate on of $q$.

We can represent the activations of procedures during the running of an entire program by a tree called on **"activation tree"**.

**Each node** in an activation tree **corresponds to one activation** and **root is the activation of the main.**

At a node for an activation of procedure $p$, the children correspond to activation of the procedures called by this activation of $P$.

The activation tree for quicksort can be written as in figure.

Use of a run–time stack is enabled by several useful relationship between the activation tree and behavior of the program.

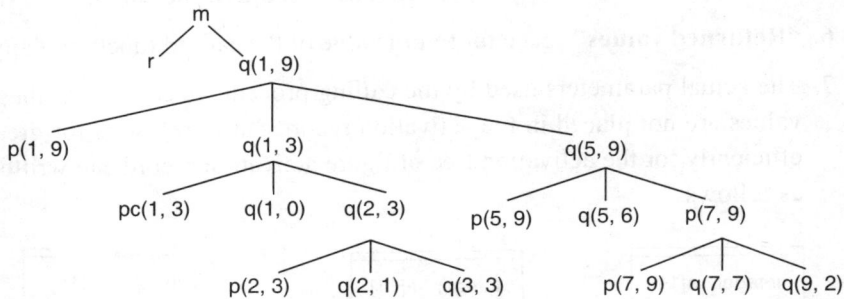

**Figure:** Activation tree for quicksort

1. The sequence of procedure calls corresponds to a preorder traversal of the activation tree.

2. The sequence of returns corresponds to a postorder traversal of the activation tree.

**Activation Records:** Procedure calls and returns are managed by a runtime stack called control stack. Each live activation has an activation record (frame). The structure of activation record will be as shown below.

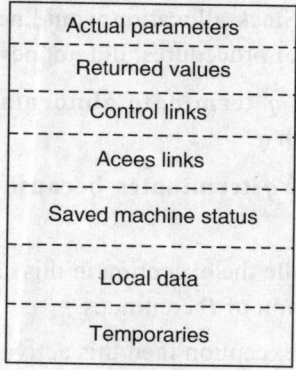

```
Actual parameters
------------------
Returned values
------------------
Control links
------------------
Acees links
------------------
Saved machine status
------------------
Local data
------------------
Temporaries
```

1. **Temporary values** such as those arising from the evaluation of expression of expressions are held in temporaries where those values cannot be held in registers.

2. **Local data** belonging to the procedure whose activation record is this.

3. A **saved machine status,** with information about the state of the machine just before the call to the procedure. This information **includes return address** and content of registers.

4. An **"access links"** is needed to locate data needed by the called procedures but found elsewhere e.g in another activation record.

5. A **control work** pointing to the activation record of the caller.

6. **"Returned values"** space for return value of the caused function if any.

7. The actual parameters used by the calling procedures commonly these values are not placed in the activation record but in registers for great efficiently for the activation tree of figure activation record can written as follows.

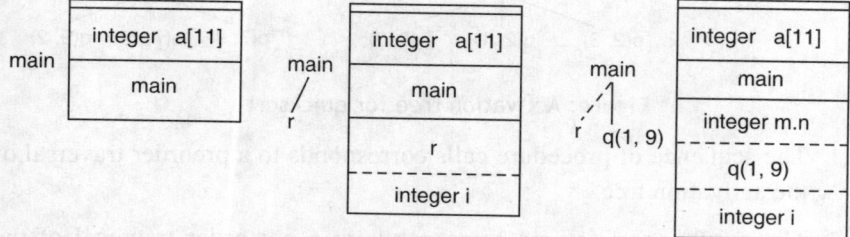

## Calling Sequence

Procedure calls are implemented by **calling sequences** which consists of code that allocates an active record on the stack and enters information into its fields.

A **return sequence** is similar code to restore the state of the machine so the calling procedure can continue its excution after the call.

The code in a calling sequence is divided between the calling procedure (the "callee") and the procedure **it calls (the "callee").**

In general if a procedure is called from $n$ different points, then portion of the calling sequence assigned to the caller is generated $n$ times.

The following principles are helpful when designing calling sequences.

1. **Values communicated between caller and callee** are **generally placed at the beginning of the callee's activation record.** So they are as close as possible to the caller's activation record.

2. Fixed length items are generally placed in the middle. Such items include the **control link, the access** links and the machine status field.

3. Items whose size may not be known early are placed at the **end of the activation record.**

4. We must locate the **top–of–stack pointer judiciously.**

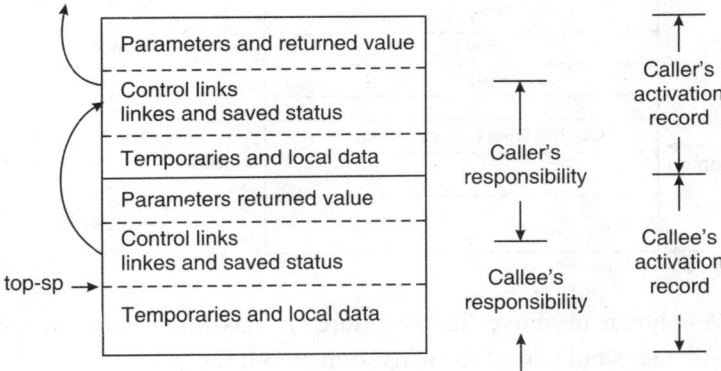

**Figure:** Division of tasks between caller and callee

A register **top–sp** points to the end of the machine status field in the current top activation record.

The **calling sequence and its** division between caller and callee is as follows.

1. The caller evaluates the actual parameters.

2. The caller stores a return address and the old value of top-sp into the callee's activation record.

3. The callee saves the register values and other status information.

4. The callee initialize its local data and begins execution.

## Corresponding Return Sequence

1. The callee places the return value next to the parameters.

2. The callee restores top-sp and other register and then branches to the return address that the callee placed in the status field.

3. Caller knows the return value, relative to the value of top-sp.

## Variable-Length Data on the Stack

The run-time memory management system must deal frequently with the allocation of space for objects the sizes of which are not known at compile time.

A common strategy for allocating variable-length array is shown below.

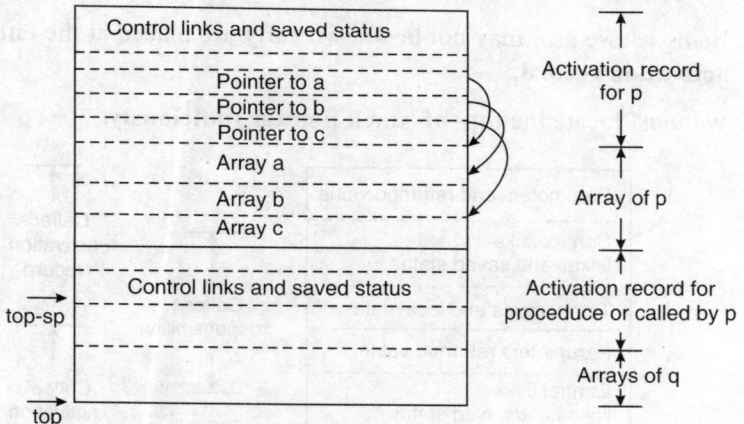

- As shown in above fig procedure '$p$' has three local arrays, whose storage is not part of the activation record for '$p$'.

- Only a pointer to the beginning of each array appears in the activation record itself.

- The activation record for '$q$' begins after array of '$p$' and any variable length array of $q$ are located beyond that.

- Two pointers **top and top-sp** are used **top** marks the actual top of stack it points to the position at which the next activation record **top-sp** is used to find local, fixed-length field of the top activation record.

## 8.3 ACCESS TO NONLOCAL DATA ON THE STACK

Access of data becomes more complicated in languages where procedures can be declared inside other procedures.

**Data Access without Nested Procedures:** For languages that do not allow nested procedure declarations, allocation of storage for variables and access to those variable is simple.

1. **Global Variable are Allocated Static Storage:** The location of these variables remain fixed and are known at compile time.

2. Any other name must be local to the activation at the top of the stack and can be accessed though the **top-sp points** of the stack.

**Benefit of Static allocation** for globals is that declared procedures may be passed as parameters or returned as results with no substantial change in the data-access statergy.

## Issues with Nested Procedures

- Access becomes for more complicated when a language allows procedure declaration to be nested and also uses the normal **static scoping rule.**

- Static scoping rule means a procedure can access variables of the procedures whose declarations surround its own declaration.

## A Language with Nested Procedure Declarations

The family of a languages do not support nested procedures. The one of the language that supports nested procedures is ML.

**ML is a functional language**, meaning that variables once declared and intiatized are not changed [array is an exception whose elements can be changed].

Variables are defined and have their unchangeable values intialized by a statement of the form.

```
val < name> = <expression>
```

functions are defined using the syntax

```
fun <name. (<arguments>) = <body>
```

for function bodies we shall use let statement of the form

```
let <list of definitions> in <statements> end
```

Most importantly, function definitions can be nested.

## Nesting Depth

All $C$ functions are at nesting depth 1. If a procedure '$p$' is defined immediately within a procedure at nesting depth $i$, then give '$p$' the nesting depth $i + 1$

Consider a sketch in ML of quick sort example.

```
fun sort (input File, OutputFile) =
Let
val a = array (11,0);
fun read Array (inputFile) = ....;
    ... a ....;
fun exchange (i, j) =
    ... a ...;
fun quicksort (m,n) =
    Let
        val v = ...;
        fun partition (y, z) =
            ... a ...v ... exchange ...
    in
        ...a...v... partition...quicksort
    end
in
    ...a...read Array... quicksort
end;
```

Here the only function at **nesting depth 1 is the sort** function which reads of integes into array and starts them using quick sort algorithm.

**read Array, exchange and quicksort** are at nesting depth 2 (two).

Since **partition** is defined immediately within a function at **nesting depth 2, it is at depth 3.**

## Access Links

A direct implementation of the normal static scope rule for nested functions is obtained by adding a pointer called the **access links to each activation record.**

If procedure 'p' is nested immediately within procedure q in the source code, then the access links in any activation of 'p' points to the most recent activation of q.

Access **links form–a chain from** the activation record at the top of the stack to a sequence of activations at progressively lower nesting depths.

**Example:** Below shows a sequences of stacks that might result from execution of function sort.

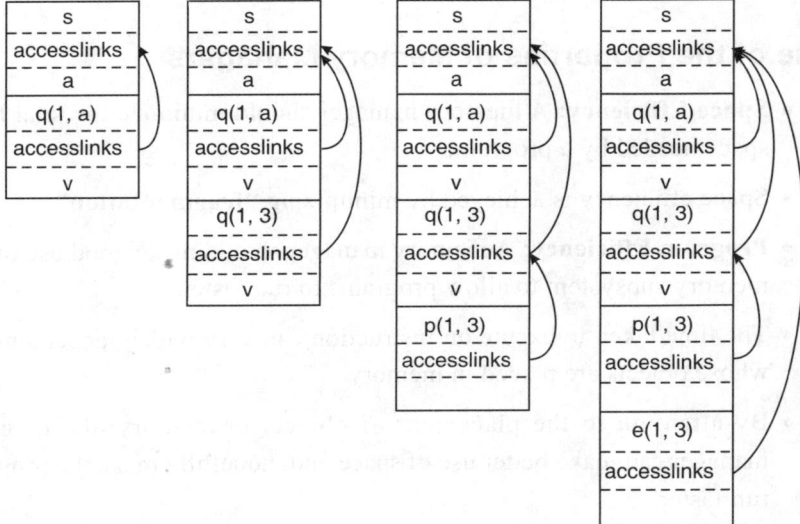

## 8.4 HEAP MANAGEMENT

The heap is the portion of the state that is used for data that lives indefinitely or until the program explicity deletes it.

**The Memory Manager:** The memory manager keeps track of all the free space in heap storage at all times. If performs two functions.

**Allocation:** When a program requests memory for a variable or object the memory manager produces a chunks of contiguous heap memory of the requested size.

- If the chunk of the needed size is available, it seeks to increase the heap storage space by getting consecutive bytes of virtual memory from the operating system.

- **Deallocation:** The memory manager return deallocated space to the pool of free space. So it can reuse the space to satisfy other allocation request.

Memory management would be simple if

(*a*) all allocation requests were for chunks of the same size.

(*b*) storage were released predictably, say, first–allocated first deallo-cated.

The memory manager must be prepared to service, in any order, allocation and deallocation requests of any size ranging from one byte to as long as the program's entire address space.

## Some of the Properties of Memory Managers

- **Space Efficiency:** A memory manager should minimize the total heap space needed by a program.

- Space efficiency is achieved by minimizing **"fragmentation"**

- **Program Efficiency:** A memory manager should make good use of the memory subsystem to allow programs to run faster.

- The time taken to excute on instruction can vary widely depending on whose objects are placed in memory.

- By attention to the placement of objects in memory, the memory manager can make better use of space and, hopefully make the program run faster.

- **Low Overhead:** Because memory allocation and deallocation are frequent operations in many program it is important that these operations be as efficient as possible.

- Have to minimize the overhead the fraction of execution time spent performing allocation and deallocation.

## The Memory Hierarchy of a Computer

- The efficiency of a program is determined not just by the number of instructions executed, but also by how long it takes to execute each of these size instructions.

- The time taken to execute an instruction can vary significantly. Since the time taken to access different parts of memory can vary from nano seconds to mili second.

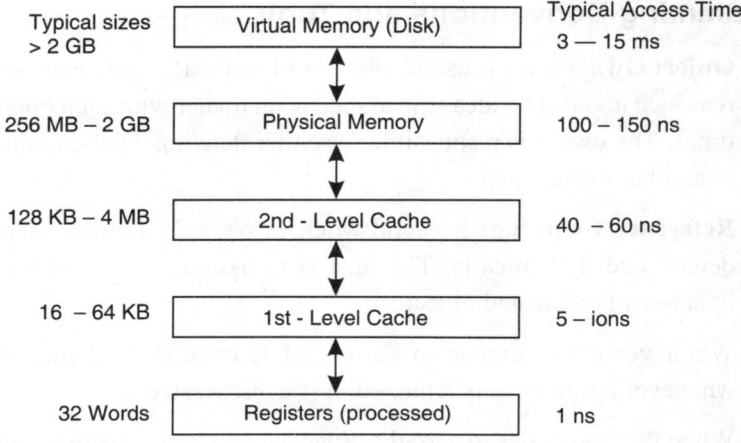

**Figure:** Typical memory Hierachy

- It is impossible to build gigabytes of storage with nonoseand access times. So all modern computers arrange their storage as a memory **hierarchy.**

- Typically a processor has a **small number of registers** whose contents are under software control.

- Next it has one or more levels of **cache,** usually made out of static RAM, that are kilo bytes to several megabytes in size.

- The next level of hierarchy is the **physical (main memory)** which is made out of hundreds of magabytes of gigabytes of dynamic RAM.

- The physical memory is then backed up by **virtual memory.** Which is implemented by gigabytes of disks.

Upon a memory access, the machine first looks for the data in the closest (lowest level) storage and if the data is not there, looks for the next higher level, and soon.

- Registers usage is managed by the code that a compiler generates.

- All other levels of the hierarchy are managed automatically caches are managed exclusively in hardware in order to keep up with the relatively fast RAM access time.

- Disks are relatively slow they are managed by the operating system with the use of "translation look a side buffer"

## Programming Conventions and Tools

- **Object Ownership:** is useful when an object's lifetime can be statically reasoned about. The idea is to associate an owner with each object at all times. The owner is responsible for either deleting a parsing the object to another owner.

- **Reference Counting:** is useful when an object's lifetime needs to be determined dynamically. The idea is to associate a count with each dynamically allocated object.

- Whenever the reference to the object is created, it is incremented, whenever a reference is removed, it is decremented.

- When the count goes to zero the object can no longer be referenced and can be deleted.

- **Region-based Allocation:** is useful for collections of objects whose lifetimes are tied to specific phase in a computation.

## 8.5 INTRODUCTION TO GARBAGE COLLECTION

- Data that cannot be referenced is generally known as **garbage.**

- Many high-level PL's remove the burden of manual memory management by offering **automatic garbage collection**, which deallocates unreachable data.

## Design Goals for Garbage Collectors

- Garbage allocation is the reclamation of chunks of holding objects that can no longer be accessed by a program.

- We need to assume that

- Objects have a type that can be determined by the garbage collector at run time.

- References to objects are always to the address of the beginning of the object never pointers to place within the object.

- **Mutator (user program)** modifies the collection of objects in the heap.

- Objects become garbage when the mutator program cannot reach them.

- The garbage collector finds these unreachable objects and reclaims their space by handling them to the memory manager which keeps tracks of the free space.

**A Basic Requirement:** Type Safety

- Unsafe languages (c, c++) are bad candidates for **automatic garbage collection.**

- A language in which type of any data component can be determined is said to be **type safe**.

## Performance Metrics

Performance metrics that must be considered are.

- **Overall Execution Time:** Garbage collection can be very slow. It should not significantly increase the total run time of an application.

- **Space Usage:** Garbage collection must avoid fragmentation and make the best use of the available memory.

- **Pause Time:** Besides minimizing the overall execution time, it is desirable that the maximum pause time is minimized.

- **Program Locality:** The garbage collector controls the placementof data and thus influences the data locality of the material program.

It can improve a mutator temporal locality by freeing up space and reusing it:

## Reachability

- All the data that can be accessed directly by a program without having to dereference any pointer is **root set.**

- A program can reach any member of its root set at any time, and any object with a reference that is stored in the field members or elements of any reachable object is itself reachable.

- An optimizing compiler can do following things to enable the garbage collected to find the root set.

- The **compiler can restrict the invocation of** garbage collection to only certain code points on the program, when no "hidden" references exist.

- The compiler can write out information that the garbage collector can use to recover all the references.

- The compiler **can assure that there is a reference to the base address of all reachable objects** whenever the garbage collector may be involved.

The set of **reachable objects changes** as a program executes. There are four basic operation that a mutator performs to change the set of reachable objects.

- **Object Allocation:** These are performed by the memory manager, which return a reference to each newly allocated chunk of memory.

- **Parometer Passing and Return Values:** Objects pointed to by [references to objects are passed from the actual input parameter] references remain reachable.

- **Reference Assignments:** Assignments of the form $u = v$ whose $u$ and $v$ are references have two effects.

  1. $U$ is now a references have to the object refered to by $v$.

  2. If the original reference in $U$ is lost then the object become unreachable.

- **Procedure Returns:** As a procedure exists, the frame holding its local variable is popped off the stack. If the frame holds the only reachable reference to any object, that object becomes unreachable.

- There are two basic ways to find unreachable objects Either **we catch the transitions as reachable** objects turn unreachable, or we **periodically locate all the reach able objects and then infer that all the other objects** are unreachable.

- **Reference Counting** is a well known approach for first approach.

- Count of references to an object is maintained as the mutator performs actions that may change the reachability set.

- When the count goes to zero, the object becomes unreachable.

- The second approach computes reachability by tracing all the references transitively.

- A **tree-based** garbage collectors marks all objects in the root set as **"reachable"** examines iteratively all the reference in reactable objects to find more reachable objects.

- This approach must trace all the references before it can find any objects to be unreachable.

- Once the reachable set is computed, it can find many unreachable objects at once and locate a good deal of free storage at the same time.

## Reference Counting Garbage Collectors

Reference count can be maintained as follows:

  1. **Object Allocation:** The reference count of the new object is set to 1.

2. **Parameter Passing:** The reference count of each object passed into a procedure is incremented.

3. **Reference Assignments:** For statement $u = v$, where $u$ and $v$ are references the reference count of the object referred to by '$v$' goes up by one, and the count for the old object referred to by is goes down by one.

4. **Procedure Returns:** As a procedure exists, all the references held by the local variables of that procedure activation record must also be decremented.

If several local variables hold references to the same object that object's count must be decremented once for each such reference.

5. **Transitive Loss of Reachability:** Whenever the reference count of an object becomes zero, we must also decrement the count of each object pointed to by a reference within the object.

## Reference Counting has two Disadvantages

It cannot collect unreachable; cyclic data structures and it is expensive.

Cyclic data structures are quite plausible, data structures often point back to their parent nodes or point to each other as cross references.

The advantage of reference counting is that garbage collection is performed in an incremental fashion.

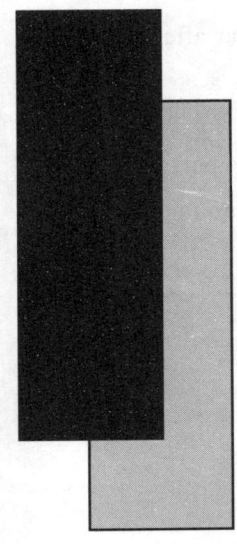

# APPENDIX

## MODEL QUESTION PAPER–I

1. (a) With a neat diagram, explain the different phases of compilation.

   (b) Discuss the different compiler construction tools.

   (c) Explain the input buffering strategy used in lexical analysis phase.

2. (a) Define the following terms:

   (i) Token

   (ii) Lexeme

   (iii) Pattern

   (iv) Handle.

   (b) Write the transition diagram that accepts the reserve words case, const, char, and continue.

   (c) Write the principle of non recursive predictive passing.

   (d) Show that the following grammar G, is ambiguous, $A \rightarrow AA \,|(A)|\varepsilon$.

3. (a) What is left recursion and left factoring, explain with an example for each?

(b) Compute first and follow for the following grammar after eliminating left recursion.

$E \rightarrow E + T/T$   $T \rightarrow TF/F$       $F \rightarrow F* |a|b|\ (\varepsilon)$

(c) Explain the different error handling strategies of the parser.

4. (a) GenerateSLR parsing table for the following grammar $S \rightarrow (L)/a$ $L \rightarrow L, S/S$.

   (b) Write the precedence function for the grammar $a.\ S \rightarrow (L)/a\ L \rightarrow L, S/S$

|   | a | ( | ) | , | $ |
|---|---|---|---|---|---|
| a |   |   | -> | -> | -> |
| ( | <· | <· | ≐ | <· |   |
| ) |   |   | -> | -> | -> |
| , | <· | <· | -> | -> |   |
| $ | <· | <· |   |   |   |

   (c) Write the algorithmfor construction of LR parsing table.

5. (a) Construct LR(1) items for the grammar G, $A \rightarrow (A)/a$.

   (b) Define synthesized attribute and inherited attribute Give the semantic rule for implementation of desk calculator with example.  (07 Marks)

   (c) Construct annotated parse tree for the expression $4 * (3 + 5) - 7$ using semantic rule for simple desk calculator.

6. (a) Write a note on activation records and its use.

   (b) Explain in detail the stack allocation strategy.

   (c) What is printed by the program assuming.

   (i) Call–by value

   (ii) Call–by–reference

   (iii) Copy–restore linkage

   (iv) Call–by–name

   Program main (input; output);

   procedure P(x, y, z)

   begin

   $y := y + 1;$

   $z := z + x;$

   end

begin

    $a := 3;$

    $b := 3;$

    $P(a + b, a, a);$

    print a

end

7. (a) Write the semantic action for

    (i) do while loop

    (ii) for loop

  (b) Define the following terms:

    (i) Usage count.

    (ii) Register assignment and allocation.

    (iii) Register descriptor and address descriptor.

  (c) Explain different loop optimization techniques.

8. (a) Generate the machine code and compute the cost for the following instruction set. Assume there are only two registers available for storing intermediate value

    $a = 1\ b = 10\ c = 20$

    $d = a + b;\ e = c + d;$

    $f = c + a;\ e = b + d;$

    $d = 5 + f$

  (b) Construct the basic block and flow graph for the following program statement begin

    $locn = -1$

    $i = 0$

    while (i < 100) do

    begin

        if $a(i) = x$ then loen = I

        $i = i + 1$

    end

  end

# MODEL QUESTION PAPER–II

1. (a) Explain the different phase of a compiler with a block diagram.

   (b) Construct transition diagram for the following:

   (i) Relational operators

   (ii) Identifiers and keywords

   (iii) Unsigned nmbers.

   (c) Construct a NFA for regular expression $(a/b)^*\ abb$

2. (a) Define Ambiguity, show that the following grammar is ambiguous:

   E → E + E/E – E/(E)/id

   (b) Given the grammar:

   E → E + T/T

   T → T * F/F

   F → (E)/id

   (i) Remove left recursion.

   (ii) For the resulting grammar, construct LL (1) parsing table.

3. (a) Determine the operating procedence relation table for the grammar:

   E → E + E|E – E|E * E|E/E| E↑ E|(E)|–E/id, assuming

   (i) ↑ is of highest precedence and right – associative.

   (ii) * and/are of next highest precedence and left associative and

   (iii) + and – are of lowest precedence and left – associative.

   (b) Construct canonical LR(1) parsing table for the grammar.

   E → E + T/T;    T → T*F/F;    F → (E)/id

4. (a) Construct LALR parsing table for the grammar: S → CC; C → cC/d.

   (b) Briefly explain the concept of syntax directed definition with an example.

5. (a) Explain L-attributed definition in detail.

   (b) Briefly explain the different data structures used for symbol table.

6. (a) Briefly explain the different types of intermediate codes with an example.

   (b) Explain the structure preserving transformation on basic blocks.

7. (*a*) Explain in detail various issues involved in code generation phase.

   (*b*) Briefly explain any five kinds of code optimization with an example each.

8. Write short notes on:

   (*a*) LEX

   (*b*) Recursive Descent Parsing.

   (*c*) Error recovery in Operator-precedence parsing.

   (*d*) DAG representation of Basic blocks.

# MODEL QUESTION PAPER–III

1. (*a*) Explain the different phases of compiler with a block diagram.

   (*b*) Construct a transition diagram for the following:

   (*i*) Relational operators

   (*ii*) Identifiers

   (*iii*) Unsigned numbers

   (*c*) Distinguish between phase and phases.

2. (*a*) Define ambiguity. Show that the grammar

   S → *ictses|icts|a*

   is ambiguous and eliminate ambiguity from the expression.

   (*b*) What do you mean by left recursion? Given the grammar,

   E → E + T|T

   T → T * F|F

   F → (E)|*id*

   (*i*) Remove left recursion and do left factoring if needed.

   (*ii*) For the resulting grammar construct LL(I) parsing table.

3. (*a*) Construct LALR parsing table for the grammar.

   S' → S

   S → CC

   C → cC|*d*

   (*b*) What is handle pruning? Explain the same with the grammar.

   E → E + E|E * E||(E)|*id*

   and the input string is *id*1 + *id*2 * *id*3 $.

4. (*a*) What are precedence functions? Give an algorithm for constructing precedence functions. From the table of precedence relations given below, construct precedence functions.

| | id | + | * | $ |
|---|---|---|---|---|
| id | | -> | -> | -> |
| + | <- | -> | <- | -> |
| * | <- | -> | -> | -> |
| $ | <- | <- | <- | |

(*b*) Briefly describe the concept of syntax directed definition.

5. (*a*) Explain the different storage allocation strategies.

(*b*) Give a scheme for runtime storage allocation for C–like languages along with the structure of activation record.

6. (*a*) Briefly explain the different types of intermediate codes, with the expression.

$a : b * - c + b * - c.$

(*b*) Explain in detail various issues involved in code generation phase.

7. (*a*) What are basic blocks? Explain in detail DAG representation of basic blocks.

(*b*) Briefly explain any five kinds of code optimization.

8. Write short notes on.

(*a*) Grouping of phases.

(*b*) LEX

(*c*) Recursive descent parsing

(*d*) Error recovery in LR parsers.

# MODEL QUESTION PAPER–IV

1. (*a*) What is compiler? Explain the different phases of compiler by considering the following statement as input.

position : = initial + rate * 60

(*b*) Briefly explain the need for multipass in compiler.

(*c*) Briefly explain a strategy to reduce the number of passes.

2. (*a*) Write a transition diagram to recognize the following set of tokens. Write program segments for start state, any one of the intermediate states and any one final state.

BEGIN

END

ELSE

Identifier

(b) What is look ahead operator? With examples show how this operator may be used to solve lexical analysis problems.

3. (a) With a schematic, explain the role of Parser. List and explain various error recovery strategies.

(b) Define left–recursion. Eliminate left recursion from the following grammar:

$E \rightarrow E + T/T$

$T \rightarrow T * F/F$

$F \rightarrow (E)/id$

Also obtain FIRST and FOLLOW symbols for the above resulting rammar.

4. (a) Construct SLR(I) parsing table for the following grammar.

$E \rightarrow T * E/T$

$T \rightarrow T + F/F$

$F \rightarrow id$

(b) Compare the relative merits and demerits of LL (1), SLR (1), LALR (1) and canonical LR(1) parsing methods

5. (a) Briefly explain the concept of syntax directed definition with example.

(b) Write a note on L–attributed definition.

(c) Give SDTS for an arithmetic expression with +, * and –, Show annotated parse tree for the input $3 + 4 * 5$.

6. (a) Explain in detail, different storage allocation strategies.

(b) With example explain different parameter passing methods.

7. (a) Briefly explain the main issues in code generation.

(b) Briefly explain any five kinds of code-optimization.

8. Write short notes on:

(a) LEX

(b) Recursive descent parser.

(c) Dead code elimination.

(d) L–attributed SDD.

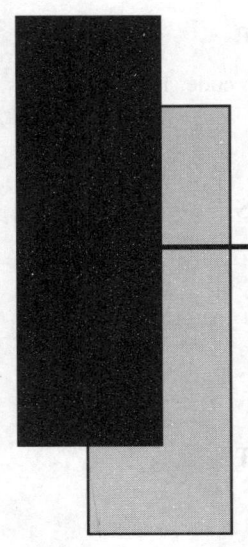

# INDEX